Integrated Mat
Management

Integrated Materials Management

R.J. Carter
MA, MCIPS, MBIM, Cert.Ed.
Director of DPSS Consultants

P. Price
BA(Hons), CPCMM, DipIIPMM, DipCA, DipHA, DipMM,
MCIPS, MIMI, MILDM, AFSIMM
Senior Lecturer in Purchasing, University of North London

THE M & E HANDBOOK SERIES

Pitman Publishing
128 Long Acre, London WC2E 9AN

A Division of Longman Group UK Limited

© Longman Group UK Limited 1993

First published in Great Britain 1993

British Library Cataloguing-in-Publication Data
A CIP catalogue record for this book is available
from the British Library

ISBN 0 7121 1038 0
ISBN (CIPS) 0 7121 1046 1

Typeset by FDS Ltd, Penarth
Printed and bound in Singapore

Contents

Part three Materials planning and control

Part seven Physical distribution management

Preface

Physical distribution management is a feature of almost every modern industrial and commercial operation, although it has for many years been mostly unexplored territory. This book is designed to open up some of the basic elements and aspects of the subject. It is also an attempt to relate logistics management to the rest of the organization.

We have based this book on *Stores Management* (R J Carter 2nd edition 1985), but have expanded the text to include new chapters on materials management, transportation, materials planning and control aspects of the subject. We have also revised and updated several of the existing chapters to ensure that the new edition provides a sound and up-to-date background to the subject.

This Handbook provides an excellent framework of notes for the student and the practitioner, and it is hoped that this book will be of real assistance to those undertaking examinations. It is useful to note that in many professional and industrial examinations an element of logistical management knowledge is required by the student and this book should be particularly useful in this area.

The book has been prepared primarily for students undertaking examinations for the Chartered Institute of Purchasing and Supply and the Association of Supervisors in Purchasing and Supply. It specifically covers the requirement of CIPS Logistics, the ASPS (First Certificate) papers in *Stores Design and Materials Handling*, *Stores Administration and Control of Stock* and the ASPS (Second Certificate) papers in *An Appreciation of Management of Materials*, *Principles of Supervision* and *Transport and Distribution*. The book would also be very useful to those students undertaking the Institute of Materials Management examinations.

The main themes of the book, i.e. the storage, control, distribution and handling of materials, could be useful to students undertaking the examinations of the Royal Society of Arts, Chartered Institute of Marketing, Association of Accounting Technicians (Level 3) and the Institute of Production Control. It should also be useful to students undertaking BTEC National and Higher National courses that contain materials based options.

1992   R.J.C.
                                                                    P.P.

Acknowledgments

During the writing of this book, we have had assistance from many organizations and individuals. We would like to express many thanks to the following: London Borough of Croydon, Lansing Bagnall, Yale Trucks, Integrated Handling Ltd, Ascros Ltd, Henly Trucks, Chartered Institute of Purchasing and Supply, Chartered Institute of Marketing, British Institute of Management, Institute of Production Control, Link 51 Ltd, Association of Accounting Technicians, Polytechnic of North London Business School, Mrs Dawn Carter, ACIB, Cert. Ed., Christine Rowat, Ian Buckle who drew the illustrations in Chapters 17 to 23.

Part one

Control of physical resources

1
Management principles

Approaches to management

1. Introduction

There are various approaches to the task of management, from F.W. Taylor's scientific management based upon the concept of management as a science and therefore being observable and predictable, through to E.F.L. Brech's.

2. Definitions of management

The following quotes represent the wide spectrum of management thinking:

(a) 'A social process entailing responsibility for the effective and economic planning and regulating of the operations of an exercise, in fulfilment of a given purpose, such responsibilities include judgement, planning, control, integration, motivation and suspension.' E.F.L. Brech (1957).

(b) 'Management must always, in every decision and action, put economic (in terms of the organization) performance first, therefore management is an economic organ in an industrial society. Every act, every decision, every deliberation of management has as its first dimension an economic dimension.' Peter F. Drucker (1968).

(c) 'Management may be thought of as the task of planning, organizing and controlling any organization or group.' Tony Proctor (1982).

(d) 'To manage is to forecast and plan, to organize, to command, to co-ordinate and to control.' H. Fayol (1916).

(e) 'The five essential managerial functions are planning, organizing, staffing, leading and controlling.' Koontz and O'Donnell (1976).

These definitions, although individual, do have common elements — the need to control, plan and organize the organization's activities, bearing in mind social and economic considerations.

The role of the stores manager

3.   The stores manager

'Stores management has got to be recognized in future as a facet of management in the same way as we already recognize production, engineering, marketing and finance.' S. Calvert (*Journal of the Institute of Production Control*, 1979).

The job of being a stores manager should begin with the concept that the stores are an essential part of the organization and that the stores manager is first and foremost an organizational manager, a member of the management team. His contribution to the management of the organization is that of controlling, planning and organizing activities within his sphere of responsibility, i.e. the stores (*see* **5**).

4.   Common problems

There are, however, some commonly encountered problems in relation to the transition of staff from the buyer's position to that of manager. Dr David Farmer FInstPS states in the *Institute of Purchasing and Supply Journal* (April 1979) that becoming a member of the management team could reveal the following problem areas:

(a) failure to delegate effectively;
(b) too much involvement with 'detail';
(c) relationships with other managers;
(d) report writing skills;
(e) decision-making;
(f) operational thinking instead of strategic thinking.

The concept of control

5. Controlling

The concept of control is central to understanding the role of the stores manager, in relation to the materials side of the organization. It is the job of the stores manager to ensure that his operation is running as efficiently as possible and that it is making a worthwhile contribution to the overall objectives of the organization. To enable resources to be utilized in the most effective manner, it is vital that management has a means of measuring the performance of individual parts of the organization. Control can only be exercised after a process of comparison between planned and actual has taken place. The control process therefore must commence with the establishment of 'standards' (*see* Fig. 1.1).

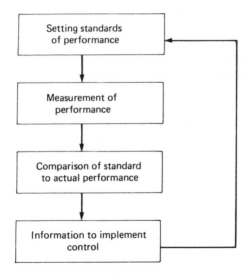

Figure 1.1   *The control process*

In relation to stores management these standards can relate to the following:

(a) stock levels (*see* 15:4);
(b) staff levels;
(c) space usage;
(d) quality control and inspection (*see* Chapter 8);
(e) materials handling equipment usage;
(f) financial control;
(g) security;
(h) stock maintenance.

6.   Methods of control
Having established a system of standards the next phase is to set up a system for measuring the performance of the department to be controlled. The following methods are the most commonly employed:

(a) budgetary control;
(b) profit centre analysis;
(c) ratios;
(d) audit;
(e) comparisons;
(f) management by objectives.

7.   Budgetary control
A budget is a financial and a quantitative statement covering a given period of time, for the purpose of obtaining a given objective. In relation to stores management the budget could relate to:

(a) operating costs;
(b) materials in stock;
(c) capital budget.

The basic advantage of a budgetary approach to control is that information is produced gradually over a period of time, therefore corrective action can be carried out during the actual measurement period. For example, the stock controller will be able to monitor the materials budget and take corrective action, thus ensuring that the overall objective of the budget is met by the end of the budgetary period.

8. Profit centre analysis

This approach to measuring performance is based upon the concept of the stores as a controller of assets and a generator of income. The stores department have, for example, the following assets:

(a) materials in stock;
(b) materials handling equipment;
(c) space.

Against this the stores department is given a notional profit, when the cost of operating the stores is set against stock turnover, e.g.

$$\frac{\text{Net profit}}{\text{Total assets employed by stores}} \times 100\% = \frac{10,000}{1,000,000} \times 100\%$$

Rate of return = 1%

The basic idea of the profit centre approach is to run the stores department as a separate business, employed by the rest of the organization to provide a service. The measurement of performances is therefore based upon the employment of assets in relation to profits and costs. If the stores manager can reduce the total assets needed to perform the service, or can reduce the costs of providing the service, then the rate of return percentage will improve.

9. Ratios

Ratios can be employed as an indication of trends, showing the relationship between two variables. In relation to stores management there are a number of useful ratios that can be calculated to indicate the performance of the stores. It is vital that any ratio analysis is carried out on a regular basis, so that comparisons can be made and trends identified.

(a) $\dfrac{\text{Materials handling costs}}{\text{Total cost of storage}} \times 100\% = $ % of materials handling costs to total costs

(b) $\dfrac{\text{Value of stock held}}{\text{Total assets employed}}$ x 100% = $\begin{array}{l}\text{\% of stock to}\\ \text{total assets}\\ \text{employed}\end{array}$

(c) $\dfrac{\text{Cost of storage}}{\text{Total organization costs}}$ x 100% = $\begin{array}{l}\text{\% of storage}\\ \text{to total costs}\end{array}$

(d) $\dfrac{\text{Operating costs of stores}}{\text{Stock turnover}}$

10. Internal audit
This is a system of detailed investigation of the stores operation. The stores are divided into sub-units and each unit is carefully examined by either internal or external auditors. The job of the auditor is to check stores records, i.e. stock record cards, bin cards, scrap and obsolescent reports, departmental expenses and stock checks. This investigation will highlight discrepancies and will indicate where more management input is required.

11. Comparisons
This is a system whereby activities and/or costs of the individual store operations are compared over a number of years. It is very important that in terms of analysis, the figures produced by comparisons have to be reviewed against changes in the value of money, scale of the enterprise and level of turnover. Some basic comparisons for the measurement of stores' performance could include the following:

(a) value of stock held 19/4–19/5;
(b) number of requisitions processed 19/4–19/5;
(c) value of scrap and obsolete stocks 19/4–19/5;
(d) value of stock check discrepancies;
(e) transport and distribution costs;
(f) materials and distribution costs;
(g) space costs;

(h) number of stores staff employed;
(i) number of nil stock situations;
(j) number of deliveries handled.

12. Management by objectives

'Management by objectives is a system that integrates the company's goals of profit and growth with the manager's need to contribute and develop himself personally' (John Humble, *Management by Objectives*, 1972). Objectives should be established in consultation with departmental and senior management, with a view to forming a number of practical and achievable objectives, which the stores management will strive to attain. By setting specific objectives, such as to reduce total stock deterioration by 10 per cent in value terms over the next financial year, management can evaluate the performance of individual managers. Therefore, the organizational objectives of reducing the costs of production are married to the manager's personal objective of reaching his target and gaining prestige and thus to intrinsic motivation.

Organization

13. Definition

Organizing can be defined as deciding what positions have to be filled and the duties and responsibilities of each position. One of the main roles of the manager is to organize the activities of his department. He must attempt to integrate and coordinate the individual sub-units within his department to achieve its overall objectives. The activities that the stores manger would have to organize could include the following:

(a) materials handling systems;
(b) storage space and layouts;
(c) deployment of labour;
(d) transport and distribution systems;
(e) training and staff development;
(f) structure of the stores department.

Planning and decision-making

14. Definitions

Planning has been variously defined. 'A technique whereby the skills of a variety of specialists can be brought to bear on the problem before the formal stage of decision-making is reached.' H. Simon (1959).

'Planning is an activity which involves decisions about objectives, plans, policies and results.' G.A. Cole (1982).

'Planning is more than just forecasting. It involves the process of choosing an objective, charting a course and moving along that course to the attaining of the objective.' Robert Fulme (1978).

From these three definitions we can see that planning contains the following basic elements:

(a) objectives;
(b) resources;
(c) methodology;
(d) communications;
(e) forecasting.

15. Objectives

The organization has to establish both corporate and functional objectives. How can an organization employ its resources in the most effective manner, unless it fully understands and defines what it means by 'effective'?

Corporate objectives relate to long-term future goals for the organization; functional objectives relate to immediate goals and targets. The stores manager should be involved in both corporate and functional objective setting (*see* 21:**4**).

16. Resources

Having established a number of objectives, the next stage is to evaluate the resources at the command of the organization or department. This can be done by establishing the strengths, weaknesses, opportunities and threats in relation to the department and organization concerned, as illustrated by John Argenti's cruciform. An example of a typical stores department's cruciform is shown in Fig. 1.2.

Strengths	*Weaknesses*
1. Skilled staff	1. Expensive overheads
2. Sympathetic senior management	2. Lack of materials management
3. Space available	

Threats	*Opportunities*
1. Security breakdown	1. Automation of central warehouse
2. Rising transport costs	2. Leasing materials handling equipment
	3. New technology

Figure 1.2 *Typical stores department cruciform*

The stores manager has to ensure that any plans made must take into consideration the resources available so as to maximize the strengths of his department and minimize the effect of weaknesses.

17. Methodology
Management have to employ their skills as experts in the relative areas of their responsibility to develop the means by which the stated objectives can be achieved.

18. Communication
A system whereby plans are effectively communicated to all those directly and indirectly involved is an essential element in the planning process (*see* 21:**7**).

19. Forecasting
In relation to planning, a high degree of forecasting is required to attempt to ensure that the plans being made will take into account changes that may occur in the internal and external environment in which the department has to function. There follows a list of internal and external factors:

(a) *External factors:*
    (*i*) Technological

> (*ii*) Political
> (*iii*) Economic
> (*iv*) Social and ethical.
> **(b)** *Internal factors:*
>> (*i*) Level of turnover
>> (*ii*) Mergers and takeovers
>> (*iii*) Outlook of senior management
>> (*iv*) Structure of the organization
>> (*v*) Capital investment.

A good example to illustrate this need for forecasting in relation to planning within the stores is shown by **(a)** the technology and **(b)** the structure of the organization.

(a) *Technology.* The stores manager will have to take into consideration the impact of low-cost computer-based stock control systems, in relation to plans for stockholding. Will the introduction of such a system mean that stockholding could be scaled down in the next few years by virtue of increased control?
(b) *Structure of the organization.* The stores manager would have to take into account any future possible alterations in the overall structure of the organization: a system of materials management (*see* 3:3) would have a direct impact upon the communication system required by the stores department.

Motivation

20. Definitions
'A motive is defined as an inner state that emerges, activates or moves and directs or channels behaviour toward goals.' Tony Proctor (1982).

Motivation is an essential part of the manager's role in the organization. It is the job of the manager to motivate the human resources that he is responsible for. A number of major motivational theories have been developed in the last eighty years, and all of these theories are designed to help the manager to understand the behaviour of individuals and groups.

21. Major motivational theories

(a) *Maslow's hierarchy of needs.* Maslow's theory is based upon two concepts: first, the 'needs' of individuals are in a hierarchy, with basic physiological needs at the lowest level and self-actualization as the supreme need (*see* Fig. 1.3). The second concept is that need equals action; the individual is motivated to satisfy these needs in a systematic way. The individual will have to deal with basic physiological needs before he tackles the higher social needs. Maslow's work has been used as a starting point for discussion on motivation since it was first put forward in 1943.

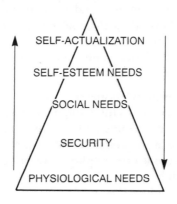

Figure 1.3 *Maslow's hierarchy of needs*

(b) *McGregor's Theory X and Theory Y.* McGregor's theory is based upon two separate 'models' of man. Having established these two models, McGregor went on to predict their behaviour and the incentives that could be used to motivate them. He describes a typical Mr X as:

(*i*) lazy
(*ii*) unambitious
(*iii*) lacking identification with organizational goals
(*iv*) easily duped.

This model of man would mainly react to an extrinsic form of motivation, i.e. wages, conditions and discipline.

Mr Y is defined thus:

    (*i*) ambitious
    (*ii*) hard-working
    (*iii*) committed to the organization.
This model of man would mainly react to an intrinsic form of motivation, i.e. promotion, praise, feeling part of the team.

    This approach to motivation has the advantage of simplicity and in some situations Mr X and Mr Y can be clearly identified. However, the complexity of man usually makes generalizations a dangerous practice.

(c) *Rensis Likert*. The basis of Likert's work is that of supportive groups: individuals work well in tightly knit groups. These groups, while motivated by economic and security motives, were also motivated by Maslow-style self-actualization. Likert came to the conclusion that successful managers combine the classical tools of management, while at the same time encouraging workers to participate in the managing of the activity.

    There are other motivational theories, all of which are useful in increasing the manager's total understanding of the behaviour of individuals and groups. Once the manager has an understanding the next step is to put together a package of incentives that will motivate employees to perform their tasks as effectively as possible.

Progress test 1

1. Give three definitions of management. **(2)**

2. What are the basic functions of a stores manager? **(3)**

3. What are the problems and difficulties facing the storekeeper who has recently become a stores manager? **(4)**

4. How could a stores manager measure the performance of his department? **(5)**

5. 'Management by objectives is a system that integrates the company's goals of profit and growth with the manager's need to contribute and develop himself personally.' Discuss. **(12)**

6. Outline two major motivational theories used by managers to control their employees. **(21)**

2
Introduction to logistics

Totally integrated supply chain management

1. Introduction

The efficient management of the physical flow of raw materials, spare parts, work in progress and finished goods from suppliers, through an organization and on to the final customer is a very complex task. It requires the integration and coordination of many different functional activities. Escalating costs, increased service levels demanded by customers and decreasing product life cycles have caused organizations to realize the importance of integrating these important but often fragmented activities. Though the need for integration is widely recognized among materials supply practitioners, an all embracing term to use to describe this activity is still being debated. Jargon such as *total physical distribution, materials control, supply management* and *production flow* are used both carelessly and interchangeably. The term most commonly used in the USA, which is also gaining ground in Europe, is *integrated logistics management.*

2. Definitions of logistics

Some of the more popular definitions are as follows:

(a) 'Logistics is the management of the physical and information flows of production and of all activities related to these flows. The physical flow of products include the movement of raw materials from suppliers, in process within the firm and the movement of finished goods to the consumer. The informational flows for products cover reports and documentation relating to goods movement.' W. Rose (1986).

(b) 'The all embracing word is Logistics, which covers the movement of raw materials from their sources to the processing point (materials management) and the movement of finished goods from the plant through various channels of distribution to the ultimate customer (distribution).' J. Gattorna (1983).

(c) 'Integrated Logistics Management is the area of administration that manages the physical flow of materials, spare parts and finished goods from suppliers, within the organization and to the final customer. It involves integrating such sub-functions as physical procurement, materials management and physical distribution management.'

3. Tasks of logistics

The logistical task of an organization is to evolve procedures that meet customer service plans at minimum cost. The logistical manager's role is to provide physical support to marketing, manufacturing and purchasing activities.

4. Integrated logistical procedures

The three areas of physical procurement, materials and distribution management have significantly diverse physical movement and information requirements.

5. Logistics and physical procurement

The term physical procurement applies to the movement of requirements from the supplier to manufacturing, assembly plants, warehouses or retail stores. It assists the goal of purchasing by making the goods available when and where required. It involves coordinating:

(a) the firm's own transport — if goods are to be collected;
(b) the hiring of transport — if a specialist firm is to be used;
(c) the selection of the most suitable movement mode — rail, road, sea or air;
(d) the packaging needed — pallets or special material;
(e) the documentation required — especially if goods are arriving from overseas;
(f) unloading facilities;
(g) initial inspection needs.

6. Logistics and materials management

Materials management involves the control of the internal flow of materials and semi-finished products between the different phases of manufacturing, raw materials stores and despatch department. Materials management coordinates:

(a) material requirement schedules;
(b) work in progress — storage and issued;
(c) management of stockyards and storehouses;
(d) internal material handling;
(e) the physical performance of just-in-time needs;
(f) the marshalling of finished goods for dispatch.

7. Logistics and physical distribution management

The physical distribution system is involved in the packaging and movement of finished goods to the customer or final user. It supports the marketing objective of customer service. They make the final product available when required, in the correct quantities and by the selection of suitable channels where appropriate. It involves coordinating:

(a) packaging;
(b) channel selection — retailer, wholesaler or straight to end user;
(c) transport — own or third party;
(d) mode selection — rail, road, sea or air;
(e) vehicle and route scheduling;
(f) unit load decisions — containers or pallets.

8. Advantages of integrated logistics

The objectives of an integrated logistic system is to minimize the operating costs of the physical materials system and to maximize customer service levels. This is achieved by analysing the cost and efficiency structures of the different sub-functions involved in logistics (physical procurement, materials management and distribution) and by trading off their respective benefits and costs, logistics can maximize total organizational effectiveness.

Benefits of total materials management should include:

(a) Improvements in:
  (*i*)   service levels to customer;
  (*ii*) company competitiveness;
  (*iii*) company image;
  (*iv*) standardization of procedures;
  (*v*)   company communications both internally and externally;
  (*vi*) less departmental empire building;
  (*vii*) allocation of responsibility where functional overlap occurs.
(b) Reductions of costs by:
  (*i*)   joint stock control of raw materials and finished goods;
  (*ii*) reduction in lead times and buffer stocks;
  (*iii*) implementation of the principles of just-in-time;
  (*iv*) improved warehouse utilization;
  (*v*)   more accurate forecasts by working from a customer demand-pull system;
  (*vi*) improved transport management.

9. Resistance to logistics management

The main problem faced by potential logistics managers is that of resistance by associated departments. Purchasing, stores, production control and transport can feel that their relative positions and status will be undermined by the formation of a logistics management system (*see* Figs. 2.1 and 2.2). This problem has to be overcome by close communication and participation, and with the education of these vital managers to ensure that they appreciate the cooperative nature of successful logistical systems.

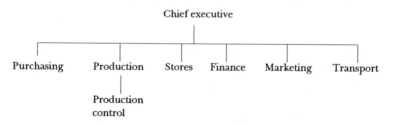

Figure 2.1 *Organizational chart (without logistical management system)*

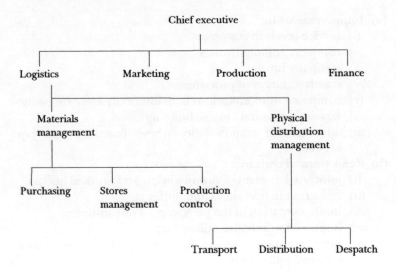

Figure 2.2   *Organizational chart (with logistical management system)*

10. Organizational comparisons

In organizations where a system of logistical materials management is employed, materials requirements will be reacted to in a prompt and coordinated manner. For example, in a manufacturing concern a large order arrives unexpectedly from overseas. In the organization with logistics management, the manager would call a meeting of representatives from purchasing, stores, production control and transport. This group will discuss the problems of meeting the order and coordinate their joint efforts towards fulfilling the order. The non-logistics management company would not be able to react in this coordinated manner. There will be a number of lateral lines of communication which could lead to hold-ups, stock-out and general delay in fulfilling the order.

Table 2.1 *Logistical integration of the supply and distribution chain*

Activity	Physical procurement	Materials management	Physical distribution
Sub-activities: Physical flow of materials	Inspection at suppliers' plant Transportation in Loading	Unloading Inspection procedures Storage Issue Internal transfer to production line to work in progress to finished goods store	Finished goods to despatch Packaging Transportation Route scheduling Load scheduling Distribution network Regional warehouse Distribution channels
	Materials handling inventory control	Materials handling inventory and production control	Materials handling inventory and sales order processing
Department integration	Purchasing Transport Finance	Quality control Stores and stockyard management Production	Despatch Transport Marketing

Documentation and information flow

Progress test 2

1. What activities are coordinated by materials management? **(6)**

2. List the main advantages of a system of integrated logistics. **(8)**

3. What activities are performed by the physical distribution section? **(6)**

4. What activities are co-ordinated by the physical distribution management? **(7)**

5. Outline the main causes of resistance to the introduction of a logistics department. **(9)**

3
Appreciation of materials management

The philosophy of materials management

1. Introduction

Materials management has a philosophy close to that of modern marketing. The marketing concept involves all aspects of marketing, i.e. market research, advertising, sales, etc. Likewise the materials management concept involves production planning, stores, purchasing and transport. In marketing the organization and all its staff have to think in a marketing-oriented way. For example: how will the customer react to this product change? What will be the effect on sales if we alter the packaging? With materials management the same principles apply. The organization and all its staff have to consider their decisions in relation to how they will affect the materials side of the business.

2. Definitions

The Chartered Institute of Purchasing and Supply defines materials management as 'the total of all those tasks, functions, activities and routines which concern the transfer of external materials and service into the organization and the administration of the same until they are consumed or used in the process of production, operations or sales.'

A simpler definition of materials management could be 'the line of responsibility which begins with the selection of suppliers and ends when the material is delivered to its point of use.' Dean Ammer, *Harvard Business Review* (1969).

Materials management is a concept which brings together under one manager the responsibility for determining the manufacturing requirements, scheduling the manufacturing process, and procuring, storing and dispersing materials. As such it is concerned with, and controls, activities involved in the acquisition and use of all materials employed in the production of a finished good.

Materials management organization

3.   Four major types
A *Harvard Business Review* survey revealed four major types of materials management organizations:

(a) *Integrated structure.* This shows the classical integrated materials management structure which accounted for 31 per cent of the companies in which a materials manager is said to exist (*see* Fig. 3.1).

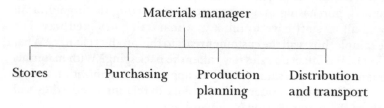

Figure 3.1   *Integrated structure*

(b) *Distribution orientated.* These are partially integrated organizations in which the distribution and traffic function, the production planning and inventory control function report together. Companies with such structures, which accounted for 23 per cent of the companies with materials managers, tended to integrate those materials functions that were closer to markets than to sources of supply in integration.

(c) *Supply orientated.* These are partially integrated organizations in which the purchasing function and the production planning and inventory control functions report together. In such companies the two materials functions that report to the same manager are closer to the supply end of the materials pipeline.

This type of materials management organization accounted

for 18 per cent of the cases in which the materials manager or the equivalent existed.

(d) *Manufacturing oriented.* This type of structure is organized around manufacturing which is in the middle of the materials flow. It accounted for 28 per cent of the materials managers in the *Harvard Business Review* survey.

4. Functions of materials management

Materials management works with all departments, the main objective being to provide the right materials to the right operating point at the right time in a usable condition and at the minimum cost. The basic functions of materials management are as follows:

(a) *Production and materials planning.* To ensure efficient use of personnel, materials facilities and capacity. This also covers assistance in both long- and short-term planning with control over the materials used and issued.

(b) *Materials handling.* With the responsibility for accepting, handling and physically moving materials to production.

(c) *Procurement of goods.* At the right time, the right quality and quantity and, of course, the right price, taking into account storage, delivery, handling costs and the maintenance of supplier relations.

(d) *Distribution.* Covering receipts, storage, despatch of packed finished goods and registration of all transactions.

(e) *Control of material cost.* Where costs arise materials management must organize reduction programmes for planning, stocks, purchasing, materials handling as well as providing an effective means of monitoring the effects of the programmes.

(f) *Communication.* To ensure a well balanced and efficient communication system between the various activities.

The main point of materials management is to satisfy the needs of all operating systems, such as the manufacturing production line, the need arising from customer demand patterns, promotional activities and physical distribution schedules. It is the operating system that the materials manager views as the customer. The manager must work around the system until everything fits and needs are satisfied.

Materials flow and control (integration)

5. Integration

Materials management contains the means for integrated control of the materials flow, the purposes of which are:

(a) to have materials available as and when required so that an even flow of work is maintained in production without excessive inventories;

(b) to optimize the input of materials according to potential sales and capacity of the manufacturing plant;

(c) to ensure that the maximum value is obtained per unit of expenditure.

To be successful the means chosen for realizing these targets must give consideration to the basic questions regarding materials and to the tasks for initiating and maintaining the materials flow.

Basic considerations in relation to materials control

The tasks associated with materials management are concerned with careful and deliberate planning and the evaluation of results. This control must be based on a clear understanding of the problems associated with the materials flow of a particular organization, for example the product complexity, the number of technical modifications and the reliability of suppliers.

6. What is required?

The kinds of materials needed are determined by identifying gross requirements from production plans, or from analysis of past materials usage which can be used for forecasting future usage rates.

7. When is it required?

This is calculated by checking which items required are already in stock or have been ordered and by calculating when the remaining requirements must be ordered to meet production schedules.

8. **How much is required?**
   This will depend on stock ordering levels.

Advantages of a materials management approach

9. **Advantages**
   The adoption of a materials management approach by the organization will generate a number of significantly valuable advantages in terms of total organizational control and materials control. The advantages are as follows:

(a) *Identification of costs* of material flow through the organization, enabling the materials manager to pinpoint rising cost areas and to take appropriate action.

(b) *A database* of materials related information which management can use to assist in all decision-making activities related to materials.

(c) *Improved total control* of the organization, thus enabling a quick response to environmental and organizational change.

(d) *Encourages and promotes* interdepartmental cooperation and coordination, i.e. production control working closely with stores (*see* 19:**14**) in its planning activities.

(e) *The appointment of a senior manager* responsible for all aspects of materials management will pinpoint total responsibility for the materials part of the business. The materials manager will be a link between the material and non-material based parts of the organization. Within a logistics organization the manager would report directly to the logistics manager.

(f) *Improved stock control* and stock turnover. The materials management system enables stocks to be reduced due to improved control and interdepartmental cooperation.

(g) *Reduced transport costs.* The close coordination between the materials based departments allows efficient use of transport services.

(h) *Improved quality of staff.* Given that the materials manager will promote team based working and will offer greater promotion and staff development opportunities, the company will attract a higher calibre of staff.

(i) *Reduced materials obsolescence.* The overall control system achieved with materials management will reduce stock obsolescence and thus reduce total material costs.

(j) *Improved quality control.* The ability to impose standards is facilitated by a common materials management policy in relation to quality control.

The advantages of materials management can be measured. It may result in less capital being tied up in stocks but usually it is not that simple. In most cases the advantages can only be seen in the long run, in the form of shorter throughput times, fewer production stoppages because of missing or bad quality materials, better customer service and a closer working environment. Departments will consult with one another in an atmosphere of trust and support, with a common will to accomplish the total materials job.

Scope of materials management

10. Departments involved in materials management

Dean Ammer states that 'there is no general agreement about precisely what activities are embraced by materials management' (*Harvard Business Review*, 1969). In view of this statement the way to proceed is with a typical materials management system, common to a number of manufacturing organizations. This is not to preclude the variations found in other organizations, but merely to act as an illustration (*see* 3).

In a modern materials management system there are four key integrated areas:

(a) Stores management
(b) Materials planning and control
(c) Purchasing
(d) Production.

Each of these aspects is covered in detail in each chapter and in the book as a whole. A matrix to indicate the contribution of each of these four basic functions is shown in Table 3.1.

Table 3.1 *Material-related functions*

Activities (examples)	Production	Stores management	Purchasing	Materials control
Ordering			X	
Materials handling		X		X
Storage		X		
Production planning	X			
Depot stocks		X		X
Stock control				X
Supplies selection			X	
Negotiations			X	
Corporate planning	X	X	X	X
Standardization		X	X	X
Stock obsolescence		X		X
Marshalling				X
Loading		X		
Security		X		
Stock records		X		X
Warehousing		X		
Supplier relations			X	
Batch control	X			
Fulfilling orders	X			

Progress test 3

1. What are the main functions of a Materials Management Department? **(4)**

2. List three main definitions of 'logistics'. **(2)**

3. Present a diagram to indicate the logistical integration of the supply and distribution chain. **(Table 2.1)**

4. What is a materials management philosophy? **(1)**

Case study no. 1:

Dadds Engineering

Dadds Engineering is a large manufacturing company involved in the production of a range of water pumps for the motor vehicle industry. The company sells direct to several large car manufacturers and also distributes via accessories shops and main dealers throughout the UK. The company has been in business for over 25 years. The founder, Fred Dadds, left the business to his only son ten years ago.

In the past five years the company has grown considerably and profits have increased steadily. Turnover continued to rise during this period and overall the company was doing well.

Peter Dadds took the role of Managing Director from his father ten years ago. The structure of the organization has changed very little over the past years. Peter feels that a successful formula should not be altered. In recent times, however, problems have arisen within the organization that have caused great concern to the management of the company.

A large and very profitable contract to supply the Kuwait Ministry of Defence with water pumps for all its military vehicles was won by the company. The Marketing Director was able to negotiate a deal with the Kuwaitis, but only by promising delivery within three months. He felt sure that the company could produce the goods on time. In point of fact the order was not supplied on time. A vital component within the pump that was provided by an outside supplier was not in stock and a delivery time of nine weeks held up the final production date by several weeks. The contract was supplied, but the Kuwait government were not impressed with Dadds Engineering.

Another major crisis that faced the company was that of obsolete stocks. Due to a recent change in EC regulations regarding the electrical insulation used in the manufacture of vehicle pumps, stocks of the cable previously used had to be scrapped. The Production Manager had been aware of the impending alteration for some months, and he was very surprised therefore to find that the buyer had in fact recently ordered three months' stock of the soon to be obsolete cable. The value of this stock ran into thousands of pounds. It also meant that stocks of the new cable were not on order and this would delay production by several weeks.

The Stores Manager, Mr Catchpole, has recently sent a memo to the Managing Director. In it he outlines the following: His staff are constantly being asked for items that he does not have in stock, whereas certain lines of stock have not been requested for months and are taking up valuable space within the storehouse. He goes on to complain that the Marketing Department demand that stocks are built up in the depots for forthcoming promotions, only to find that the finished goods are not ready or that transport does not exist to move them into the depots.

Peter Dadds has become more and more aware of these operational problems, and the overall profitability of the company has begun to suffer because of these inefficiencies. He has decided to call a meeting of the senior managers to discuss these current problems and hopefully to find some solution.

Discussion question

1.   How could a materials management style approach assist this company?

Part two

Components of a materials management system

4
Stores administration

Stores management

1. Definition

The stores in most organizations is an area in which all kinds of materials needed for production, distribution, maintenance, packaging, etc., are stored, received and issued. The stores function is therefore basically concerned with holding stocks. However, stores management covers a great deal more than just these aspects, and includes the following activities:

(a) Holding, controlling and issuing stocks
(b) Control of all storehouse, stockyards and outside storage
(c) Materials handling functions
(d) Quality control activities
(e) Training of stores staff
(f) Clerical administration of stores operations.

2. Types of materials held in stock

The following is a generalized list of typical items to be found in a medium-sized productive operation:

(a) Raw materials
(b) Component parts
(c) Packaging
(d) Spare parts
(e) Tools, gauges, jigs
(f) Work in progress
(g) Finished stocks
(h) Maintenance materials.

However, the range, value and complexity of items held by

any particular stores will depend upon the size and complexity of the operations involved. Different types of organizations have different types of items in stock. For example, a *production* operation will have raw materials, component parts, work in progress and packaging and associated materials. A *distribution* operation will have finished stock, component parts and part-completed work. An engineering and maintenance operation will have spare parts, tools, equipment, and cleaning and servicing materials.

Because of this wide variation in the kind of items that can be found in any stores, the storekeeper needs to have a wide working knowledge of a great number of material types and operations.

3. Basic functions of stores

The modern stores has a wide variety of functions that it has to perform as efficiently as possible. The way in which stores management carries out these tasks will be reflected in the overall efficiency of the organization. These functions include the following:

(a) To store and supply all the materials and related services to ensure continuation of the operation;

(b) To store, control and issue all work in progress and part-completed items;

(c) To store, control and issue all tools, equipment and spare parts needed by the operation of the organization;

(d) To receive, store, control and salvage all scrap and excess materials produced by the organization;

(e) To ensure that adequate health and safety precautions are taken in relation to the whole stores operation, in conjunction with the safety officer;

(f) To control (in cooperation with the training department) all training and staff development within the stores area.

Relationship between stores and other major departments

4. The concept of service in relation to stores operations

The stores, by virtue of its function, must be seen as providing a service to the rest of the organization in which it operates. The standard of that service will affect the overall efficiency of the organization. The relationships between stores and the other major departments within the organization are therefore very important. Although stores is providing the service, it needs a certain amount of participation and information from other major departments to ensure that the service provided is efficient and meets the needs of the organization in every sense.

The need and duties of the other departments in relation to stores are discussed below.

5. Production

As this is obviously one of the most important users of the stores service, stores management has to ensure that all materials needed for the continuation of production are available as and when required.

Production management's part in this relationship is to ensure that adequate warning is given to stores about the need for materials, together with information about the type and quality required, future demands and also the performance of the materials issued.

6. Distribution

The relationship here is very important when stores management has control of finished stocks, which have to be distributed to depots and warehouses throughout the organization's distribution network. Stores management has to ensure that adequate stocks are available in correct quantities and marshalled ready for loading on to the method of transport employed.

Distribution is responsible for supplying stores management with up-to-date information about the needs and wants of the distribution system and it must make every effort to give stores management adequate notice of loading quantities, destinations, types and marshalling points, to ensure an efficient service from the stores system (*see* 24:1).

7. Engineering and maintenance department

The engineers are responsible for ensuring that the plant and machinery operated by the organization is kept in working order and is performing at its designed efficiency. Stores management has to ensure that all the necessary spare parts, tools and equipment are in stock or easily available from suppliers' stock. The engineering department will often work to an engineering schedule (a timetable of engineering activities covering two or three months). A copy of this schedule must be given to the stores manager so that stocks can be checked and items bought in that will be needed during the time period covered by the schedule. This will ensure that the items required by the engineers will be available as and when they are required, thus avoiding the situation of stripped down machines being left for weeks awaiting spare parts.

8.   Quality control and inspection

Quality control is the department which is responsible for administering the standards (*see* 8:6) set by the organization in relation to all the materials both used and produced by the organization. Inspection is a very important part of the process. Stores management has to ensure that all deliveries of goods are held aside until checked and passed by quality control, and must set up a system for informing quality control that items have been delivered. All items checked and subsequently rejected have to be held by stores. During this period, stores has to ensure that the stock labelled 'for rejection' is not allowed to become part of the acceptable working stock. Problems of rejected stock being used in production can be very costly in terms of loss of output and reputation.

9.   Purchasing department

The links between the stores and purchasing in terms of their activities has always been very close. In many cases these two departments are united under the heading of 'materials management'. Where two separate operations do exist, the relationship between them is vital. Purchasing is responsible for buying all the goods and services needed by the organization. Purchasing relies on stores for a wide variety of supportive activities. Purchasing needs stores to keep it informed about the levels of stocks at any given time, and it is up to stores to keep purchasing up to date as to the total stock situation. This will enable purchasing to ensure the stocks are procured and that a balanced and economic flow of goods and services is provided.

Purchasing, because of its physical separation from the stores area and the factory floor (many purchasing offices are not actually on the production site), relies on stores for up-to-date and accurate information, based on factory and user feedback to the storekeeper, about the performance of goods and services it is providing. This information about the performance of stock can be very important in ensuring maximum efficiency of the purchasing operation and its evaluation of the materials purchased.

Stores must also remember that it is the purchasing department which is responsible for the buying of goods and materials and all that it involves, so stores must resist the temptation to become directly involved with suppliers, unless directed by the purchasing department. It can cause problems if stores management makes decisions regarding the delivery, quality, progressing and selection of goods without the full background information that the purchasing department will have. The organization that employs the 'materials management' approach to its stores and purchasing operation will tend to suffer less from this kind of problem.

10. Sales department
The relationship between stores and sales is a very important one. Stores is responsible for ensuring that all stocks held for sale are stored, issued and controlled as efficiently as possible. The sales staff will often rely on stores to ensure that finished stock is available as and when required; they will also require stores to ensure that marshalling of stock is carried out and that the process of stocking up in relation to sales promotions and other marketing activities is carried out effectively. Stores may also be responsible for the control of spare parts and accessories used in connection with the finished product, which have to be supplied as and when required by the sales department. Stores management must also be aware of the forecasts of future sales, so as to be able to make plans in terms of stock levels, storage space, outside warehousing and staff levels.

11. Maintenance department

Stores has to ensure that all the materials, tools, spare parts and equipment needed by the maintenance department are in stock as and when required. This will include the general maintenance items, e.g. cleaning materials, paints, carpentry tools, etc., as well as the more specialized items used in ventilation systems, heating systems and other elements of the operation. To ensure that these items are in stock, stores must be aware of all the long- and short-term maintenance plans, as produced by the maintenance department. In some cases, specialized materials will have to be ordered in advance of need and stores management will therefore need to have a complete knowledge of all plans, dates, requirements and possible consequences of maintenance.

12. General accounts department

The relationship between stores and accounts covers several very important areas. Accounts relies on stores for information concerning the value of the stock held, and about items damaged and therefore to be written off the asset list. The accounts department will often ask stores to confirm the receipt of goods as invoiced, especially in the case of doubt or query. Stores also provides a continuous supply of data regarding the use of stock in the operations and therefore aids the accounts department in its function of cost allocation to particular batches or jobs as carried out by the operation function.

Duties and responsibilities of stores management

13. Introduction

There is a very wide range of duties and responsibilities that stores management has to perform at various times and stages of the storehouse operation. All are very important to the overall efficiency of the organization and its objectives.

14. Economy

One of the basic duties of stores is to ensure that all operations within the stores system are performed as efficiently and as economically as possible. The concept of economic levels of stock is part of this responsibility (*see* 15:1). This duty to ensure minimum costs should be clear to every member of the stores team.

15. Receipt of stock

It is the duty of the storekeeper to receive and handle all the items delivered to the store, to check the documentation (delivery notes, packing notes, etc.), and to inform purchasing management of all goods received.

16. Inspection

It is the duty of stores to inspect and check all the deliveries made to the store. These checks include such factors as quantity, type, quality, damage and shortage. In many cases suppliers will not accept responsibility for damaged goods unless they are reported within a specified number of days of delivery. Information arising from such inspections has to be passed on to purchasing.

17. Storage of stock

It is one of the basic duties of stores to unload and store all the goods delivered to the store. Storage of materials entails the correct locations of goods in connection with suppliers' instructions and requires skill and knowledge on the part of stores staff, bearing in mind that some materials need particular conditions of storage, e.g. must be kept dry, etc. It is the duty of stores to ensure that goods do not suffer damage or deterioration because of inefficient storage.

18. Identification and location of stock

It is the responsibility of stores management to formulate and update a system of stores coding, so as to follow efficient identification and location of all goods and services held within the stores operation. It is also the duty of stores to ensure that, if the item required is not available, then a suitable and authorized alternative is recommended (where it exists).

19. Security of stores

It is the duty of stores management to ensure that security is maintained at all times within the stores buildings and stockyards. The security element of the store manager's job covers not only theft, but also damage, fire and spillage. It also includes ensuring that all doors, windows and stockyard fencing are secure.

20. Stocktaking and checking

The stores manager is responsible for organizing, supervising and collating all stock checks carried out by the organization. He will be required to formulate counting sheets, allocate staff, check results, investigate discrepancies and produce final figures for use in the final accounts.

21. Issue and despatch

It is the duty of stores to ensure that the goods and services required for operation are issued as and when required, bearing in mind the need for proper authorization and strict clerical control of all issues of stock. The issue process should be smooth and efficient. It is often the issue of stock procedure that determines the status of stores throughout the whole organization.

22. Stock control

It is the responsibility of stores management to ensure that the process of stock control is performed within the stores section. The stores manager must ensure that the basic aims of stock control (*see* 15:20) are achieved. Stores must analyse the information concerning production, sales and distribution needed to maintain the stock control system.

23. Stock records

It is the responsibility of stores management to ensure that adequate and up-to-date stock records are maintained for every item held in stock, whether on site or in a depot or warehouse. These records must provide the kind of information required to control and maintain the levels of stock established, i.e. level of stock, order levels, code number, suppliers' reference, etc.

24. Materials handling

One of the basic jobs of any stores team is the handling of all materials, quickly and safely. Moving goods from the store to the factory or warehouse is a very important duty of the stores manager and his staff.

Progress test 4

1. What are the basic functions of the stores? **(3)**

2. List the types of materials held in a typical industrial stores. **(2)**

3. Outline the nature of the relationship between stores and distribution. **(6)**

4. Outline the nature of the relationship between stores and purchasing. **(9)**

5. What are the main duties and responsibilities of the stores department? **(13–24)**

5
Physical aspects of stores management: stockyards

1. Definition

Stockyards are usually open storage areas used for the storing of various non-perishable goods, that is, materials that will not deteriorate or perish when exposed to the elements over long periods of time.

2. Types of materials suitable for stockyard storage

Because of the exposed nature of a stockyard, it obviously provides excellent storage for materials that are destined to spend their working lives in open or exposed conditions (e.g. concrete paving stones, sand, shingle, etc.). However, it also provides storage for other materials as follows:

(a) *Stoneware*, e.g. concrete slabs, paving stones, bricks, construction materials.

(b) *Heavy iron and steel casting*, e.g. drains, piping, bridge units, lamp posts.

(c) *Heavy duty electrical cable*, e.g. of the type used to carry high voltage electricity in underground conditions.

(d) *Outdoor machinery*, e.g. tractors, cars, lorries, drilling equipment, cranes, etc.

(e) *Scrap and waste materials*, e.g. filings, turnings, obsolescent stocks, chemical waste and by-products.

(f) *Coal, cokes and other fuels*, e.g. stored in drums.

Location and construction

3. Location

Stockyards are usually set aside from the rest of the stores installations and connected by a link road. In some cases stockyards are some distance from the main store and may be part of the organization's distribution system, acting as a constant source of stock to outlets within the area. Smaller unit stores may also have a small stockyard within their boundaries.

4. Factors affecting location

The decisions relating to the location of stockyards have to be taken by senior management, with specialist advice from stores management. There are a number of factors that will influence the location decision.

(a) *Cost of land* in the immediate area or surrounding districts. This will affect whether or not the stockyard is set up close to the present store or, in the case of high local land prices, at a site some distance away.

(b) *Space available* within the precincts of the organization itself. If space is not available and cannot be purchased or developed, then the yard will have to be set up some distance away.

(c) *Transport connections* between the main store and the stockyard. These have to be adequate for the amount of stock movement involved. Depending on the requirements of the organization or, indeed, its suppliers, a stockyard may need to be near a major transport link.

(d) *The size and construction* of the stockyard. The larger the stockyard the more likely it is to be set up out of the inner city area.

(e) *The type and character of the materials* to be stored. For example, highly dangerous materials would have to be stored away from the rest of the organization's installations and would also have to be away from centres of population in case of accidents.

5. Construction of stockyards

One of the main advantages of a stockyard is low expenditure and running costs in return for a large storage capacity. One of the reasons for this cost is that construction is so inexpensive. A stockyard only requires a sound base, secure fencing and good strong gates, unlike complex stores buildings which require foundations, walls, roofing, ventilation, heating, etc.

6. Methods of stockyard construction

There are basically four methods of constructing the base of a stockyard. The advantages and disadvantages of each are discussed in **7–10** below. Which method is used will determine both the cost of construction and the type of material that can be stored.

7.   Simple fencing-off of waste land

This is the cheapest form of stockyard, needing no outlay for a base. Of course, it limits the yard to the storage of only scrap or obsolete materials and will also restrict the pallet loads, owing to the sinking of materials-handling equipment when dealing with heavy loads on unsupported surfaces.

(a) *Advantages:*
  (*i*)   Very cheap to construct.
  (*ii*) No maintenance required.
  (*iii*) Can be easily removed in the future and set up in another location.

(b) *Disadvantages:*
  (*i*)   Very limited in the type of materials that can be stored.
  (*ii*) Equipment will quickly become bogged down in adverse weather conditions.
  (*iii*) Difficult to manage and locate stock.

8.   Gravel surfaces

These are very popular with many organizations especially for storing low value stock in large quantities when limited resources are available. The gravel surface will support a certain amount of weight.

(a) *Advantages:*
  (*i*)   Still quite cheap to lay down.
  (*ii*) Can be relocated reasonably easily.

(b) *Disadvantages:*
  (*i*)   Will still not support heavily laden equipment and pallets.
  (*ii*) Tends to become waterlogged in bad weather conditions.

9.   Tarmac surface

This is by far the most popular form employed for stockyards. The tarmac surface is very strong and will support quite heavy loads in all weather conditions. Many firms employ tarmac as a permanent stockyard base.

(a) *Advantages:*
  (*i*) Excellent storage.
  (*ii*) Easily laid out and marked for a location system (*see* **18**).
  (*iii*) Easily maintained and repaired.
(b) *Disadvantages:*
  (*i*) Quite expensive when compared with methods **7** and **8**.
  (*ii*) Subject to damage, especially in very hot weather, with heavy loads causing indentations and holes in the surface.

10. Concrete surface

This is by far the most stable and strong of all the methods described. It is able to deal with the heaviest loads and will be operable regardless of the weather conditions. Concrete is often used where very heavy loads are to be stored and heavy materials-handling equipment will be employed (e.g. heavy cables, construction equipment, plant).

(a) *Advantages:*
  (*i*) Able to cope with materials in terms of weight placement.
  (*ii*) Easily laid out and marked for efficient location and selection.
  (*iii*) Usable all the year round.
(b) *Disadvantages:*
  (*i*) Very expensive compared with the other methods listed.
  (*ii*) A very permanent structure that would be most expensive to pull up and rebuild.

Benefits and problems

11. Advantages of stockyards as a means of storage

Stockyards have various advantages as storage areas of certain materials. Most of the benefits relate to the cost of both construction and operation.

(a) *Relatively inexpensive* to set up and surface, compared with the cost of building a new storehouse of similar capacity.
(b) *Ideal for storing non-perishables* and unusually bulky and heavy materials or equipment, at a very low cost per unit stored.
(c) *Ability to use heavy handling equipment,* e.g. diesel-powered (*see*

Fig. 18.6), without the problems of ventilation associated with such equipment within the storehouse.

(d) *Low energy consumption* in terms of lighting (only used in the evenings or winter period) and heating, which is not required apart from the stockyard office and other internal installations within the stockyard area.

(e) *Low maintenance costs* in terms of repairs and replacement of fittings compared with those of the storehouse.

12. Operational and organizational problems

Stockyards also have a variety of problems and faults associated with them. The basic problem, from which all the subsequent problems arise, is the lack of stores management involvement in the setting up and running of the stockyard. Because the stockyard tends to be divorced from the stores building and is an open-air operation, the basic stores crafts of neatness and careful planning tend to be forgotten.

The following are some of the faults of a typical stockyard:

(a) *The incorrect surface* for the type of materials being stored and handled. It is a false economy to surface with gravel and expect the stockyard to cope with heavy loads in all conditions.

(b) *Inadequate security* in terms of fencing and alarm systems allowing easy access by 'unauthorized persons' into the storage area. It is a false economy to spend large amounts of money on a sound fencing system only to neglect holes and breaks which appear subsequently in the fence.

(c) *Waterlogged surfaces* owing to the lack of good drainage facilities and designs. This will make working in the stockyard more difficult and more dangerous, especially in the winter when surface water can turn to ice. In addition, it should be noted that deterioration of even highly resistant materials can be increased by constant contact with water.

(d) *Inadequate or non-existent artificial illumination system* in terms of floodlights or spotlights for use in the hours of bad light or darkness. This is especially important where materials are handled at all times during the 24-hour period and at all times of the year. Good lighting makes accurate selection of materials possible and will help to reduce the accident rate.

(e) *Inadequate links* between the stockyard and the main

transportation medium employed. In most cases this entails a link to the main road. Many organizations make the mistake of providing resources for an excellent stockyard but failing to ensure that links with the main transport method are adequate. The result is that the stockyard can become isolated from the rest of the storage system in adverse weather conditions or when heavy vehicles become stuck.

(f) *A complete lack of logical and efficient location and marking system* within the stockyard. Many stockyards are used as a dumping area for all types of materials, and the tendency is therefore for goods to be stored without any thought to frequency of usage or utilization of space.

(g) *Inefficient and neglected stockyard control centres* such as the gatehouse, which should be centres for documentation, control and location plans, leading to loss of control over the storage and selection of stock. Such neglect arises from the general lack of supervisory control from which stockyards tend to suffer.

(h) *Rotation codes tend to be ignored* because of lack of control and the difficulty of correct selection in a badly laid-out yard.

Layout and organization

13. Introduction

To enable the stockyard to operate efficiently and effectively a logical and workable yard design must be designed and implemented. Some of the factors to be considered are discussed in **14–18** below.

14. Frequency of usage

Materials to be stored must first be classified in relation to the frequency of usage. The materials are usually grouped into three logical sections:

(a) high usage rate;
(b) medium usage rate;
(c) low usage rate.

The principle is that materials that are constantly being issued and delivered to the stockyard should be placed near the entrance/exit, thus reducing the handling times of these high usage materials and minimizing travelling time. The logic is followed through in relation to the other categories, i.e. medium and slow moving materials being progressively further from the point of entry (*see* Fig. 5.1).

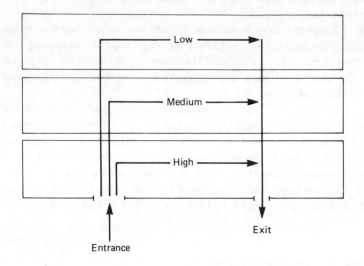

Figure 5.1 *Stockyard layout*

15. Allocation of adequate gangway

It is vital that every section of the stockyard should be totally accessible for the handling equipment employed by the stores. To enable this requirement to be met, a complex system of gangways must be devised. The gangways must fulfil the following requirements:

(a) Width must be sufficient to allow easy movement of handling equipment safely and quickly.

(b) A one-way direction system must be introduced along these gangways to prevent accidents and blocked gangways that could be caused by a two-way system.

(c) Care must be taken to ensure that gangways are not duplicated (i.e. two or three going to the same location) as this would be a waste of expensive storage space.

16. Entrances and exits

These must be so located as to ensure a one-way traffic flow system, thus reducing delays and hold-ups. In many large stockyards the entrance and exit gates are side by side and the control centre or gatehouse is situated between them, enabling materials to be recorded on delivery and issue. The gates at the entrance and exit must be secure, lockable and wide, and in some cases high enough to allow the largest vehicle employed to pass through.

17. Control centre (gatehouse)

This must be in a position of central control, able to exercise a degree of observation over the main areas of activity within the stockyard. The control centre must have a number of resources at its disposal to ensure that it will be able to perform the functions of controlling and recording the movement of stock in relation to the stockyard. The following are the resources required by control centres:

(a) *Telephone link* with the main stores installations and offices (i.e. stock control, stock records, materials handling, etc.).
(b) *Adequate filing equipment* for the documentation involved in delivery and issue of stock.
(c) *Basic office equipment* and stationery (i.e. typewriter, pens, booking forms, etc.).
(d) *Trained and responsible staff* to man and control the control centre.

18. Location systems

To ensure that stock can be stored in and selected from the stockyard as quickly and efficiently as possible, a logical and workable stock location system is required. The location system will ensure that the stockyard controller is able to locate any item in the stockyard at any time and therefore direct the materials handling resources in the correct direction. A master copy of the store location plan should be kept in the control centre, usually on a large board-type visual aid, which can be easily referred to and employed.

19. Equipment required by the stockyard

The typical industrial stockyard needs a certain amount of basic equipment to ensure efficient operation. Obviously the type and amount of equipment required will depend upon the size of the yard and the materials being handled. However, the following are some items of equipment which can in general be considered essential:

(a) *Mechanical handling devices.* There are usually fork-lift trucks or pallet trucks and these are used mainly within the stockyard itself for storage and issue of stock in bulk (*see* 18:4 & 5).

(b) *Manual handling equipment.* There will always be a need for small hand-operated handling devices (e.g. pumps and trucks) for the marshalling of small loads and orders and for use when mechanical devices are not working (*see* 18:6–19).

(c) *Security equipment.* This includes locks and chains as well as the keys to basic electrical alarm systems.

(d) *Fire-fighting equipment.* This usually takes the form of extinguishers, fire blankets, hose reels, etc., and the organization's fire instructions and details as to how to deal with the kind of fires the materials stocked could produce (e.g. petrol, chemicals, scrap, etc.).

(e) *Racking equipment* for pallets.

Stockyard management

20. The stockyard's role within the overall distribution system

By distribution we mean the process of getting the products of the organization from the place of production to the point of consumption. Stockyards which are used to hold the organization's finished product have a vital role to play in the distribution system in the following ways:

(a) Stockyards can be used as a 'topping-up' centre, where goods are stored in bulk from the place of production and distributed to customers in the local area.

(b) Emergency stocks of goods are often held in small stockyards up and down the distribution network to be used in the event of sudden high demand or in emergencies such as adverse weather conditions, which make movement over long distances impossible.

(c) Stockyards can be used as a marshalling area where goods are collected from various parts of the organization's productive system, sorted into customers' requirements and despatched to centres of demand.

21. Stockyard integration into the organization's distribution system

For stockyards to play a useful part in the distribution process there has to be integration between the stockyards, storehouses and depots throughout the system. By integration we mean that coding systems, location codes, stores procedures, materials handling equipment, etc., must be uniform. This will ensure that a stockyard will not be managed any differently from a main storehouse or depot, just because of its open construction.

22. Management of stockyard operations

Stockyards need to be carefully and professionally controlled and managed if they are to provide the organization with the full potential storage capacity at the minimum cost per unit. A vast amount of capacity is wasted in many stockyards because of bad or no management. Stockyards, because of their construction, do tend to be left to their own devices as far as stores management is concerned.

To avoid this waste and to ensure full use of resources, the stores manager should consider the following management points in relation to any stockyard:

(a) *Overall placement of pallets, bins, drums, etc.* must be neat and logical to avoid accidents and wasted space.

(b) *The staff* who are involved in running and supervising the stockyard must not be isolated from the rest of the stores staff, as often happens. Such isolation leads to slack control and low morale.

(c) *Management involvement* and resources must be provided to ensure adequate overall control of the stock and operation and also to ensure full integration into the supply management system as a whole.

(d) *Up-to-date and well-maintained equipment* is vital if the stockyard is to operate efficiently.

(e) *Security systems* provided to protect the main stores and other installations must be extended to cover the stockyard as well.

(f) *A sound and logical stock location system* is vital to the efficient operation of the stockyard.

(g) *Supervision of all deliveries and issues* of stock is vital if control of storage is to be established and 'dumping' of materials prevented. This can only be achieved by a policy of constant manning of the stockyard and control centre, with management backing.

23. Stockyards and the cost of storage

There can be no doubt that for certain types of materials the stockyard provides very inexpensive and efficient storage, provided that the basic principles outlined in this chapter are followed. If they are not, stockyards can become very inefficient and costly in several ways.

(a) Accidents will be of a high frequency in badly organized stockyards and could cost a great deal in terms of lost man-hours.

(b) In badly laid-out and disorganized stockyards, there is a tendency for certain types of stock to become isolated behind large and heavy units, thus entailing the need for manual labour to locate and issue some stocks.

Progress test 5

1. What factors need to be considered when deciding on the location of a stockyard? **(4)**

2. Outline the main methods of stockyard construction. **(7–10)**

3. What are the advantages of storing certain materials in a stockyard? **(11)**

4. What are the common faults of a stockyard? **(12)**

5. What kinds of materials handling equipment are required by a typical stockyard? **(19)**

6. Describe the role of stockyards in relation to the overall distribution system. **(20)**

Case study no. 2:

Warehouse control system at the British Shoe Corporation

By Paul Docknee, Logical Industry Ltd, February 1992

Reproduced with the kind permission of the Institute of Materials Management

British Shoe, Europe's biggest footwear retailer, is a subsidiary of Sears plc. British Shoe's warehouse at Leicester is the centre of a distribution system supplying stock to some 2,400 high street outlets. These include Freeman, Hardy and Willis, Trueform, Curtess, Dolcis, Saxone, Manfield, Cable and Co., Shoe City, Lilley and Skinner and Olympus Sport.

The Leicester warehouse is one of the largest single storey warehouses in Europe with storage for seven million pairs of shoes. Each week about 1.1 million pairs are delivered from the 850 manufacturers worldwide and a similar number are despatched to the branches in the UK using British Shoe's fleet of 120 lorries (a mix of rigid, articulated, double height and trailer type). The warehouse has to be highly mechanized to handle this turnaround.

There are 11 miles of electronically controlled conveyor systems, a fully automatic sorting system activated by laser scanning beams and round the clock shifts to assure the continuous operation of the warehouse from Sunday evening to midday on Friday.

The key to successful operation of the warehouse is a system developed by the systems house Logica for scheduling, optimizing and controlling the picking operations.

Prior to the installation of the system, the old procedures at the warehouse required manual picking of goods to small roll cages. Picking lists, holding data on what was required by individual branches, were generated by British Shoe's IBM mainframe.

Often branches only required a single pair of particular size, colour and style combination. As the warehouse stocks a large number of styles, picking trips required operatives to walk great distances. When the picking trip was completed, there would be a 100 per cent manual accuracy check performed by someone else. Errors would be keyed into the IBM mainframe system which would then produce correct delivery notes. The disadvantages of the approach were the long distances that had to be covered on foot and the stock that had to be held as individual pairs of shoes.

Key objectives

To counter this, British Shoe's management set three key objectives for the warehouse operation to become more competitive: improve the efficiency of the picking operations, reduce shelving and provide the same level of accuracy at reduced cost.

Some two years were spent by British Shoe's Distribution Development Department investigating and simulating possible solutions. A significant improvement in efficiency of picking was indeed needed. One conclusion was merging the stock requirements for a number of branches. This produces the problem of sorting for branches, which dictates the need for a sorting machine.

The economics of costs justifying the provision of a sorting machine, its maintenance and operatives against the inefficiencies of the old picking operation are complicated. However, computations showed there were some savings and British Shoe opted for the sorter approach.

As the company's IBM mainframe is orientated to data processing applications, it was considered necessary that a warehouse management system should be installed in the warehouse to interface between the IBM host and the sorting control systems. The contract to provide this was awarded to Logica Industry under a competitive tender.

Approach to development testing

Development of the system started in July 1988; it went live in May 1990. From an early stage it was known that any testing involving the sorting machines would be difficult because errors could be introduced from many sources.

With this in mind, Logica developed software to simulate/monitor the interfaces with the IBM mainframe and the sorter control systems. This enabled an acceptance test to be developed, which allowed the full functionality to be tested without connection to the sorters or the IBM system. The approach proved to be very worthwhile. The complexity of the algorithms used in the system and the nature of the data led to a large amount of effort being spent preparing data for test purposes. Special utility programs were written to generate test data.

Performance

From the outset it was known that the applications program had to be written efficiently to meet the performance objectives. With performance in mind, it was necessary to do regular performance tests with realistic quantities of data, the data being provided over a modem link from

British Shoe's mainframe. With only a single Micro VAX to do both testing and development, contention quickly arose. Performance testing had to be scheduled in the evenings.

The greatest challenges were found in programs which generated the picking trips and the sortation plans. These programs needed to execute as fast as possible. The data processed by these programs is dependent on the departure schedule of the lorries. The operations staff therefore prefer to execute the programs as late as possible to pick up any changes to the schedule. The programs typically process 50,000 branch order records each time they execute and are responsible for minimizing the walking distance for picking operatives and for balancing the workloads on the sorters.

The algorithms involved are complex and involve a great deal of sorting. On the first day of live operation, it was pleasing to see the effectiveness of the algorithms. Typical picking trips which, under the old system, would have taken an operative over an hour to complete, were finished in less than half the time. Also, instead of picking individual boxes of shoes, they picked cartons.

Systems operation

Based on a Digital Equipment Micro VAX II computer, the Logica system sits between the IBM 3084/3091 mainframe and two sorter systems. Each sorter consists of a Philips' VME computer controlling a network of 68000-based single board computers (SBCs) which perform the low level control. The sorter software was developed under UNIX in c.

Communications with the IBM host is via a DECnet/SNA gateway using Digital's data transfer facility which provides a high level, high performance interface. Communication with the VME systems is via high speed RS232 links using a protocol specially developed to provide high capacity. Each sorting machine has 23 SBCs controlling operations. There is one SBC for each infeed and one for each bank of destination lanes. There are 112 destination lanes on each sorter.

The IBM mainframe generates the stock requirements for its retail outlets on a daily basis. Up to 224 retail outlets can be fulfilled in a single picking session. The IBM-generated data is transferred to Logica's system which is then responsible for scheduling and controlling the picking operations in the warehouse to meet the departure schedule of the transport department.

The Micro VAX system merges the requirements of the outlets to generate picking notes which minimize the distance walked by the picking operatives according to an algorithm specially prepared by Logica. It is often possible to pick cartons of shoes instead of individual boxes. This provides savings as fewer cartons need to be opened and shelved.

The items picked are transported in picking trolleys to the two sorting machines ready for sortation. The contents of the trolley are unloaded onto infeed conveyors fitted with laser barcode readers, which allows stock to be identified and located in the sortation plan which defines the destination chute to which it is to be sorted. The sortation plan is prepared by the warehouse system simultaneously with the picking notes.

Mispicked stock not required in the sortation plan is sent to special chutes from which it will be reshelved with the aid of a shelving report detailing the location of the stock in the warehouse and the optimum route to walk.

Stock sorted to the destination lanes is loaded on to roll cages and wheeled directly onto the lorries. The final results of the sort are used to generate delivery notes which detail the stock being despatched to the retail outlets. The allocation of picking notes to operatives is recorded on the system and error rate information is gathered, thereby allowing management to monitor the operation's efficiency.

Logica designed the warehouse system with a high resilience to failure. The application implements its own form of disc shadowing for all application data.

The IBM mainframe produces data for 24 hours worth of sorting. If the IBM complex suffers a breakdown, or the link with Micro VAX goes down, the warehouse system can survive for one day, continuing with warehouse operations. If the Micro VAX goes down, sorting can continue for over two hours.

Recovery from a single disc failure is ten minutes. The system will also tolerate power failure and employs check pointing to allow British Shoe to pick up from the point the system stopped. This is handled entirely automatically on start up. A system failure at British Shoe's central warehouse would have a direct impact on its shops and sales. To cover this, 24-hour support is provided during the six days the warehouse works through modems and terminals located at Logica Industry's Leatherhead offices.

System benefits

- More efficient operation through a significant reduction in the distance walked by warehouse staff when collecting stock and in the time and labour required to open cartons and place the contents on shelves.
- Increased company efficiency and improved accuracy in distributing to stock retail outlets.

- Accurate management information for better control of the total operation.
- Automatic checking of stock collected from the shelves at a stage early enough to allow corrective action to take place before the lorry departs.
- Improved utilization of bulk picking trolleys used for transporting stock around the warehouse.

6
Physical aspects of stores management: Stores buildings

1. Importance of stores buildings

Stores buildings are the key to any stores system: they are the basis of all stores operations and activities within the organization. The size and scope of stores buildings will differ between organizations according to the following factors:

(a) Size and complexity of the operation involved.
(b) Resources and capital available for building and conversion.
(c) Siting of existing operations.
(d) Future plans and expectations of the organization.

Because of the importance to the stores and the organization itself, any major decisions regarding the stores buildings must be very carefully and professionally considered by both stores and senior management.

2. Functions of stores buildings

The functions of stores buildings vary according to the needs of individual organizations. The following are some of the more common functions:

(a) A large central store will act as the distribution and collection point for all stock.
(b) Stores buildings will provide storage for all materials including work in progress, finished stock and raw materials.
(c) The stores building often contains the administrative and management resources (i.e. offices, issue counters, delivery bays, etc.) within its area.
(d) Quality control and inspection operations are often performed within the confines of the stores building.
(e) Materials handling equipment is often used and stored within

the stores building. The charging of trucks can take place in designated areas of the store.

Types of building and equipment

3. Single-storey stores buildings

These are probably the most common and are very widely employed. As the name suggests, the store is built on one level, without stairs or upper floors. However, many single-storey stores use mezzanines to provide a degree of upper storage. Single-storey buildings have several basic advantages.

(a) They are relatively cheap to construct and maintain owing to the simple design and the lack of upper floors.

(b) Having everything on one level improves the logistics of materials handling and the natural flow of the materials through the store.

(c) Ventilation and the other basic services (electricity, water, gas; etc.) are easier to install and operate.

(d) The use of the ground floor only enables great weights to be stored, without the problems associated with multi-storey buildings and the weight limitations on upper floors.

The basic disadvantage associated with single-storey stores buildings is that of space. Many organizations operate within a confined area and do not have the ability or the resources to purchase large plots of land for such a development.

4. Multi-storey stores buildings

These are used mainly in areas of high density population where land and resources are not available, or in situations where the organization itself is based on a multi-storey site and the individual floors are served by different sections of the store. The multi-storey stores has the following advantages:

(a) The multi-floor environment enables great flexibility for alternative use of storage space (e.g. offices, production facilities) should the need arise.

(b) Separation of areas of stock by a system of floors can be an aid to security and fire precautions in that an outbreak of fire could be contained on one level without damaging the rest of the stock.

(c) Modern building techniques allow for quite heavy loads to be handled on the upper floors.

(d) Multi-storey buildings are well suited to handling small units of high value (e.g. electronic components) in an inner city area.

The basic disadvantages of a multi-storey store are the high capital outlay on construction and the subsequent costs of running the building.

5. Storage equipment within stores buildings

Obviously, the type of storage equipment employed will depend a great deal upon the construction of the store and the materials being stored and handled. There are several basic approaches to the problem of storage systems.

(a) *Open-plan systems*. This describes a system of no real permanent storage equipment and the storage area is used to store mainly palletized materials. In some cases an organization may employ a system of *pallet-racking* whereby the ability to stack pallets on three or four levels is obtained (*see* Fig. 17.2).

(b) *Shelves and racking*. These are very common indeed, especially in older buildings designed and constructed before the widespread use of mechanical handling devices. Shelves and racking are used to store a large variety of materials and items, from small units to steel piping and tyres, depending entirely upon the products involved.

(c) *Racking*. Racking can be the sole medium of storage if the store is being used to hold large amounts of materials like timber, piping, metal sheets, etc.

(d) *Combined system*. A combination of all these different methods of storage is the most common situation in which stores management finds itself operating. Most organizations have a wide variety of stock and therefore need diverse means of storage.

Purpose-built and converted stores buildings

6. Purpose-built stores installations

The term 'purpose-built' relates to the situation where the organization involved has designed and constructed a stores building bearing in mind its own individual needs and operational requirements. Purpose-built stores are usually associated with the large organizations which have the resources to embark on such a project.

However, smaller organizations can acquire a 'purpose-built' store on the open market, provided it has been designed for basically the same operation as the purchaser's. For example, an organization storing a large amount of heavy palletized materials would require a large open-plan store, whereas the holder of numerous small manufactured units may need a storage area of several storeys and numerous closed and open shelves.

7. Advantages of purpose-built stores installations
The following are some of the operational advantages of purpose-built stores:

(a) Stores management has the opportunity to ensure that the most efficient layout design is produced, in relation to materials handling and storage.
(b) The latest techniques, innovations and stores developments can be incorporated in the basic design requirements. For example, the use of computerized materials handling systems requires the laying down of 'guide tracks'. This kind of work is best carried out during actual construction.
(c) The building will provide the organization with exactly what its needs dictate. There should be no wasted space, and future requirements should be allowed for, thus reducing the problems of expansion in later years.

8. Disadvantages of purpose-built stores installations
These include the following:

(a) *Expense.* Designing and constructing a purpose-built store involves a great deal of time and money.
(b) *Conflicting interests.* These can arise between stores management and other departments (e.g. finance and production).
(c) *Misjudgment.* Any misjudgment about the real needs of the organization could result in a great waste of resources.

9. Converted stores buildings and installations
As organizations develop and expand the need for storage

space and handling facilities expands in proportion. Therefore many organizations find themselves having to convert buildings from some other use to that of stores buildings. These buildings can range from old factories to large residential houses, depending on the size of the operation and the property available. This is a very common situation and one in which many stores managers are forced to operate.

10. Disadvantages of converted stores buildings

The following are some of the disadvantages of using buildings not primarily designed for the purpose of storage:

(a) *Environmental conditions* needed to store the materials may not be correct, so expensive equipment may need to be installed (e.g. for frozen food, damp-free conditions, etc.).

(b) *The materials handling and storage systems* may not be suitable for use within the converted area (e.g. level floors are needed for many electric trucks) and the problem of access via doors and entrances is often a major problem in relation to converted buildings.

(c) *The needs of the organization* will obviously not have been taken into consideration at the original design stage.

(d) *Further expansion* may be restricted by factors outside the control of the organization, e.g. local government planning permission.

11. Advantages of converted stores buildings

These include the following:

(a) They are relatively cheap to acquire, either by outright purchase, or by lease if the organization lacks the capital to buy.

(b) The organization has the option of moving its stock to another location in the future should its demands change.

(c) Careful planning and layout of converted buildings can produce very useful storage facilities.

12. Sources of buildings for conversion

There are many sources from which the stores manager and his organization may be able to secure suitable storage accommodation. These sources will include the following:

(a) *Local authorities* have a great deal of property within the organization's local area.

(b) *Nationalized industries* with local operations, e.g. British Rail or the Post Office, may have property under-utilized and therefore available.

(c) *Private companies* in the area may also have space, or a building that they no longer need and may be willing to lease or sell.

(d) *Central government* may also have property which could be purchased or leased for storage of materials.

Hiring outside warehouse space

13. Reasons for hiring

In some situations the organization may decide to hire its storage needs and not become involved in either building or conversion projects. The motives for hiring warehouse space are as follows:

(a) *Stock level variations* associated with seasonal products which only need storage for a short period of time. Expensive constructed buildings would therefore only be used for a relatively short time.

(b) *Lack of resources* on the part of the organization either to construct or to buy the stores buildings it requires.

(c) *Temporary changes in demand* causing a drop in sales and an increase in stocks, beyond the normal capacity of the organization's own stores buildings.

(d) *Local government planning permissions* may have been refused for a proposed construction within the organization's own property.

(e) *Future demands* of the organization may not be fully known and therefore the organization may decide to hire until the situation becomes clear and the correct decision can be made.

14. Problems of hiring outside warehouse space

There are several problems associated with the hiring of outside warehouse space and each of these has to be considered by the stores manager before any decision is made.

(a) *Location* of the warehouse in relation to the organization.

(b) *Transport links* and travelling time between the main stores and the outside unit.

(c) *Cost of storage* charged by the warehouse.

(d) *Whether the conditions of storage* are suitable for the materials involved.

(e) *The terms and conditions* of the hiring agreement as they affect the stores and the organization.

15. Factors to be considered when hiring warehouse space

Before any materials can be stored in an outside warehouse, a contract or agreement has to be formulated and signed between the two parties involved. It is vital that this agreement is carefully studied by stores management before any arrangement is entered into. The factors to be considered will include the following:

(a) *The actual cost of storage* must be clearly determined and an agreement as to the *nature* of the costs should be reached, e.g. is the cost for the whole storage regardless of usage, or only for the space used?

(b) *Notice of termination* required by both sides has to be clearly laid down.

(c) *Responsibility for stocktaking* must be clearly laid down.

(d) *Responsibility in terms of stock damage* and insurance must be clearly laid down.

(e) *Exact environmental conditions* under which the stock must be handled and stored must be agreed.

(f) *Responsibility for stock control* and stock records while the stock is being stored must be agreed.

(g) *Provision of labour and materials handling* equipment must be clearly laid down.

Construction, location and layout

16. Factors affecting the design and construction of a new stores

Any decision relating to the design and construction of a new store must be made with the advice and opinion of the stores manager. The following factors must be considered:

(a) *Volume of stocks involved.* This should also reflect future demands as well as the present.

(b) *Nature of the stocks involved.* In most cases a wide variety of stock will be stored. Special sub-stores and storage sections may be required where specific environmental conditions can be maintained.

(c) *Value of the stocks involved* and security systems needed (e.g. alarms, doors, CCTV).

(d) *Materials handling systems* already employed by the organization and the compatibility of the new stores with these systems (e.g. an organization employing diesel-powered trucks may not be able to operate such trucks within a stores building).

(e) *Loading bays* required within the new store. This will depend upon the rate of issue from stocks, the method of transport employed and the frequency of deliveries to customers.

(f) *Goods-in bays* required. This will depend upon the frequency of deliveries, the transport method employed by suppliers and the method of packaging.

(g) *Ancillary services* and accommodation within the main store will need to be allocated space and this will therefore reduce the overall capacity of the new installation. Such services will include:

(*i*) stores offices (stock records, stock control, general administration);

(*ii*) toilets and washroom facilities;

(*iii*) rest room and in some cases a canteen facility.

(h) *Main method of transport* employed by the organization and its suppliers. This will have a direct effect upon design and construction of new stores buildings.

(i) *Environmental conditions* needed and the type of ventilation, heating and lighting systems required to maintain these conditions.

(j) *Labour resources* needed to operate the new stores installation.

(k) *Capital and land available.*

17. Factors affecting the location of the new store

There are several vital factors that will affect the location decision regarding the new stores building. Again, it is very important that stores management is involved in the decision-making process at all stages.

(a) *Land available* within the existing operational area will obviously be first choice, but if such land is not available then a location nearby needs to be found.

(b) *Local government planning permission* needs to be obtained before any construction work can commence.

(c) *The cost of land* within the existing location of the organization may force the construction of the store outside the area.

(d) *The basic principle* behind stores buildings is that they must be as near to the main productive or distributive unit as possible to enable costs to be reduced.

18. Costs involved in design, construction and operation of stores buildings

There are a great many costs involved in the stores building project. Each of these costs must be carefully examined to ensure the economic feasibility of the project and the organization's ability to operate the store. The costs will include the following:

(a) *Construction* costs and the cost of all installations.

(b) *Rates* levied upon the new building by the local authority.

(c) *Cost of maintenance* and depreciation.

(d) *Cost of materials handling* equipment required.

(e) *Cost of storage* equipment needed.

(f) *Energy costs* in relation to gas, electricity and fuels.

(g) *Cost of labour* needed to operate the store.

(h) *Administration* and management costs.

(i) *Security costs* in relation to outside security organizations, alarms, special locks, fire-fighting equipment and insurance cover premiums.

(j) *Cleaning costs* in relation to floors, offices and pest control.

(k) *Transportation costs* in relation to goods to be delivered to customers.

19. Regional aid

In some instances, central government can provide financial assistance for organizations which wish to move from areas like the south-east to other, depressed areas of the country, to help provide employment. The organization may consider the possibility of moving its whole operation to a new site and gain the advantages of this aid.

20. Stores building layout

One of the basic factors that affects the efficiency of the whole stores operation is that of main building layout. As the main store is the key to the stores system, it must reflect in its layout the needs of the organization, if it is to be effective. When designing the stores layout the following factors must be taken into account (*see* also Fig. 6.1):

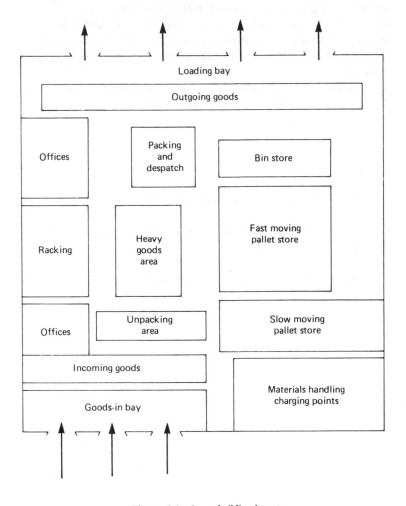

Figure 6.1 *Stores building layout*

(a) *The capacity required* for the various methods of storage employed. A typical breakdown could be 20 per cent bins, 60 per cent pallet racking, 10 per cent shelves, 10 per cent racking.

(b) *The frequency of issues* for each stock classification, thereby stabilizing the position of fast, medium and slow-moving stocks in relation to the materials handling and stock issue.

(c) *The location of office accommodation* in relation to strategic points of control (e.g. issue sector) within the new store.

(d) *The maintenance and charging points* for electrically powered materials handling equipment employed within the new store.

(e) *Gangways and access* required to allow materials handling of all materials held.

(f) *Size and number of main loading and delivery bays* required within the store, depending upon the frequency of deliveries and issue of stock.

Progress test 6

1. Outline the two main types of stores buildings. **(3, 4)**

2. What types of storage equipment are usually found within the stores building? **(5)**

3. What are the advantages of a purpose-built storehouse? **(7)**

7
Stock receipt procedure

Stock receipt documents

1. Introduction

Stock receipt involves all the materials and items supplied to the store, whether from internal transfer (i.e. from another part of the organization) or from external sources (i.e. delivery from suppliers). Both must be strictly controlled to ensure efficient stores management and smooth operations.

A comprehensive set of documents has been developed to enable this control to be maintained. Each of these documents has an important and specific role to play. Although documents will be designed by individual organizations to accommodate their own needs, the logic behind them remains constant. The main documents are described in 2–7 below.

2. Reorder notification

This is produced by the stock record section and is sent to purchasing, who in turn will place an order with the appropriate supplier, after going through the purchasing cycle (*see* Fig. 13.1). Stores is therefore aware that a delivery of stock will eventually come about, although it may be some time before the goods actually arrive at the stores.

3. Purchasing copy order (*see* Fig. 7.1)

This is issued by the purchasing department, and is usually a carbon copy of what has been sent to the supplier. It will therefore contain information regarding the following:

PURCHASING ORDER				Date

To _____

Please supply the following items

Item	Code no.	Description	Quantity	Price
Methods of delivery				
Delivery date				

For and on behalf of Jones Ltd

Figure 7.1 *Purchasing copy order*

(a) code number and description of the goods;
(b) quantity ordered;
(c) method of delivery;
(d) required delivery date;
(e) price;
(f) date of the order being placed.

This document is kept on file by the stores section, as it provides confirmation that stock has been ordered from suppliers.

4. Advice note

This is issued by the supplier contracted to supply the stock ordered by purchasing. It is issued when the goods are despatched by the supplier and is designed to provide the following data:

(a) confirmation that the order will be delivered;
(b) a provisional delivery date and time;
(c) method of delivery to be employed by the supplier;

(d) quantity of goods that will be supplied;
(e) the code number and description of the stock concerned.

5. Delivery note (*see* **Fig. 7.2**)
This document is usually supplied with the goods as they are delivered; it states what the supplier has actually delivered to the store. However, it must be carefully checked against the stock unloaded, to ensure that the figures and detail on the delivery note are accurate. It is the responsibility of the stores manager to check delivery notes and sign them as correct or not as the case may be. The delivery note could be described as the most important stock receipt document, as it contains the following information:

Jones Ltd

DELIVERY NOTE

Date ____________

To

Address

Please accept delivery of the following items

Item	*Description*	*Code no.*	*Quantity*	*Price*

Method of delivery

Goods received by (signature) ____________

Figure 7.2 *Delivery note*

(a) quantity;
(b) type;
(c) colour;
(d) code;
(e) date;
(f) costs.

6. Carrier's consignment note
This is used when the supplier has contracted-out the actual physical delivery of stock to an organization in business for that purpose (e.g. British Rail, Road Transport Services, etc.). Such organizations provide their own form and delivery note so that control of what is delivered can be maintained and claims for non-delivery properly processed. In most cases the goods delivered will have both a supplier's delivery note and a carrier's consignment note.

7. Internal packing note
This is used to carry out a more detailed check of the stock delivered once the parcels, boxes, drums, etc., have been broken down for storage. The packing note lists what is actually within each unit delivered. It should give specific data about quantities, types, sizes, colours, specifications, etc.

Stock receipt cycle

8. Introduction
The receipt of stock should follow a standard and logical sequence of events. Each stage of the stock receipt cycle is very important and must be carefully controlled and supervised by the stores. The stages of the receipt cycle are set out in **9–19** below.

9. Notification of order being placed by purchasing
This will inform stores that goods have been ordered and a provisional date and method of delivery established. Stores management can therefore make provisional plans in relation to the stock receipt system.

10. Confirmation of delivery
This enables the stores manager to make definite arrangements for the delivery of a specific amount of stock by a confirmed method of delivery.

11. Stock allocation
Once the delivery has been confirmed steps must be taken to ensure that sufficient space is allocated for the new delivery (this

may mean stock rearrangement). Space allocation is vital if double handling is to be avoided (17:7).

12. Labour allocation

The unloading of stock will require some degree of manual handling in almost every situation. In some cases a large number of staff may be needed, and plans must therefore be made to ensure that when the delivery takes place labour will be available.

13. Materials handling allocation

This must also be planned to deal with the delivery. Certain types of materials and packaging will obviously require various specialized materials handling equipment to unload and store them properly (e.g. palletized goods will require fork-lift trucks).

14. Scheduling of deliveries

Scheduling will enable deliveries to be dealt with using the full resources of the stores operation. The ideal schedule will provide a steady stream of deliveries during the stores working day.

15. Delivery of goods

At this stage of the cycle the goods actually arrive at the store. The delivery note is checked against the stock supplied. If stores is not able to check a load owing to pressure of work, industrial action, etc., the delivery document must be signed and the word 'unchecked' must be written. This is so that any claim for shortage or damage will not be complicated by a signature on the delivery note accepting the stock.

16. Unloading and inspection

This is dealt with more fully in 8:3.

17. Storage of deliveries

In some cases, deliveries will have to be broken down into smaller units and then stored on the shelves, bins, racks or whatever storage equipment is suitable. It is vital at this stage that goods are placed in their correct storage location, otherwise the whole issue and checking system will be adversely affected.

18. Notification of damages, shortages or errors

Such notification should be sent directly to the following sections:

(a) Purchasing;
(b) Production planning;
(c) Quality control;
(d) Stock control and stock records.

19. Notification of delivery

Notification in relation to accepted stock should be sent to the departments listed in **18** above. All these sections need to be informed so that they can adjust their records accordingly and note the increase in stock.

Other aspects

20. Special deliveries

In some instances there may be a need to provide special arrangements for certain types of deliveries and materials. The special arrangement could be to accommodate a delivery out of normal working hours; for example, a delivery of a major piece of equipment may take place during the night to avoid traffic. In such cases a team of storemen will need to be made up to work the hours and receive the goods.

21. Special handling

Some materials may require very special handling on receipt into the store (e.g. explosives, chemicals, etc.). This will require careful planning on the part of the stores management to ensure that all preparations and safety measures are taken to reduce the risk of accident or damage.

22. Importance of communications between purchasing and stores

In relation to the receipt of stock, sound and meaningful communications between purchasing and stores are vital. Purchasing must keep stores fully informed about all developments concerning the delivery of stock. Often changes in delivery schedules are made because of factors beyond the control of the supplier or buyer, but unless stores is advised, a great deal of preparation and work will go to waste and stores will be working to a schedule that has no real meaning, making management of the whole operation very difficult.

It must also be noted that it is vital for stores to inform purchasing of any faults, shortages and errors made by the supplier so that purchasing can contact the supplier immediately and arrange a new delivery. If this is not done, purchasing may well assume that all is correct and take no action.

23. Internal transfers

This is the term used to describe the process of moving stock from one location within the organization to another. Each location (e.g. depot or warehouse) may have its own stock record and stock control system, and means of controlling all transfers must therefore be enforced.

The internal transfer note is the standard document used to transfer stock and check all deliveries against. It is very similar to a supplier's delivery note (*see* **5**) in its function.

Progress test 7

1. What range of data would you expect to find on a standard advice note, delivery note and packing note? **(4, 5, 7)**

2. What are the stages in the stock receipt cycle? **(9–19)**

3. Why does the storekeeper need to be informed about materials requiring special handling? **(21)**

4. Why are communications between purchasing and stores important in relation to stock receipt? **(22)**

8
Inspection, quality control and standardization

Inspection

1. Introduction

Responsibility for inspection varies from company to company according to the nature of the organization and the technicalities of the merchandise. The following questions need precise answers when a system for inspection of incoming goods is devised:

(a) What special inspection requirements are necessary?
(b) What specifications are to be followed?
(c) What are the facilities required to coordinate and cooperate with user departments?
(d) Are bonded stores required for deliveries of certain goods?
(e) What action is to be taken when goods are rejected?

2. Inspection by stores

Because of stores' traditional inspection role, the link between stores and quality control must be a strong and useful one. Many organizations rely completely on stores to check and monitor all goods delivered into stores. The trend today is for stores and quality control to work closely together within the inspection role, since both stores and quality control have a part to play in that procedure.

3. Role of stores in quality control

The stores has a very important part to play in the quality control operation, as follows:

(a) *Inspection of all materials* delivered to the stores. This inspection must be made against the predetermined levels of acceptability. There are two basic inspection methods:

(*i*) 100 per cent method — all items are tested;

(*ii*) sampling methods — only a sample of each batch delivered is tested.

(**b**) *Supply of samples* of every delivery to the quality control section so that regular checks and tests can be made on each delivery, thus maintaining consistency of supply quality.

(**c**) *Notification of rejection*. When goods are rejected by stores, quality control must be informed immediately, as must purchasing, production and planning.

(**d**) *Holding of reject stocks* in one area set aside for that purpose. This will ensure that faulty materials are not used in production, which would subsequently cause faulty output.

(**e**) *Correct storage* of materials to ensure that materials delivered to the company which are acceptable should remain so and not be damaged in storage.

Quality control

4. Introduction

The reputation and survival of an organization depend upon satisfying the customer's needs. Poor quality can lead to a loss of credibility, and increased costs due to scrap, rework and late deliveries which are caused by the need to repeat tasks that were not 'right the first time'.

5. Total quality control (TQC)

The object of TQC is to prevent waste by not producing defective products in the first place. TQC was developed by the Japanese in the 1970s . It insists that everything is important in the goal of first-class quality. The relationship between supplier, buyer and the ultimate customer must be integrated to prevent poor quality rather than the more traditional approach to detect the goods that do not meet specification. The materials management function has an important role to play in quality control.

Aims and scope of quality control

6. Definition

Quality control is the process of setting standards of acceptability for the goods purchased and produced by the organization and basing the acceptance or rejection of materials upon those standards.

7. Specifications

A specification is a detailed description of any given item. The details in a specification are as follows:

(a) size
(b) dimensions
(c) performance
(d) characteristics (colour, texture, form)
(e) quality
(f) chemical analysis
(g) functions.

Once the specification has been drawn up, all goods supplied to the store will have to meet the requirements of the specification, otherwise they will be *rejected*.

8. Rejection

If goods are found to be below the standard set by the organization, they will not be accepted into the stores. This is called rejection of stock. Once an item has been rejected a careful procedure must be followed:

(a) *The goods are double checked* to ensure that real cause for rejection exists. This usually means a senior member of the stores staff becoming involved.
(b) *The quality control department* must be notified so that it can inspect the items and confirm the rejection order.
(c) *Purchasing* must be informed so that it can contact the supplier to arrange for the faulty items to be collected or returned.
(d) *Production planning* must be informed so that it will be aware of a shortage of stock in certain areas which may affect its production programmes.

9. Quality control department
Many organizations have their own quality control department whose sole function is to monitor the standards and quality of the goods used and produced by the organization. The trend is for more and more companies to employ professional quality control staff to ensure consistency of quality and output.

10. Aims and objectives of quality control
These are as follows:

(a) To set and monitor standards of quality for all items handled by the organization.
(b) To eliminate the possibility of faulty production becoming distributed and sold to the consumer which might damage the organization's reputation.
(c) To liaise between all the departments involved in setting standards (*see* **12–15**) to ensure that all standards set are acceptable and workable to all those concerned.
(d) To ensure the quality and performance of all items delivered into the store from supplies and production sources.

Establishment of quality control standards

11. Introduction
To enable quality control to function, the organization must establish a system of standards based on its own needs and objectives.

12. Factors that influence the standards of quality control
The stringency or otherwise of quality control standards will depend upon the following factors:

(a) *Company policy* in relation to its reputation and productive quality. A company which is facing strong competition in relation to quality of products will need very stringent quality control standards if it is not to fall behind its rivals.
(b) *Complexity of the items involved.* The degree of quality control inspection will depend a great deal upon the type and nature of the goods involved. Highly specialized and technically advanced

materials will need a high degree of specialized skill and knowledge on the part of the quality control inspectors.

(c) *Agreement between the major departments* involved in setting standards. It is vital that all the departments which have to live and work with these standards accept them. The acceptance is best achieved by each department being represented at the standard-setting stage.

13. Method of establishing quality control standards

There are several methods employed by organizations for setting quality control standards.

(a) *Boardroom directives.* A decision is made at board level as to the quality of the material handled. This procedure has the disadvantage of not having resulted from consultation with the line managers involved and so tends to lead to a failure to implement controls by the sections actually working under them.

(b) *Standards set by quality control.* Such standards tend to be more acceptable, but again the lack of consultation may lead to problems. Quality control should exist primarily to advise on setting standards and to ensure they are implemented.

(c) *Joint consultation approach.* This is the method that normally enjoys the greatest success within most environments. The departments concerned will be brought together at regular intervals to discuss, and subsequently agree on, the detailed standards outlined by company policy.

14. Departments involved in establishing standards

Where a joint consultation approach is adopted, the following departments should be involved:

(a) *Production.* By virtue of the fact that this department has to work with the materials purchased for use in production, its interest lies in a high quality of input, as this will improve productive output by reducing delays arising from rejected materials, and will also improve machine output.

(b) *Marketing department.* Because marketing has to sell the products produced by the company in the market-place, its interest lies in the best possible quality of output in terms of finish, performance, design and packaging.

(c) *Design department.* Designers have to be involved in the setting of standards because it is their responsibility to see that the requirements in terms of quality and performance, as demanded by the customers and the company, are met.

(d) *Customers.* The customers are indirectly involved in setting standards in as much as, if the goods produced by the company are inferior to other brands, customers will not buy them.

(e) *Quality control.* The role of inspectors and monitors of quality make it vital that quality control is involved at every stage of the procedure for the establishment of standards.

(f) *Stores management.* In many instances stores is the first line of defence against faulty materials being introduced into the system, because stores has traditionally held the responsibility for the inspection of all materials delivered to the store (*see* **3**). This has now been developed to include a more stringent series of inspections of both 'brought in' and 'own production' items, in liaison with the quality control department.

(g) *Purchasing.* This department must be involved at every stage of the establishment procedures to ensure that:

    (*i*) it is fully aware of the needs of the company in terms of quality and price of materials purchased;

    (*ii*) it will be able to provide all information as to the availability of the specification proposed and also its effect upon the overall cost of production and thus ultimately the sale price.

15. Conflict of interests in quality control

In the establishment of acceptable standards, one often finds a conflict of interests between the departments involved. These conflicts can have several sources, as follows:

(a) *The production department* may show an unwillingness to be tied to strict standards of productive output that can, in some cases, cause delays in output.

(b) *Marketing* is unwilling to accept increased prices arising from increased costs of improving quality, yet at the same time it demands the highest quality of output to increase sales.

(c) *Purchasing* realizes the need for high quality materials to be purchased and supplied, but by the same token is committed to keeping costs down.

Standardization

16. Definition
Standardization means reducing the numbers of very similar items held in stock, thereby reducing the overall stockholding of the organization.

17. Factors that increase stock variety
Stock variety can increase over a period of time and, without investigation, may long remain undetected. The following are some of the factors that lead to duplication of items:

(a) *Staff turnover* in both the purchasing and stores departments often leads to stock lines being duplicated because of an initial resistance to change on the part of new stores and purchasing staff.
(b) *Personal preferences* of the users. Many heads of departments have their own preferences and may demand that stocks of certain items must be purchased and stored.
(c) *One-off demand* for a certain variety of item that may only be needed for one occasion is unwittingly maintained in stock thereafter.
(d) *Changes in availability* at certain times may encourage organizations to hold more than one variety of an item to safeguard against a nil-stock situation.

18. Quality control and standardization
Because quality control is mainly concerned with the examination of materials and the monitoring of standards, many items that have an unnecessarily high degree of variety can be spotted and eliminated with all the advantages that brings.

19. Advantages of increased standardization of stock
These include the following:

(a) *Reduced storage space used.* Because of the reduced variety, less overall stock will be necessary.
(b) *Reduced stores administration.* Because of a reduced variety of stock, less stores administration will be required in terms of stock, records, stock control, inspection, checking and issue, computer time and documentation.
(c) *Improved stock control.* This results from the fact that more

attention can be paid to the control of stock when the varieties involved are reduced.

(d) *Reduced overall levels of stock.* For example:

Pre-standardization
Stock line: Stationery

Item:		Stock	
Varieties:	(*i*)	Smiths Super black	£200
	(*ii*)	Parkers Classic black	£300
	(*iii*)	Jones black	£200
	(*iv*)	Phillips Universal black	£150
		TOTAL STOCK	£850
		Value	£850

After standardization
Phillips Universal black biro

	TOTAL	£600
	Value	£600

Stock saving: £250

This can be repeated throughout the whole stockholding of many organizations and vast savings in capital tied up in unnecessary stock can be achieved.

(e) *Improved service from the suppliers.* The resulting competition among suppliers should mean both better prices and better service for the organization.

(f) *Improved establishment of standards.* Once the items in stock have been standardized, the setting of standards is greatly improved, because both stores and quality control have only one standard to set and monitor for each item held, rather than a system of standards for every variety, which would lead to a lack of conformity in implementation.

20. Disadvantages of standardization

There are certain disadvantages arising from the standardization of stock that must be considered. There will be more involved in some organizations than in others, depending on the operation and needs of the company.

(a) *Reduced flexibility.* Once the varieties have been standardized, sudden shortages of that particular line may cause supply problems.

(b) *Reduced choice for the user.* It may be felt that the variety that was previously used was best for the job.

21. Standardization process
Standardization involves the following procedures:

(a) *Identification of stock duplication.* This is often achieved when stores coding has been completed and similar code numbers warrant investigation (*see* 9:**21**).

(b) *Selection of standard item.* Once a duplication has been discovered, the next stage is to select the best of the range in relation to usage, price, performance, etc. It must be able to meet all the needs of the present stock variety. In these instances the so-called 'universal' or 'all-purpose' type of item tends to be selected in an effort to meet all the requirements placed upon the item involved.

(c) *Calculation of total stock requirements.* The next stage is to establish the revised level of stock for the item involved. This can be obtained by reference to the stock record system (*see* 14:**2**). The total usage of the item, regardless of variety, will indicate the overall level of demand for the item concerned. For example:

Parkers	(actual usage)	£75
Smiths	(actual usage)	£150
Jones	(actual usage)	£100
Phillips	(actual usage)	£275
	TOTAL	£600

22. The role of stores management in standardization
Stores management is in a unique position to assist the process of standardization and also help prevent excess variety being created in the stocks held. This can be achieved in the following ways:

(a) *Discouraging users* from ordering non-standard issue items wherever possible. This can be done by recommending, and in some cases actively promoting, the standard stock item.

(b) *Informing the users of the costs* involved in holding a wide variety of stocks and the effect upon the organization's profitability.

(c) *Constantly reviewing the stock records* to locate possible sources of stock standardization.

(d) *Discussing with purchasing* the subject of standardization and the possible items on the market that could be used to reduce stock variety.

23. The role of materials management in standardization
Materials management is in a unique position to assist the process of standardization and also help prevent excess variety being created in the stocks held. This can be achieved in the following ways:

(a) *Discouraging users* from ordering non-standard issue items wherever possible. This can be done by recommending, and in some cases actively promoting, the standard stock item.

(b) *Informing the users of the costs* involved in holding a wide variety of stocks and the effect upon the organization's profitability.

(c) *Constantly reviewing the stock records* to locate possible sources of stock standardization.

(d) *Discussing with purchasing* the subject of standardization and the possible items on the market that could be used to reduce stock variety.

Progress test 8

1. What are the factors that influence the setting of quality control standards? **(12)**

2. Describe the main methods of establishing standards. **(13)**

3. Which departments need to be involved in the process of setting standards? **(14)**

4. What are some of the possible conflicts of interests in the setting of standards? **(15)**

5. What is the role of stores management in relation to quality control? **(3)**

6. What are the advantages of increased standardization of stock? **(19)**

7.   What are the key questions that need to be asked when inspecting incoming goods?   **(1)**

Case study no. 3

TQM — The Rolls Royce experience

By Ken Janes, Controller of Production Assurance, Rolls Royce, January 1991

Reproduced with the kind permission of the Institute of Materials Management

Rolls Royce has been involved with quality from its very beginning and, by the nature of its products, has always been required to meet exacting regulatory and airworthiness requirements.

The total quality concept was considered by Rolls Royce in 1987 as part of a drive to increase further the quality awareness within the company and implement a programme of operational improvement.

The initiative for introduction of the programme initially came from the Product Assurance Group which realized that it was essential, if the programme was to succeed, for the concept to be launched from the top of the organization. This was achieved by the arrangement of a seminar chaired by the managing director with his 50 most senior executives in attendance.

The agenda for the seminar took the form of an address by the managing director followed by an explanation of the total quality concept by an external consultant. This was followed by an address by the director of product assurance which outlined the current product assurance performance.

The second part of the seminar took the form of a series of presentations given by the executive group directors, outlining their current programmes for product assurance improvement.

The engagement of an external consultant, having experience of total quality management in other major companies, had the advantage of providing a valuable independent flavour to the proceedings.

Steering Committee sets goals

Following the seminar, a steering committee was appointed to consider the launch of the total quality management programme. The Steering Committee comprised executive directors, senior managers and the external consultant. The main task of the Steering Committee was to define the meaning of total quality in Rolls Royce and to establish corporate goals.

It was established that, in Rolls Royce, total quality would mean the *continuous improvement of customer satisfaction*.

The corporate goals were agreed as follows:

- To provide an awareness of total quality in all employees.
- To improve operational effectiveness by the elimination of waste.
- To improve customer satisfaction contributing to increased market share.

Having established the strategy for TQM, the steering committee examined several possibilities for the way forward and the following questions were considered:

- Should total quality management be organized on a corporate basis, or should it be undertaken by the individual company groups? (*See* Fig. 8.1.)
- Should external consultants be used?
- Should the central steering committee continue to organize the programme?
- What is the relationship between total quality management and product assurance.

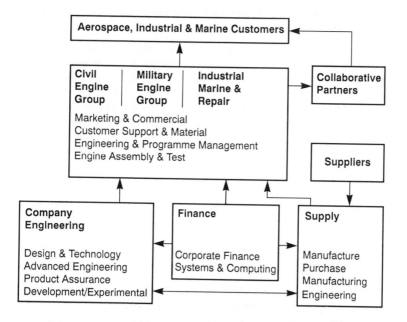

Figure 8.1 *TQM — Rolls Royce*

This latter issue of the TQM relationship to product assurance was a key issue in the talks.

The way forward

The Steering Committee finally decided on the following approach for the way forward:

- Individual group strategies would be adopted.
- The group directors would be responsible for their programmes and would report progress through their business meetings.
- The progress of the company total quality programme would be monitored centrally.
- It was necessary to keep total quality separate from product assurance. Total quality and product assurance have two separate objectives. Product assurance is a contractual requirement. Total quality is a company initiative in pursuit of excellence.
- The use of external consultants would only be used where specific internal resources were not available and the company would develop its own total quality expertise as the programme proceeds.

As the programme progressed, total quality facilitators were appointed in the major groups of the company. These individuals were established in full-time positions and are responsible for running the programme within their individual groups.

The use of promotional material was a feature in the total quality initiative. Posters, newsletters, handbooks and brochures were produced by individual groups to promote the activities being pursued. The newsletters, in particular, provided a vehicle for the facilitators to communicate with all personnel within their specific areas.

The programmes for the individual corporate groups were tailored to suit the particular group requirements and focused on the areas where most benefits could be obtained.

Certain groups adopted diagnostic task forces as a means of developing the programme.

Numerous individual task forces were created as a follow-on dealing with specific projects using techniques such as cause and effect diagrams and departmental task analysis.

All the groups implemented total quality awareness training and the supply group extended this to their supplier network.

Integrated teams were set up between engineering and manufacturing to achieve a match of process capability and specification, resulting in a simultaneous engineering concept.

As the programme developed, it was recognized that the operational improvements arising from the total quality initiative required management at the highest level. In engineering, this resulted in the formation of a total quality improvement board.

External resources have been used to a significant extent in promoting training for total quality awareness. Manufacturing systems engineering techniques were used in the introduction of the cell concept within the supply group.

The progress of the TQM programme is reported to the Rolls Royce Industries Board by the individual group directors. Cost savings associated with the total quality initiative are monitored in the individual group operational statistics. The overall company position is monitored centrally by the corporate product assurance group through a total quality master plan. This plan is reviewed by the company board.

The total quality concept is a company objective and a policy statement is included in the company product assurance manual.

It is important to remember that:

- Total quality short-term actions are a prerequisite in support of long-term goals.
- Total quality is a journey, not a destination.

9

Stores identification

Stores coding

1. The need for stores coding

Because of the complexity of the modern industrial organization, the range and type of items held in stock by that organization are correspondingly complex. This means that a system has to be developed that can identify and classify the wide range of items held in stock, quickly and efficiently. 'Common' names (e.g. table, chair, pump) serve well enough in everyday work, but cannot be used in the context of stores management because of the following difficulties:

(a) Common name terms are very limited and not very descriptive.
(b) Often an item has more than one common name, and this can lead to confusion and mis-issue.
(c) Many items are of a highly technical nature and would require a great deal of explanation in common language.

Because of the problems of using only common language terms, stores management has come to the conclusion that *codes* must be developed that are able to identify all the items held in stock, without the use of long descriptive and complex definitions (we all use some form of 'coding' in everyday situations, e.g. EC = European Community).

2. The types and forms of coding systems

Each organization has its own needs and resources, and this will influence the type of coding system employed. The following are some of the more common systems:

(a) *End-use coding.* This is where the item is coded by virtue of its end-use in terms of the operation or product. For example, in assembly line operation items are end-use coded by way of the item on the production line — a Ford Escort production line will have a complete range of stocks (wheels, engines, gearboxes, fittings, etc.) all stored in a designated area for use only in connection with that production line.

(b) *Colour coding.* This is a system based on the use of colours to code and identify items held in stock. It can be a very effective means of identification, but it has the major disadvantage of being very limited in its range. Once the basic distinct colours (i.e. red, blue, black, white, yellow, green, etc.) have been used it can no longer be employed. This type of colour coding is used mostly in connection with chemicals and in timber stores.

(c) *Supplier's code.* This is where the stores employs the coding system of the supplier of the goods. However, it can be very confusing when more than one supplier is involved or when the logic of the supplier's system is not understood.

(d) *Nature of the item.* This is where each type of item held in stock is classified and coded according to the item's basic nature and make-up. It is the most widely employed system in modern stores management. The advantages of this method are discussed in **3** below.

3. Advantages of 'nature of the item' coding

The logic of nature of the item coding (*see* **5**) is applicable to any coding situation and it is the most common method of identifying and classifying the stock held. It has several advantages over the other systems that have been mentioned (*see* **2**).

(a) It can be used *to cover every item in stock*, regardless of type or complexity.

(b) Because of its logical step-by-step formula it can be *easily translated* into the item's full name by the storekeepers and the other departments who use and work with the code. In some cases a series of digits are employed in stores coding, but it is not so easy to translate that type of coding system.

(c) *The flexibility* of this type of coding ensures that any new type or range of items introduced into the store can be covered and coded by this system (unlike the more restricted colour coding systems).

(d) *It meets the needs of the organization*, because of its ability to be as complex or as simple as required by the type of organization involved. Whether a major corporation or a small family concern, each will have its own needs and resources.

4. Factors to be considered when introducing a stores code

Several important factors have to be carefully considered before a coding system is introduced into the stores system.

(a) *The range and type of stock to be coded.* The more complex and variable the items held in stock are, the more flexible and complex the code will have to be.

(b) *The staff and resources available to introduce and update the stores code.* A very complex system will need a great deal of time and skill to introduce and maintain. Stores personnel will require specialized training if the system is to be successful.

(c) *Will the system be computerized or manual in its operation?* The role of computers in stores management is a fast growing one and numerical stores coding is essential for efficient computer data storage. (*See* 23:**11**.)

5. Construction of a stores code

Having established the need for a stores code, and the basis on which it is to operate, the next step is its construction. The various needs of individual companies make it impossible to produce a system to cover every situation. However, a basic system can be designed to illustrate the underlying logic and mechanism of the stores code.

The system of coding based on the nature of the item (*see* **2(d)**) requires the gradual classification of each identifiable feature of the item and the incorporation of that feature into the code itself. Such a system allows any item to be coded, and anyone who understands the code will be able to identify the item from its code number. In the following example, the goods to be coded are copper rods.

(a) *Stage 1.* What basically is the item to be coded? Under what major heading can it be situated (e.g. raw material, component part, finished production, electrical)? The item to be coded is obviously a basic raw material, so we can give the first part of its code as:

RM

(b) *Stage 2*. Having established the basic heading under which our copper rods fall, the next step is to determine what type of raw material it is. In this case it is a base metal, and the next part of the code could therefore be **M**. We now have:

RMM

(c) *Stage 3*. Having classified the type of raw material, the next stage is to identify the code and the type of material. The code could now read:

RMMC

(d) *Stage 4*. Having established what type of material the item is, the next stage is to identify the code and form of the item (e.g. bars, nuggets, rods, etc.). The code could now read:

RMMCR

(e) *Stage 5*. Having established the form in which the item is stored, the next stage of the coding process will involve the identification and coding of any grade, class, type, etc., A, B, C grade, or by a number, e.g. 1–10. If in our example the item concerned has a grade number of 'A', the code would now read:

RMMCRA

(f) *Stage 6*. The final stage of the coding process involves the identification of sizes, dimensions, weights, performance, etc., as shown in the item's description. In our example the item is shown in metres, and this information must be included in the code reference. The final code for our copper rods, Grade A, 6 m x 5 mm diameter will therefore be coded as:

RMMCRA 6 m x 5 mm

Further examples of the nature of the item coding are shown in Fig. 9.1.

(a)	C/P	=	Component part
	E	=	Electrical
	SP	=	Spark plug
	N17	=	Type/specification
	16 mm	=	Size

Code for 16 mm N17 spark plug is (C/P.E.SP.N17.16 mm)

(b)	RM	=	Raw material
	T	=	Textile
	N	=	Nylon
	A	=	Grade/type
	R	=	Rolls
	16 m x 200 m	=	Size

Code for nylon material in rolls of 16 m/200 m grade A is
(RM.T.N.R.A.16 m x 200 m)

(c)	P	=	Packaging
	C	=	Cellophane film
	B	=	Colour film blue
	A	=	Grade/type
	R	=	Rolls
	0.5 mm x 100 mm	=	Size

Code for rolls of cellophane blue, packaging grade A is
(P.C.B.A.R.0.5 mm x 100 mm)

Figure 9.1   *Examples of the nature of coding*

6.   Stores vocabulary

Once the stores code system has been devised and introduced, the information in relation to the code, i.e. the logic of the code and the full descriptions of the items held, has to be stored and must be accessible to the departments who need to have a working knowledge of the code system. This information is kept in the 'stores vocabulary' or 'catalogue', which is a book or file that contains the code numbers of all the items held in stock and its full description. It is vital that this system is kept up to date and covers all the items held in stock.

The following are some of the potential users of the code who may need a copy of the stores vocabulary:

(a) Purchasing department.
(b) Suppliers.
(c) Production and other 'user' departments.

(d) Accounts and invoice checking (the code reference can be used on invoices and delivery documents).

7. Characteristics of an efficient coding system

A coding system will always be judged by results, that is, the efficient and successful identification and location of the item required. However, this criterion is that of the 'user' who normally is only interested in obtaining the correct item of stock. From the overall stores management point of view, other factors decide the efficiency of the coding system.

(a) *The code must cover every item held in stock.* A system that does not do this may not cover a new item, which could lead to control problems.

(b) *Flexibility.* Because of the dynamic nature of modern industrial stores, many new products are being stocked and produced every year and there are changes in design, packaging and performance. All these alterations and variations have to be covered by the basic coding system, which must therefore be expandable to accommodate increases in stock, range and scope.

(c) *Consistent format and logic of the system.* It is very important that once the basic logic of the system is established (e.g. **RM** = raw materials, **S** = stationery, etc.), it is carried on throughout all coding. Some organizations make the mistake of creating a code for one part of their stores operation and then find they are operating several different coding systems, thus causing confusion and errors.

(d) *The system employed must meet the needs* of the organization that is employing it. Obviously, different firms with different problems and needs will have a vast range of coding systems. However, the basic point that must be remembered is that the system must meet the needs of the firm, whatever they may be. For example, the coding system employed by Ford would be far more complex than that used by a local distribution depot, even though the basic logic may be the same.

8. Role of other departments in stores coding

Because of the fact that other departments, outside the stores, will need to use the code, they should be involved and consulted during the coding process, thus ensuring the workability of the code. The following are some of the factors to be discussed with other departments:

(a) Logic of the code employed (i.e. whether colour, end use, nature of the item or any other).

(b) Common classifications and headings under which the stock will be coded.

(c) Channels of communication to ensure that stores is made aware of any new items to be held in stock.

(d) Which departments will need to have a copy of the stores vocabulary, e.g. Production, Distribution, Engineering, etc.

Advantages of stores coding

9. Introduction

We can see from the points made so far in this chapter that stores coding is a very expensive and time-consuming process, involving a great deal of effort and control. To justify this effort certain tangible advantages have to be expected from the employment of a stores coding system. A number of possible advantages are outlined in **10–18** below.

10. Simplicity

A long and complex requisition need not be completed, for by using a simple series of letters and digits the exact item required can be communicated to the storekeeper, thus saving time and effort.

11. Accuracy of selection

Having been given the exact code number for the item required, the storekeeper will be in a position to select and issue the item without the possibility of a mis-issue, providing that the code reference quoted is correct. This is a great advantage in relation to highly technical or complex items which may appear visually to be identical, but which often have vast internal differences and performances. Such differences will be identified and isolated by the stores code.

12. Stores marking

A coding system prevents duplication of effort, not only in

relation to selection procedures and authorization, but also in terms of stores marking and labelling. The use of a code reference will help the storekeeper to mark-up his storage area quickly and efficiently.

13. Assistance to purchasing

The purchasing function can be greatly assisted in its operation by the use of a stores coding system. One of the basic responsibilities of stores management is to keep Purchasing informed about levels of stocks and goods needed to be purchased. When the stores operates a coding system, purchasing is also given a copy of the 'stores vocabulary' or 'catalogue' (*see* **6**) which will contain all the information needed to understand the requests made by stores, again saving the use of long, descriptive requisitions.

14. Reduction of errors

Because of the exact nature of a stores code and its basic logical approach, it is quite difficult to make an error in identification, unlike the process of completing a long and complex written request in which mistakes are much easier to make.

15. Assists the supplier

In some cases a copy of the code could be sent to a major supplier, who would then be able to supply the items ordered, with purchasing simply using its code reference. This extra use of the code would help to save time and effort at all stages of the purchasing cycle (*see* Fig. 13.1) and thus reduce the administrative costs of ordering.

16. Basis of a stores location system

Because of the logical classification system used by the stores code, it lends itself very well to the process of stores location, whereby each section of the store has a certain type of product held within that area. This information will be stored in both the stores vocabulary and the stock record cards. When a user comes to the store for an item, the code number will be used to identify and locate the item required.

17. Standardization

The process of standardization of stock is greatly assisted by the use of a stores coding system, especially when used in connection with a computer system (*see* **18**).

18. Computers and stores coding

For a computer system to operate efficiently and effectively it must be able to locate and identify on its files the items held in stock, so that transactions for stock records, stock control and storage can all be processed as soon as possible. The development of the role of the computer in stores management has led to increased attention being paid to stores codes. Computer operations are greatly assisted by the use of a logical coding system. Because of the logical way in which computers operate they are able to identify quickly the item in question, once given its code number.

Data is stored in computers in certain forms, e.g. punch cards, punch tape, and magnetic tape and disc. The cost of holding information is based on the number of letters or digits actually fed into the computer. The cost of storing information will therefore be reduced when a code reference is used to describe the goods, rather than its full literal description.

Other advantages of stores coding in relation to computer systems are that it assists the process of 'direct input capture' (*see* 23:**10(c)**), and aids the process of computer programming and operation.

Stores coding and standardization

19. Definition

The term 'standardization' describes the process of reducing the variety and variation of the type of items held in stock, so that items of a similar design and function will be eliminated from the stock, leaving only one type of item to do the job required.

20. Advantages of stock standardization

The process of standardization has several major advantages for both stores and the organization as a whole.

(a) *Reduction of overall stock levels.* Standardization may mean that several medium sized stocks can be replaced by a proportionally smaller large stock. For example, a range of 4 items each with a stock of 100 (total stock 400) might be replaced by a single stock of 250 of a selected single item.

(b) *Reduction of stores administration.* Because of the reduction in the range of items, fewer stock record cards will need to be updated, there will be fewer bin cards and issue notes, less computer time will be needed, and there will be less stock control and reductions in the other administrative functions and documents associated with holding stock.

(c) *Improvement in quality control.* This is because the established level of acceptability will be simple to administer where a reduced range of items in stock is produced by standardization.

(d) *Increased competition for contracts among suppliers.* This will happen because of the reduction of types of items purchased and the increased value of the contract to be won. This should lead to better prices and better service from suppliers.

(e) *Increased control.* There will be increases in the overall stores management control of the whole stock situation, including the operation of stock control and stock obsolescence.

21. The application of stores coding to standardization
    Because of the logic or nature of the item coding, items that are very similar in nature, and thus function, will have very similar code references. Therefore, when the code references are compared, very similar codes can be investigated to establish whether or not the items involved are basically the same and, if so, whether standardization can effectively take place. In many stores the range of items held is so wide and they are kept in so many locations, that without the stores code to highlight similar products, duplication of stock would be much greater.

Progress test 9

1. Why do we need stores coding?   **(1)**

2. What are the main methods of coding?   **(2)**

3.   Describe the stages in the coding process.   **(5)**

4.   Describe the data stored in the store vocabulary.   **(6)**

5.   What are the main advantages of a stores coding system?
(9–18)

6.   What are the advantages of stock standardization?   **(20)**

10
Security and safety in the stores

Scope and importance of security

1. Definition
One of the most important aspects of stores management is security, which covers not· only theft and fraud, but also stock deterioration, damage, location and special storage. Mike Comer of Network Security Ltd states 'Security is a management responsibility.'

2. Methods of stores security
There are two main methods by which the security of the stores can be attempted. The advantages and disadvantages of each are discussed in **3** and **4** below.

3. Security services
This means making use of specialized organizations that supply a trained team of security guards and other personnel to guard against theft.

(a) *Advantages:*
  (*i*) Trained staff are able to cope with difficult situations.
  (*ii*) 24-hour cover is available if required.
  (*iii*) It reduces the damaging effect of conflict between members of the company's own staff.

(b) *Disadvantages:*
  (*i*) Very expensive service.
  (*ii*) Security staff do not become involved in stock loss other than theft or fraud.
  (*iii*) Friction can arise between the organization's staff and

management because of outside intervention in cases of theft.

(*iv*) Trade union defence of members involved in thefts will be far stronger in cases where security services are involved.

(*v*) A high security staff turnover makes it difficult to build relationships with them.

4. Stores management security

In every store the storekeeper and stores manager are ultimately responsible for the stock held in their charge. In view of this, most organizations rely on the stores management to control stores security.

(a) *Advantages:*

(*i*) Stores staff will have specialized knowledge to call upon.

(*ii*) This method builds up good relationships and trust between the organization and its staff.

(*iii*) Good security is in the stores staff's own interests.

(*iv*) Stores management will be held accountable for stock loss.

(*v*) Stores staff will be able to cover the aspects of deterioration, damage and special stores.

(b) *Disadvantages:*

(*i*) Large-scale theft involving stores staff may not be uncovered.

(*ii*) Stores management would not be fully trained in security techniques.

5. Reasons why stores security is vital

Storehouse security is vital for several reasons, all of which reflect both the value of stock and its operational role within the organization.

(a) *Stock records* become meaningless as a means of stock control if stock is lost and not recorded. The calculated level of stock indicated by the stock cards will bear no resemblance to the actual stock held.

(b) *Stock control* of any sort becomes impossible unless stock records data is reasonably accurate.

(c) *Production planning* relies on stock being available against a predetermined plan. If stock is not secure then these plans will need constant reforming with all the losses in output and efficiency that involves.

(d) *Stock represents a major part of the organization's capital or money,* therefore any stock lost because of theft, fraud or damage will have to be replaced, which will increase the organization's costs and reduce its profits. The value of stock lost every year is impossible to calculate, but the figure must run into millions of pounds to which must be added the loss of profits and revenue arising from production hold-ups and lost contracts. Good security will therefore reap definite financial rewards.

Stores management and security

6. Responsibilities of stores management in relation to storehouse security
The stores manager has a direct responsibility for stores security in all the areas in which materials are stored, marshalled and handled, namely:

(a) stores buildings
(b) stockyards
(c) stock sheds
(d) marshalling points
(e) work in progress stores.

The wide range of responsibilities and duties of the stores manager in relation to stores security are discussed in **8–13** below. Each of these responsibilities demands great care and attention to ensure a comprehensive security cover.

7. Security policy
It is vital that the organization has a uniform security policy, which should include the following points:

(a) appointment of a senior manager with overall responsibility for security;
(b) allocation of a reasonable budget to cover the costs of security;
(c) consistent enforcement of the stated company penalties for theft, from the shop floor to the manager;
(d) regular discussions at managerial level regarding security.

8. Custody of keys

The stores manager is responsible for all the keys and locks used within the stores area, and he should therefore ensure that the following rules are observed:

(a) All keys should be numbered so that the correct key can be matched to the correct lock quickly and efficiently.

(b) All keys should be registered in the central security log by the overall security department.

(c) Individual members of the stores staff should be made responsible for certain keys and must be accountable in terms of stock losses.

(d) Keys taken from the central key bank (where all the stores keys should be held) must be booked out to those who take them and similarly signed back when they are returned. This will enable all keys to be accounted for at any time.

(e) The number of duplicate keys must be kept to a minimum to ensure adequate control, although a degree of duplication is necessary for operational and emergency factors. However, any duplication of keys must be strictly controlled and only undertaken after consultation between all parties involved.

9. Security of installations

The stores manager is responsible for ensuring that all the installations under his control are secure. These installations will include the following:

(a) *Stores buildings*. The storekeeper must ensure that all doors, windows, skylights, entrances, shutters and other possible means of entry are secure to prevent unauthorized persons from entering the stores buildings. Such 'no entry' should also apply to pests, e.g. rats, mice, birds, foxes, etc., as these vermin can cause a great deal of damage.

(b) *Stores offices*. The stores manager must ensure that all cupboards, cabinets, filing systems, desks, etc., are locked. Valuables must not be left in the office as this will encourage unauthorized entry and theft. Office doors must be locked when the office is not in use.

(c) *Stockyards*. The stores manager must ensure that the stockyard is secure. This will include inspection of fencing to ensure complete coverage. All break-ins or damage to the fencing must be repaired as soon as possible and the stores manager must contact the maintenance department and request repairs. The stores manager will also ensure that the stockyard gates and all locks are secure, as well as the stockyard office.

(d) *Work in progress stores*. The stores manager is responsible for all work in progress stores. All stock held must be secure and correctly recorded.

(e) *Marshalling areas*. These are often the most difficult to secure because of the need for a high degree of access by other departments (e.g. loading, materials handling, etc.). In some instances lockable pallet cages can be used to secure stocks that need to be mobile. Pallet cages are pallets with metal cages fixed on top with a lockable entrance.

Regular inspection of all installations is vital to maintain security. In some cases of 24-hour store usage, the stores team may inspect all installations at regular periods, especially during the hours of darkness.

10. Control of entry into stores installations

The stores manager must ensure that no unauthorized persons are allowed to enter the stores area. This restricted entry is for the following reasons:

(a) to prevent theft of stores;

(b) to prevent persons who should not be in the stores being injured by, for example, stock falling off fork-lift trucks.

Many stores construct counters to ensure that unauthorized persons cannot easily enter the stores. In the case of more open areas, such as stockyards, a system of pass cards can be employed. Such cards are issued by management only to those persons who should be in the store at any given time. In some instances entry to stores can be controlled by an electronic sensor and the pass cards are specially coded only to allow entry by the holder.

11. Marking of stock

It is the responsibility of the stores manager to ensure that certain materials held by the store are marked in some way to identify their ownership and origin. This applies especially to items of equipment or items which are of high value and therefore more liable to theft or misuse.

There are two reasons for marking stock. First, it discourages theft, in as much that marked stock cannot easily be sold or used outside the organization and therefore the store may lose a degree of its attraction for theft. Secondly, it ensures that, if stock is stolen and subsequently recovered by police or other agencies, the latter will know to whom the goods rightfully belong and thus will arrange for them to be collected. A great deal of stock is recovered every year by police but, because of the lack of identification, not all of it is returned to the organization from which it was stolen.

The marking of stock can be achieved in several ways, as follows:

(a) *Colour marking by paint or dye*. The colour is often related to the organization's trade mark and will therefore be easily associated with the company if the stock is stolen and subsequently found. For example, the Yellow Cab Company could use yellow to mark its spare parts.

(b) *Trade marks*. Many organizations use the method of embossing or engraving their name and trade mark on items of equipment to identify it as belonging to them.

(c) *Dye marking*. This has been used in the case of very valuable items of stock. It enables the police and the organization's officials to check members of staff and suspects: if the item is touched by hand the dye will be transferred on to the hands of the thief, indicating his involvement in the theft.

12. Fire precautions

These are very important in relation to stores security and it is the responsibility of stores management to ensure that all precautions necessary are taken so that all equipment and procedures are employed properly. Industrial fires cost organizations hundreds of millions of pounds every year, and loss of life and high insurance premiums all add to make fire prevention vitally important as part of the storehouse operation.

(a) *'No smoking' signs* must be clearly placed in all parts of the store, regardless of the materials being held. One of the major causes of fires is cigarettes and matches carelessly discarded. The storekeeper must ensure that the 'no smoking' rule is maintained.

(b) *Fire-fighting equipment* must be in strategic positions throughout the store's installations and must be regularly inspected and maintained. The following are some of the types of fire-fighting equipment:

    (*i*) *Extinguishers* (gas-operated foam dischargers). Different types of these have been developed to deal with different kinds of fires and they should be located according to their application.

    (*ii*) *Hose reels.* These are for dealing with major conflagrations and are often linked to a large tank or mains supply.

    (*iii*) *Sprinkler systems.* These are designed to saturate a given area with water or chemical foam in case of fire in a large area. Sprinklers are controlled by a thermostat and smoke sensor so that a given amount of smoke or heat will trigger off the sprinkler system,

    (*iv*) *Fire blankets.* These are made of a fireproof fabric and are used to smother very small fires or, in some cases, to wrap around a fire victim whose clothes have caught fire.

    (*v*) *Fire buckets.* These are standard fire-fighting equipment in every installation. The buckets are usually filled with sand and are used to extinguish very small fires.

(c) *Alarm systems* must be used in all stores to ensure that any outbreak of fire is detected and the alarm raised. The storekeeper must ensure that there are no obstructions covering the alarm unit. Alarm systems are usually linked to all parts of the organization and a central board in the security office indicates where each alarm is situated.

(d) *Fire drills* must be properly organized and clear fire instructions must be placed on the notice board and other places within the store. These instructions must give precise directions as to the actions to be taken in the event of fire, especially if the materials stored are of a highly flammable or dangerous nature.

(e) *Regular inspections* by the local fire brigade's prevention officer will help to ensure a safe and efficient system.

(f) *Fire doors and emergency exits* must at all times be kept absolutely clear and a clear passage along gangways must be maintained to facilitate quick exit from the store in case of fire.

13. Segregation of high-risk materials

Most stores find it more efficient and cost-effective to store all so-called 'high-risk' materials, such as petrol, oils, chemicals, explosives, spirits, etc., in a store specially designed for that purpose. Such a store is usually placed a reasonable distance from the main buildings of the organization. Segregation has the following advantages:

(a) Expensive fire-fighting and prevention equipment can be concentrated in areas where it most likely to be needed and will therefore provide better fire cover.

(b) In cases of fire in the main store, it will not be able to reach the high-risk stock and therefore the risk of a large-scale conflagration is greatly reduced.

(c) Fires in the high-risk stores can be left to burn themselves out if need be because it is separated from the main building.

(d) Application of the '20/80 rule' (*see* 15:**25**) will show that concentration of efforts to prevent fires in a small high-risk store will benefit the whole operation in terms of overall fire risk.

14. Knowledge of materials

Part of the storekeeper's job is to have a sound knowledge of the materials and items he is dealing with. Such knowledge will include all the basic characteristics of a material, and its behaviour in given conditions and circumstances. He must also be able to recommend alternatives (if they exist) to items requested but not stocked. To be able to do this the storekeeper must have experience and in some cases training.

The following are reasons why storekeepers must have knowledge of materials:

(a) *Application of the materials* issued by the stores will often be guided by the advice of the storekeeper. Operatives will expect him to have a working knowledge of materials held and their daily usage and application characteristics.

(b) *Production processes* involved must also be known by the storekeeper so that allocated issues (*see* 12:**2**) can be made properly and the correct materials issued for a particular part of the process.

(c) *Work in progress* is held by the store and therefore the storekeeper must have a knowledge of what parts will be needed to be placed on the shopfloor in relation to the work in progress held.

(d) *Handling of materials* also requires a great deal of materials knowledge to ensure that materials are handled and moved properly to minimize the danger of damage. Many items have special handling instructions that need to be understood and related to the method of handling employed (fork-lift truck, pallet truck, crane, etc.).

(e) *Inspection of materials* and quality control operations (*see* 8:3) require that the storekeeper has a sound knowledge of materials and will know what to look for in relation to faults, damage and substandard stock when either delivered to the store or issued by it.

(f) *Units of issue* are also a very important part of the storekeeper's material knowledge, especially in relation to the recent changes in measurement from imperial to metric. It is vital that the storekeeper has a sound knowledge of all units of issue for the material he holds in stock, to ensure that correct amounts are issued and used.

(g) *Dangerous materials* need specialized handling and care if the risk of fire, explosion or contamination is to be minimized. In many cases the segregated stores which hold high-risk materials will be managed by a storekeeper who has been trained and is experienced in handling such materials and will know how to store them properly to reduce the risks.

Deterioration

15. Costs of deterioration

Vast amounts of valuable stock are ruined every year in stores because of bad storage and the subsequent deterioration that takes place. All materials will deteriorate eventually, but the period of time involved and therefore the useful life of the materials can be greatly extended if steps are taken to prevent deterioration caused by inefficient storage and handling. The stores manager has a vital role to play in preventing deterioration of stock.

The following are some of the reasons why prevention of deterioration is important:

(a) The value of stock lost every year owing to bad storage is huge and will affect the organization's operational costs.

(b) Vitally important items, that are needed at a vital point of production, can deteriorate as a result of bad storage and may cost a company a great deal in lost output.

(c) The administrative costs of ordering are increasing rapidly. Every time stock deteriorates it has to be ordered again and therefore the cost of ordering is doubled and sometimes even trebled before the goods are actually used.

(d) Materials which have a degree of deterioration which is undetected may find their way to the organization's production system and could be sold to the customer. This could lead to stock being rejected and returned by the customer, resulting in a loss of reputation on the part of the organization.

(e) Recent proposed reforms in consumer protection laws could mean that organizations will be far more liable to legal action if the goods and services they provide are at fault and cause damage, regardless of how slim the connection between the item and incident may be. In the USA claims for 1 million dollars are quite common.

16. Factors that cause stock deterioration

There are many factors that can contribute toward stock deterioration, including the following:

(a) *Faulty storage areas* that allow damp to enter via broken windows, leaking roofs and badly fitting doors.

(b) *Failure to follow supplier's storage instructions* as provided on the packaging or delivery documents.

(c) *Storage of materials* in incorrect conditions of temperature or humidity.

(d) *Faulty or careless handling* of materials that leads to breakages and in some cases the opening of airtight seals designed to prevent deterioration.

(e) *Contamination of materials* by storage of certain types of materials in close proximity (e.g. storage of oil drums alongside food stuffs).

(f) *Damage* inflicted during storage by careless handling.

(g) *Failure to follow stock rotation code* and therefore allowing old stock to be left unused while newer stock is used.

17. Stores management and prevention of deterioration

There are several ways in which trained and experienced

stores management staff can attempt to prevent materials deteriorating in any store.

(a) *Conditions of storage installations.* Checks should be made to ensure that all storage installations are clean and damp free and a regular inspection should be carried out of all doors, windows, ventilators, etc., for signs of leakage. In cases of damage, immediate arrangements must be made with the maintenance department to effect repairs.

(b) *Suppliers' instructions.* Strict adherence to suppliers' storage instructions will ensure a greatly extended stock life. In many cases suppliers use a series of self-explanatory signs or codes designed to communicate, visually, the important conditions of storage and handling.

(c) *Temperature and humidity.* Stores managers must ensure that conditions of temperature and humidity are correct for the goods being stored. They must also ensure that these conditions are maintained constantly and that materials requiring similar conditions are stored together to concentrate the efforts and resources involved.

(d) *Handling.* Materials handling is a major element of the stores 'mix'. Proper materials handling is vital to reducing damage and breakages and to preventing deterioration. This aspect of the stores manager's work can range from ensuring that staff follow simple handling instructions given by the supplier (e.g. 'fragile, handle with care') to supervising the issue and loading of complex chemicals in close proximity.

(e) *Supervision.* Supervision of all storage and handling of materials by trained and experienced staff reduces the risk of bad storage or faulty handling.

Health and safety

18. Common causes of accidents in the store

The incidence of accidents in stores will depend partly upon the materials stored, but will also be greatly affected by the way work is organized and by the working environment. The following are some of the causes common to most stores:

(a) *Incorrect manual handling* of materials causing strain, muscle damage and long periods of sickness.

(b) *Faulty equipment* that suddenly breaks down at a vital moment.

(c) *Poor storage conditions* in the form of bad floors and unstable racks, shelves, bins and general fittings.

(d) *Storage and handling equipment overloaded or misused* against manufacturer's specifications.

(e) *Lack of supervision* within the stores resulting in bad stores practice, untidiness and carelessness.

19. Statement of safety policy

A statement of safety policy should be issued by the management of the stores to give a clear indication of responsibilities and policies in relation to safety. The following statement is a typical one from a modern and well-organized store:

Purchasing and Supplies Section
Statement of Safety Policy — Stores

(a) The policies contained within the Corporate and Departmental Statements of Safety Policy and those matters referred to herein will be implemented to provide the means for all stores employees to work in a safe environment. The organization and arrangements for the time being in force for the implementation of the policy will be described in this statement.

(b) The Purchasing and Supplies Manager has overall responsibility for ensuring that there are safe conditions of work within the stores, that sufficient information, instruction, training and supervision is available to enable hazards to be avoided, and that each employee may contribute to his own safety and health at work. He will take all reasonable steps to meet those responsibilities as set out in his terms of reference and will issue codes of safe practice which must be adhered to at all times.

(c) *On a routine basis* the responsibility is assigned to the Stores Supervisor as set out in his terms of reference. He will make periodic visits to the various stores within his control and will ensure that particular attention is paid to the provision and maintenance of the following:

> (*i*)   machinery, plant, equipment and systems of work that are safe and without risk to health;
>
> (*ii*) safe and healthy arrangement for the handling and use of materials;
>
> (*iii*) adequate welfare facilities;
>
> (*iv*) a clean and tidy work place.

(d) It is the intention of the Purchasing and Supplies manager to *highlight hazards* to safety and to compile lists of known hazards together with details of preventative and (where appropriate) emergency action to be taken. These sheets will be posted on the stores notice boards and will be issued to Union Stewards and Safety Representatives. All employees must report immediately any accidents or unsafe or hazardous working conditions to their supervisor. In the event of absences by the Stores Supervisor, the Purchasing and Supplies Manager will assume routine responsibility.

(e) *All employees are reminded of their own duties* under sections 7 and 8 of the Health and Safety at Work etc. Act 1974, and in particular it is their duty to take all reasonable care for the health and safety of themselves and those working with them and around them who may be affected by their acts or omissions at work.

Everyone must report immediately to their supervisor any *dangerous or defective* plant, machinery, equipment or stores and any unsafe working systems or environment. All accidents should be reported immediately to the appropriate supervisor who will ensure that the Accident Register is completed together with the accident report forms which should be forwarded to the Purchasing and Supplies Manager as soon after the accident as is practicable and certainly within twenty-four hours.

(f) *Protective clothing and equipment* provided for use must be worn when carrying out those functions for which they were issued.

(g) *The Department Safety Officer* will assist with advice and help as required and will coordinate the Sections' efforts with the rest of the Public Services and Works Department.

(h) The procedure for dealing with any question arising out of any points set out in this statement is to be dealt with as laid down in the *Procedure for Dealing with Grievances*.

(i) Failure to comply with the Health and Safety at Work Act and with the instructions set out above will result in *disciplinary action* being taken, in accordance with the Council's disciplinary procedures.

Purchasing and Supplies Manager

20. Codes of safe practice

Stores management should also issue statements giving detailed guidance on safe practices and procedures to all members of the stores staff. The following is a typical code of safe practice:

Health and Safety at Work
Code of Safe Practice — Stores

It is essential in order to achieve and maintain a safe working environment that all employees follow the procedures set out below.

Under section 7 of the Health and Safety at Work etc. Act, all employees are reminded:

(a) to take reasonable care for health and safety of himself and of other persons who may be affected by his acts or omissions at work; and

(b) as regards any duty or requirement imposed on his employer or any other person by or under any of the relevant statutory provisions, to cooperate with him so far as is necessary to enable that duty or requirement to be performed or complied with.

Materials handling

(a) Do not lift a weight that is too heavy for you.

(b) Protective gloves and footwear must be worn when rough, sharp or heavy objects are being carried. They should also be used for carrying rubbish.

(c) The floor surface should be checked and made free from obstruction, grease or unevenness before carrying.

(d) When lifting manually always obtain a correct hold, keep a straight back, chin in, arms to the body and correct balance with knees bent.

(e) Mechanical lifting devices must be maintained and examined regularly.

(f) Know the weight being lifted and select tackle of adequate strength.

(g) Give clear signals and keep out from under the lifting device.

(h) Use the correct equipment and correct number of men for the job.

(i) Move only as much as is safe at one time.

(j) Have one person in charge in a team operation, and ensure that every man knows his job.

(k) When loading a vehicle, ensure the load is stacked correctly and securely.

(l) Ensure that the load does not obstruct your vision.

Storage

(a) Check the floor load capacity.

(b) Do not stack against walls. Spread the load evenly.

(c) Do not lean a stack against the one next to it.

(d) Stack straight, avoid overbalancing, and do not exceed seven foot high, manually.

(e) Ensure that gangways are adequate and free from obstruction.

(f) Do not overload racks or bins.

(g) Barrels and drums should be stacked on end.

(h) Materials should not overhang the sides of pallets or jut out into gangways.

(i) Move materials as little as possible, and when possible use mechanical aids, and travel the shortest distance.

(j) Care should be taken when handling flammable or corrosive materials, gases and fluids, and these items should be stored in a special building or container.

(k) When using ladders, use the right one for the job and examine it first for good condition. All ladders should be lashed at the top or supported by a second person at the bottom. Extreme care is required when carrying ladders in confined spaces.

(l) Fire-points, electrical points and exits must be clear of obstruction.

(m) Manufacturers' instructions as to the safe use, handling, storage or servicing of goods must be strictly adhered to at all times.

Stores discipline

(a) Be a good housekeeper — tidiness is essential. Everything should be put in the right place as soon as possible.

(b) Floor surfaces should be kept clean and spillage cleared up immediately.

(c) Good behaviour is important. No horseplay, running or unauthorized riding on trucks.

(d) Do not open doors carelessly.

(e) Take care when pulling hand trucks. Avoid hitting persons or objects.

(f) Only smoke in the messroom, not in storage areas.

(g) Protruding nails, loose floorboards and sharp edges should all be reported and dealt with without delay.

(h) Care must be taken when vehicles are backing into storage areas.

(i) Hand tools — knives, scissors, hammers, etc. — should be handled sensibly and when not in use put in a safe place. They should be maintained in good repair and used in a good light.

Fire precautions

(a) Escape doors must not be locked while persons are employed in the building. Means of escape are to be kept free of obstruction at all times.

(b) All combustible materials should be stacked to allow ventilation and easy access. They should also be kept away from heat, hot pipes, electric lights and fuse boards.

(c) Heating appliances must be based on incombustible hearths and away from combustible materials.

(d)   Fire points should be clearly distinguished and easily accessible.

(e)   Fire extinguishers and equipment must be checked by one storekeeper regularly.

(f)   Broken or ineffective electrical equipment should be repaired without delay.

(g)   Electric cables must be kept off the floor.

(h)   Electrical installations should only be made by the electrical division.

(i)   In the event of fire, sound the alarm and report to your supervisor. If possible tackle the fire with an extinguisher or asbestos blanket. Then evacuate the building and close doors and windows.

Protective clothing

(a)   Protective clothing must be worn when fumes, dusts, flying particles, falling materials, handling hazards and corrosive or poisonous substances are likely to be encountered.

(b)   The following clothing is available to stores personnel:
  (*i*)   donkey jackets;
  (*ii*)   bib and brace overalls;
  (*iii*)   gloves;
  (*iv*)   goggles;
  (*v*)   steel toe-capped boots;
  (*vi*)   helmets;
  (*vii*)   warehouse coats.

(c)   Disciplinary action will be taken against an employee who fails to use protective clothing where its use is essential.

Health

(a)   The stores building should be inspected from time to time to ensure that it is maintained in good condition. Particular attention should be paid to the roof, gutters, drainpipes and drains.

(b)   The walls and windows should be kept clean.

(c)   Toilets must be clean and adequately equipped, clothing accommodated and drinking water provided.

(d)   Refuse must be collected regularly.

(e)   Stairs should be well lit, treads in good repair and hand-rails adequate.

(f)   Lighting and heating in working areas should be adequate.

First aid

(a)   First-aid boxes will be available at every store and inspected regularly by the storekeeper to ensure that they contain all regulation equipment.

(b) In the event of an accident:
- (*i*) telephone for help, and report to your supervisor;
- (*ii*) do only what is necessary to put the casualty in a comfortable position;
- (*iii*) do not move the casualty more than necessary before the arrival of trained personnel;
- (*iv*) do not give the casualty anything to drink;
- (*v*) talk quietly — act calmly.

(c) As soon as practicable inform Management, complete the accident report and enter details in the accident book.

Progress test 10

1. What are the two main methods of ensuring that the stores are secure? **(3, 4)**

2. Outline some of the reasons why stock security is so vital. **(5)**

3. Outline the responsibilities of the stores manager in relation to security. **(6)**

4. What are the main elements of a security policy? **(7)**

5. Give an outline of sensible fire precautions that should be taken within a typical industrial store. **(12)**

6. Why is it important to separate so-called 'high-risk' items from the standard stock? **(13)**

7. How can stores management help to reduce stock deterioration? **(17)**

Case study no. 4

ABC Ltd

Figure 10.1 shows the layout of ABC Ltd's warehouse. Examine it closely and comment upon the design in terms of:

(a) safety;
(b) security.

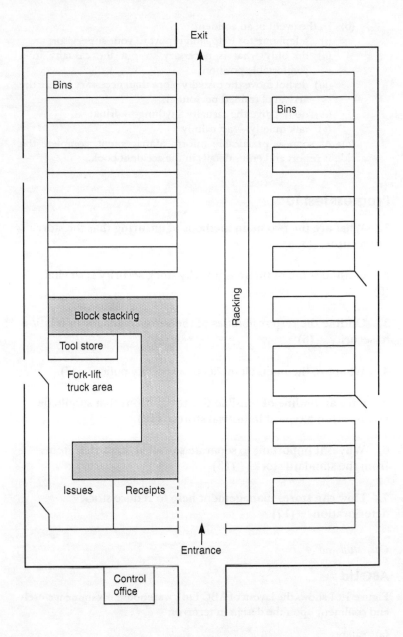

Figure 10.1 *Layout of ABC Ltd warehouse*

11
Stock obsolescence and redundancy

Definitions

1. The process of obsolescence

Stock which is described as obsolete is that which no longer has any use or value to the organization that holds the stock. The stages in the process are as follows:

(a) obsolescent;
(b) obsolete;
(c) redundant;
(d) scrap.

This process can be very costly and wasteful for the organization.

2. Obsolescent

This is the term used to describe the stock that will soon be of no use or value to the organization that has it in stock. This usually happens because of a change in the method of production or technological change that means that, for a period of time, the organization will have to use two lines of stock, the new line being gradually phased in as the old is phased out. For example, the organization may decide to change from one form of packaging to another. The old packaging will still have some use until the changeover is complete.

3. Obsolete

This is the next stage of the process, when the stock becomes completely worthless to the organization. This is not to say that another organization which has not adopted the changes which made the stock obsolete may not be interested in purchasing the stock for its own use. However, in most cases, such changes reflect a major alteration in methods or materials by an industry, and companies engaged in that industry change very quickly over to the new material and therefore the market for the old stock is greatly reduced.

4.　Redundant

This is when the stock in question is completely useless to both its owner and other organizations. If we look at the development of the silicon chip, for instance, we can see that very soon all other traditional electronic circuits will be redundant.

5.　Scrap

At this stage, the stock is sold off for the value of the materials it is produced from, rather than any value in its own right.

6.　Scrap management

Research by Bird and Clopton has shown that in some instances a scrap management policy could reap financial benefits for the organization. To achieve these savings the following must be considered by stores management:

(a) *Sell-back agreements.* To what extent could the original supplier be encouraged to buy back materials that are no longer required by the organization? In some situations the supplier will be able to reprocess materials and will therefore be willing to buy them back.

(b) *Marketing of scrap materials.* The organization should actively seek to market scrap materials, rather than just accept a spot price.

(c) *Encouraging other departments within the organization to accept and use second-hand equipment.*

Factors that produce obsolete stocks

7.　Introduction

There are several factors that can cause stock to become obsolete and most of these are outside the control of the organization itself. It is inevitable that, in our highly advanced technological society, obsolescence will occur. This is added to the problems of changing consumer demands and tastes and can lead to stocks becoming obsolete in a relatively short period of time. The factors that cause stocks to become obsolete are summarized in **8–11** below.

8. Changes in the methods of production

The organization often finds that new and more efficient methods of production are being introduced throughout an industry. This will result in the organization having to consider a change in its existing stock of raw materials, parts and packaging stocks.

9. Technological changes

In today's highly technological environment, major steps forward are being made in all areas of industry and commerce. The most striking example is that of the microprocessor revolution in electronics. The effects of the silicon chip are dramatic and far-reaching. Stocks of traditional electronic goods are being made obsolete by very rapid development in this field.

10. Changes in customer demand

A change in the consumer's buying habits or tastes will lead to obsolete stocks. There are several factors that can cause a change in customer demand.

(a) actions of major competitors (e.g. prices, quality, advertising);
(b) changes in the customer's own production system and methods.

11. Alterations on the part of the suppliers

In some cases a supplier may decide to halt the production of an item which the organization has incorporated into its original design. If this halt in production is very sudden, then any part-finished work or work in progress held in stock could be in danger, unless a suitable alternative supply can be located.

12. Rationalization

The organization may decide that a period of rationalization is required. This could lead to stocks of certain items becoming redundant as that part of the operation is run down. Obviously, management will attempt to minimize stock losses.

Waste reduction and obsolete stock procedures

13. Reduction of stock waste

It is vital that stores management takes steps to minimize the effects of stock becoming obsolete and redundant. Stock represents the organization's money and therefore must not be wasted as a result of excess redundant stocks. The store manager can reduce the amount of stock wastes in various ways.

(a) *Ensuring that working stocks are kept at a level* low enough to reduce the risk of obsolete stocks should a change come about (especially materials and equipment of a high-risk nature, e.g. electronics, plastics, etc.).

(b) *Constantly reviewing stock movement frequencies* (via the stock record system). A falling rate of usage in certain items could indicate that they have been superseded by another item held in stock.

(c) *Being aware of changes* in techniques and demand within the industry. This helps the stores manager to forecast the useful life-cycle of the stock held, and will forewarn him of major changes and other implications.

(d) *Maintaining communications* between stores and the other major departments involved. Changes in sales, designs, methods and operations must all be known to the relevant departments and stores must ensure that they are kept informed of all developments that could affect the life-cycle of the stocks held. A breakdown in these channels of communications will lead to large and expensive amounts of stock becoming scrap.

(e) *Maintaining special contact* between stores and purchasing to ensure that changes communicated to purchasing, in terms of new orders, are passed on to the stores.

(f) *Making arrangements to dispose of obsolete stock* immediately the decision is taken to declare the stock obsolete. This will enable the stock to be sold off at a reduced price, but with some return. Delay will reduce the saleability of the stock dramatically and therefore the price and return.

14. Factors that affect the decision to declare stock obsolete

There are several factors that will affect management's decision to declare stock obsolete. In most cases the decision is really about the timing of the changeover, rather than the change itself, which has been made unavoidable by external factors.

(a) *Value of stock involved.* If the organization finds that it has a very large, expensive stock of the item it will be forced to delay the change for as long as possible.

(b) *Alternative use.* Use of the stock in another capacity or areas within the organization may mean that redundancies can be avoided or at least reduced.

(c) *Action of competitors.* If competitors have already changed over and are taking away the organization's sales, then the organization has no alternative but to follow suit immediately and stand the loss.

(d) *Non-scrap items.* It may only be that the rate of usage of the item has dramatically reduced, rather than that the item needs to be completely scrapped, as in the case of spare parts for products produced by the organization. In this situation the organization may decide to hold the stock for a long period and stand the cost of storage.

15. Obsolete stock equation

This is a simple equation that can be used by stores management to estimate the amount of stock that could become redundant in a given situation. The equation is as follows:

$$\frac{\text{Total stock}}{\text{Rate of usage per week}} = \text{Stock in weeks}$$

Obsolete stock = Stock in weeks – Weeks to changeover

For example:

$$\frac{1,000}{100} = 10 \text{ weeks}$$

Obsolete stock = 10 – 4 = 6 weeks

Or 600

The sources of data for the obsolete stock equation are as follows:

(a) *Total stock:* stock record cards.
(b) *Rate of usage:* stock records and user departments.
(c) *Changeover date:* user/purchasing.

16. Obsolete stock procedure

Because of the amount of money involved in stock obsolescence and redundancy, it is vital that a procedure to deal with the problem is laid down and followed to ensure control. The procedure is as follows:

(a) Management decision to declare stock obsolescent.
(b) Arrangements made to dispose of surplus stock or scrap.
(c) Stock written off the total value of stock held and stock records and stock control adjusted accordingly.

17. Redundancy report

Once it has been established that stock is completely redundant and has to be written off as a loss, a redundancy report form must be produced and forwarded to the finance department. This report must include the following data:

(a) item's code number;
(b) full description;
(c) amount of stock involved;
(d) book value of stock;
(e) means of disposal (scrap, sold off, given away, etc.).

18. Role of stocktaking in redundancy

During stocktaking items of stock and equipment can be recognized as having become obsolete or redundant but not recorded or disposed of. This is especially likely in very large stores buildings where bad layout tends to leave small amounts of stock isolated and hidden. Once the stock has been discovered it can be investigated and dealt with as outlined in the previous paragraphs. Obsolete stock which is taking up storage capacity is costing the organization money that it need not spend.

Progress test 11

1. What is meant by 'obsolescent'? (2)

2. Describe the factors that can create obsolete stocks. **(8–11)**

3. How can stock wastage be reduced? **(13)**

4. What is the obsolete stock equation? **(15)**

5. Describe the procedure for dealing with obsolete stocks. **(16)**

6. What kind of data would a typical stock redundancy report contain? **(17)**

7. How can stocktaking contribute towards the reduction of the costs of obsolete stocks? **(18)**

12
Issue of stock

The issue function

1. Definition

The 'issue' function of stores management is the process of reacting to the demands of users for goods and services held within the store. The success of this function is often taken as a measure of the efficiency of the whole stores operation.

2. Types of issues

Because of the size and complexity of modern business, many stores hold a great variety of items and therefore different types of issue classifications exist to cover this variety.

(a) *Replacement issues.* This is where an item of equipment or a supply of goods has been broken or·has become worn out or obsolete. In this case the authorization for a new issue is the exchange for the old piece of equipment.

(b) *Imprest issues.* These are items that are required by the user to be constantly on hand, and therefore the user will need constantly to top up his supply. In some cases the items are held in small, outlying unit stores.

(c) *Loan issues.* These are usually tools and equipment that are required by certain departments for special jobs. The stores will lend the equipment needed. Such loans are controlled by means of the person borrowing the items signing out the tools and signing them back in again in the stores 'On Loan' book.

(d) *Allocated issues.* This is when stock has been allocated by the production plan (*see* 19:8) to a certain operation in a given department or section (e.g. production, engineering, packaging, etc.). In these cases the formal production planning document acts as the means of authorization.

(e) *General issues*. These are the general items of stock needed by various departments within the operation for the day-to-day running of the company. They could range from engineering spares to packaging materials.

(f) *Capital issues*. These are the major pieces of equipment purchased and issued by the company. In many cases, large capital items will not be held in stock, so that purchasing will buy the item and it will be issued as soon as it is delivered to the factory. Capital issues will always involve senior management in the issue process.

(g) *Issue of dangerous materials*. In cases where highly dangerous materials are being handled, a special issue procedure has to be followed to ensure that proper precautions are taken against possible damage. This usually involves the senior storekeeper becoming involved in the actual issue process.

Control of stock issues

3. Importance of control

The stock held by the company represents a great deal of the organization's money and resources. Control of the issue of that stock is therefore vital if losses are to be avoided.

4. Methods of controlling issue of stock

The basic principle behind the control of stock is that of *authorization*; that is to say, a system or procedure that will ensure that only certain stock is used by certain people for certain activities within the operation. Authorization of issues can be based on several systems.

(a) *Financial limits*. This is where the stores is given a list of persons, each of whom is allowed to request stock from stores, up to a given stock value limit. This system is not very common and does have certain drawbacks as follows:

    (*i*) it means keeping the stores up to date on the value of stock involved;

    (*ii*) it involves the work of updating the list of authorized persons and their financial limits;

(*iii*) it does not always prevent misuse of stock.

(b) *Position within the organization.* This is where members of the staff are able to request stock on the basis of their position within the company. For example, a manager would be able to request a greater amount of stock than a supervisor. These limits would have to be given to the stores.

(c) *The function within the organization.* This provides more close control of stock because it restricts staff to requesting only those items and services that they require in relation to their job or function within the operation, e.g. an electrical engineering foreman can only request related materials up to a given financial limit.

(d) *Free issues.* Many firms have found that it is more 'control effective' to have less control of the very small and inexpensive items of stock and concentrate on the more valuable items held in the store. This follows the concept of the '20/80 rule' which states that in relation to stores, 80 per cent of the total value of stock is represented by only 20 per cent of the total items of stock held. This has proved very effective in many stores.

5. Problems associated with control systems

There are certain problems that arise in most organizations which make the operation of these kinds of control systems difficult.

(a) *Updating of lists of authorized persons.* Because of the constant movement of staff as a result of promotions, resignations and transfers, formal lists of persons who are able to request stock and sample signatures are very difficult to maintain properly and tend to become out of date very quickly.

(b) *Designation of the number of persons who can authorize a request from stores.* This is a serious problem facing stores management. Too few members of staff designated can cause delays in the issue of stock. This is because if the designated members of staff are not available, production may be held up until one arrives to authorize the request. If, on the other hand, too many people are designated to authorize requests, then control will be seriously weakened, because stores will be unable to keep track of who can and who should not request stock.

(c) *Updating financial limits.* Inflation has caused many firms to abandon or greatly increase the financial limit controls on the request of stock, mainly because regular increases in the price of items means that goods and services vital to individual members of staff are constantly being moved out of their request range.

(d) *Flexibility and control conflict.* In any control system there tends to be a conflict between the need for a strict control of stock issued and the day-to-day operational needs of the organization. This conflict can be the cause of many shopfloor problems. Stores must be aware of such problems, and must ensure that every effort is made to issue the stock required.

6. Documentation

To enable the issue of stock to be successfully monitored and controlled, specialized control documents have been developed.

(a) *The issue note (see* Fig. 12.1) This is the basic control document used by most organizations. It comes in many different forms and will contain details relevant only to the organization involved. However, all issue notes do have certain common features that can be identified and listed, in relation to the scope of information contained within the form:

	ISSUE NOTE	Date
	Stock required	Goods issued to
Code no.		
Description		
Quantity		
Cost of stock issued		
Authorization Signature		

Figure 12.1 *Issue note*

(*i*) item required;
(*ii*) quantity requested;

    (*iii*) code number;
    (*iv*) department which has requisitioned the item;
    (*v*) date of the transaction;
    (*vi*) cost of issue;
    (*vii*) correct authorization.

We can see from this list that correct completion of the issue note by the requisitioner is vital if the correct item is to be issued quickly and efficiently.

(b) *Production programme* (*see* 19:**7**). This document is produced by the production planning department and will give details of all production activities over a given period of time. It enables stores to ensure that the correct items and services required for production are readily available. In relation to authorization, the production programme is 'authority' in itself and stores must react to production changes accordingly. Information contained on the production programme includes:

    (*i*) amount of materials required;
    (*ii*) type of items required;
    (*iii*) timetable of requirements;
    (*iv*) possible alternative programmes.

Issue procedures

7. Introduction

There is definite series of events that occur between the original need for a particular item of stock and its final issue to the requisitioner.

8. Need

The user has to decide what he needs and the type, quality, specification and amounts involved.

9. Compilation of issue note

The issue document has to be properly completed, giving fullest possible details of the goods required.

10. Authorization

The requisitioner must then locate the appropriate member of staff designated to authorize issues from stock and seek his approval and signature.

11. Requisitioner's check

The person designated to authorize the given issue of stock will be obliged to study very carefully the type and details of the issue to ensure that demand is 'real' and that the limits imposed by the organization are kept.

12. Presentation to stores

Once the issue note has been checked and authorized it will be presented to the stores for delivery. Stores is obliged to check all the data contained and verify the reliability of the authorization given.

13. Identification

Stores will then identify the items required, usually by the code number or reference by which the item has been classified. This is achieved by using the details contained in the issue note and the information held within the stores vocabulary (*see* **9:6**).

14. Selection

Once the item required has been identified it can be selected from the store. The method of selection employed will depend upon the form of stores organization and the type of goods required. There are in fact two main types of selection system as follows:

(a) *Sectional selection.* Each member of the stores team is made responsible for the selection and issue of certain items from certain sections of the store. This has the advantage of the development of detailed knowledge of particular sections of the store. However, it has the main drawback of workload distribution, in as much as, at certain times, some members of the stores team will be idle while others working on sections with high usage items will be constantly at work.

(b) *Flexibility selection.* Each member of the stores team can be called upon to select and issue any item held within the stores area. This has the main advantage of more efficient work distribution and more effective use of staff resources.

15. Issue of stock required

Once the items have been selected, delivery or collection can take place. Items may be collected by the requisitioner if the goods are readily available and can be transported. In some cases, departments may order a large selection of items that may need several days to be selected and marshalled together for collection or, in some cases, delivery to the point of consumption. Delivery of items often takes place when large amounts are involved and the materials handling function is under the direct control of supply management.

16. Cost allocation

Every item used in the running of the operation has to be costed against a certain batch of production, or against a department's budget, to ensure that the costing department will be able to allocate the material costs to each stage of the operation and therefore be able to determine the true cost of production. To enable them to do this the issue note must be 'priced', that is, the value of each issue is indicated on the issue note and it is then forwarded to costing for allocation.

17. Notification to stock records and stock control

It is very important that once materials have been issued, both stock records and stock control are advised in writing. This will ensure that all stock record cards are updated and that an accurate picture of the total stock situation can be maintained. Notification to stock control will ensure that sufficient supplies of all materials are maintained.

18. The role of computers in the issue of stock

Because of the rapid development of computer technology in relation to stores management (*see* 23:4) many organizations are using computers to improve the quality of issue control. This can be achieved in the following ways:

(a) *Direct computer input*. A specially coded card can be issued to authorized personnel who will then use these cards to obtain stock from stores. This will decrease the possibility of misuse and it will also directly update the stock records system if linked to the computer.

(b) *Updating lists*. Immediate update of authorized issue personnel will also be possible when issues are controlled by computer.

(c) *Improved identification of requirements.* A computer is able to locate and identify very quickly and accurately a certain code number against the item's given description.

(d) *Automation.* In some cases the whole issue of stock has been automated and items can be selected from stock and issued simply by providing the correct codes and signals for the computer.

Progress test 12

1. List the main types of issues that a typical store would handle.   **(2)**

2. What are the main problems associated with issue control systems?   **(5)**

3. Outline the basic issue procedures.   **(7)**

4. What are main control systems for the issue of stock?   **(3)**

Part three

Materials planning and control

The scope and purpose of materials control

1. Definition

Materials control is the process of ensuring that the stock held by the organization is supplied to those parts of the operation that require items (i.e. production, distribution, sales, engineering, etc.), bearing in mind the factors of time, location, quantity, quality and cost.

2. The concept of materials control

In modern supply management, materials control is the real control function; it encompasses all the basic aims of the materials management operation. The basic concept of materials control is quite simply the right material, in the right quantity, of the right quality, at the right time and place. Having said that, the element of *cost* in relation to materials control also plays a vital role. The aims of materials control have to be achieved, but bear in mind the limitations of cost, of which there are many regarding stocks held (*see* **3**). Gus Gillespie, a Canadian writer in the field, states 'In these days of high interest rates, technological change, vigorous competition and shifting market bases, the cost of inventory mismanagement has become prohibitive' (*Modern Purchasing,* 1982).

3. Costs involved in holding stocks

There are several basic costs incurred by any organization which holds stocks of materials.

(a) *Interest on capital tied up.* When an organization builds up stock it has, first, to purchase that stock from suppliers. In many cases the goods will have to be paid for before those goods are processed by the organization, sold, and profit earned. Therefore there is a gap between the organization paying for the stock and the final selling of the finished item. This has the effect of committing a great deal of the organization's money which will not earn any interest and cannot be used for any other purpose, until the goods are actually sold. If the period of time is a long one, it can be very costly and can lead to cash flow problems for the organization.

(b) *Materials handling costs.* When stocks are held by an organization they have to be stored and handled by the stores staff. This will include the use of expensive materials handling equipment, storage facilities and labour time.

(c) *Stock maintenance.* Stocks have to be stored in certain conditions, depending on the items involved (e.g. warm, dry, cool, etc.). Such 'environmental' needs have to be met if deterioration of the stock is to be avoided. This can result in the building of special storehouses, or the introduction of heating, ventilation and lighting systems, all of which are very expensive.

(d) *Administration of stores.* When goods are held in stock there is a great deal of administrative work involved, including control of stock receipts, issues, stock record cards, bin cards, etc. All these duties take up resources in the form of space, labour, skills and time.

(e) *Insurance of stock.* Because of the amount of money tied up when stocks are held, it is vital that the organization has adequate insurance cover, so that in the event of a fire, flood or accident, the company will be able to claim from its insurers sufficient funds to replace the stock lost. Therefore the more stock is kept, the more money is tied up and so the insurance premiums will rise accordingly. Insurance is very expensive indeed, so much so that most companies are only covered for a certain amount of stock loss, hoping that a total loss will not come about.

(f) *Obsolescence costs.* Materials held in stock may become obsolete and thus will add to the total costs of storage (*see* Chapter 11).

(g) *Security of stocks.* Materials are cash and need to be stored in secure conditions, but security systems such a CCTV are expensive to buy and install. Stock losses to theft are added to the total cost of storage.

4. Balance between service and economy in material control
It has been shown in **3** that to hold and control stock is a very expensive business, but stocks are necessary to ensure that the

operation can continue. Materials management has to attempt to balance the need for a good reliable service in terms of a constant supply of materials against the need to provide that service without committing vast amounts of the organization's money, thus reducing profits and risking cash flow problems. This is one of the reasons why stock control is such a difficult task for materials management.

In Japan, stock management is based upon the 'just-in-time' approach. This involves a policy of holding stock at the very minimum so as to reduce total costs. This is in contrast to UK organizations that tend to adopt the more traditional 'just-in-case' approach to materials management, that is having excessive stocks to cope with demands that may or may not materialize.

5. Reasons why organizations hold stocks

Having come this far, the next question must be, if holding stock is so expensive, why do it? Why not simply rely on a daily delivery of stock? The reasons are set out below.

(a) *Unreliable deliveries of stock.* Most organizations find it impossible to rely totally on any of their suppliers to deliver every order exactly on time, every time an order is placed. Few suppliers could boast that they had never been held up by strikes, transport delays, bad weather or administrative errors.

(b) *Bulk discounts.* By holding more stock than is needed in any one production period (e.g. weekly), the organization is able to buy in large quantities. Thus the purchasing department can obtain a more advantageous price when, because of bulk buying, the supplier will have a cheaper unit rate. In a company which spends millions of pounds every year on stock, such discounts can make a great contribution to overall levels of profit.

(c) *Reduction in operational risk.* Because more stock than is needed is held, there is less risk of a 'nil stock' situation coming about which could then stop production. If a supplier does fail to deliver the goods needed, the factory can still be supplied from stock. The cost of stopping production because of nil stocks can be very high indeed. In addition, to fixed costs, there will be:

(*i*) loss of profit;
(*ii*) loss of sales;
(*iii*) loss of reputation as a supplier;

(*iv*) the cost of employing labour who cannot produce.

(d) *Reduced purchasing cycle.* The purchasing cycle (*see* Fig. 13.1) is the sequence of events that has to be gone through before an item is finally delivered to stock. When an organization holds a high stock, the number of times this cycle has to be gone through is reduced. This cuts down the use of management and administrative resources and thus reduces the cost of ordering (i.e. typing of orders, postage, negotiations, telephone calls, progressing, invoice checking, payments).

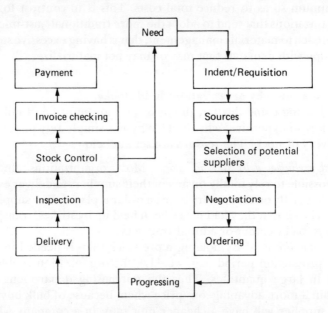

Figure 13.1 *The purchasing cycle*

(e) *Appreciation of stock value.* In times of high levels of price inflation, the holding of stocks, purchased at a certain price, can help to protect the organization from price increases.

(f) *Increased flexibility of output.* By holding a certain amount of reserve stock, the organization will be in a position to increase its level of output should an increase in demand come about (e.g. from changes in tax laws, fashions or habits).

(g) *Advantage of low seasonal prices.* There are some products that are only available at certain periods of the year and therefore the organization must purchase all its needs at one time (e.g. cotton, sugar, etc.). In some cases the price of the product varies according to world markets, currency changes or climatic conditions. By holding a large stock the organization will be able to buy when prices are low and thus reduce the cost of production. It should be noted that a common problem with stock control is that of 'bargain buys': materials that are purchased and stocked for reasons of low price, rather than need.

6. Aims of materials control

Obviously every organization has its own needs and requirements, which have to be met by its stock control system. However, if we look at stock control in terms of the average medium-size production and distribution organization, we will obtain a complete picture of stock control and its aims.

(a) *Supply a constant flow of materials to the operation.* The basic aim of stock control is to ensure that items needed for production, maintenance, engineering, distribution, etc. are in stock and ready for use. The correct quantity of stock required must be readily available.

(b) *Ensure correct quality of stock required.* Stock control is responsible for ensuring that the correct type and quality of stock needed is always available for use in the operation. The type and quality of the item required will be set by the user, purchasing and quality control. It is up to stock control to ensure that the specification set is the one that stores will issue.

(c) *Distribute stocks.* Distribution of stock can relate to both pre-production and finished stocks, and to goods held in other parts of the country or other parts of the factory complex. It is an aim of stock control to ensure that the goods needed for the operation are at the point of consumption. This can involve transportation of stock from site to site, all of which must be controlled and organized by stock control.

(d) *Time factor.* Having fulfilled the previous requirements of the task of controlling stock, the stock control system must also ensure that the required stocks are available at the correct time.

(e) *Supply information for control of production.* Stock control has to advise production planning about what to produce, in order to keep up established levels of the organization's finished stock, and must also advise on the amount of production, maintenance and distribution that can be carried out in the light of the working stock held.

(f) *Control obsolescence of stock.* Stock control is responsible for ensuring that all the stocks held by the organization are being used at a regular rate and therefore have not been superseded by a new or redesigned item. It can happen that items in stock are made redundant by changes in design, technology and the law. It is the job of stock control to ensure that the stock left which cannot be used in the operation is at a minimum.

(g) *Control stock rotation.* Stock rotation is the process of ensuring that materials are used in the correct order, and in accordance with their shelf-life or 'sell-by' date. This ensures that all stock issued is in the correct condition.

7. Factors that affect the levels of stock held

The stock control system is responsible for the correct establishment of stock levels for every item held in the store. When these levels are being established certain basic operational factors have to be considered and then reflected in the final stock figure. These factors are discussed below.

(a) *Operational need.* This relates to the amount of stock needed by production, sales, distribution, maintenance and other departments over a certain period of time (e.g. weekly or monthly). The figures will be affected by overall demand and sales forecasts. In many cases information relating to stock usage in the past is supplied by stock record cards.

(b) *Shelf-life of stock.* If an item has a very restricted shelf-life (e.g. fresh fruit) then the amount of stock that can be held will be controlled by its actual shelf-life period, unless special storage facilities can be arranged.

(c) *Delivery period.* This relates to the time taken for the supplier to produce, despatch and transport the goods needed to the store. The period of time will affect the level of stock needed to be held. Sufficient stock has to be purchased to last between one delivery and the next. The delivery period will depend on several important factors, as follows:

   (*i*) Are the goods imported?
   (*ii*) Are they ex-stock?

(*iii*) Do they have to be produced from an original specification?

(*iv*) How far will the goods have to be transported?

(d) *Buffer stock.* Buffer stock refers to the extra stock a store holds to cover any unforeseen hold-ups in delivery or sudden changes in demand. The buffer stock will vary in size depending on how reliable deliveries are and on the operational risk involved. In many organizations 25 per cent of the minimum stock level is regarded as being an adequate buffer or emergency stock.

(e) *Capital available.* This is always a very important factor when establishing the level of stock held. If funds are not available to finance the stock level first established, it will have to be reduced.

(f) *Storage capacity.* The amount of stock that can be held will be restricted by the actual physical capacity of the stores operation. In some cases where a special store is needed (e.g. a refrigerated store) for items that need special storage, e.g. meat, fresh vegetables, explosives, chemicals, etc., then the actual space available to store such items will be strictly limited by the capacity of the store. In some cases excess stock can be stored in outside warehouse units (*see* 6:**13**).

8. Sources of information for materials control

Stock control is a system that is primarily involved in making decisions which affect many elements of the operation. To enable these decisions to be made accurately and effectively the stock control system needs to have a constant flow of relevant and up-to-date information, including the following:

(a) *Corporate production programmes and schedules.* Information is needed relating to what the company intends to produce, the amounts, type and quality of item, and the production period.

(b) *Sales forecasts.* The sales department produces a forecast of what it believes will happen in terms of what the company will sell. This information is needed by stock control to establish levels of finished stock as well as pre-production stock. Stock control has to ensure that materials are available to meet present and future demand.

(c) *Distribution plans.* Stock control needs information on the distribution of stock in relation to transportation, depot capacity and demand. Stock control will use this information to ensure

stock is in the correct location. This information is usually supplied
by sales and transportation and the local depot involved.

(d) *Engineering programmes.* The basic function of the engineering
department is to service and maintain the plant and equipment
employed by the company. This is usually carried out according
to a predetermined programme, and therefore certain items
(spares, new machinery, etc.) will be needed at certain times. Stock
control will be given a copy of the engineering programme to
ensure that stock is available.

(e) *Maintenance.* The maintenance department, which is
responsible for general maintenance and care of the plant, will
also produce a programme of forthcoming events. A copy of this
should be given to stock control so that stores of essential materials
can be held.

(f) *Production planning.* This is a department which produces the
production programme. A copy of that programme should be sent
to stock control so that all necessary materials (raw materials, work
in progress, components, packaging, etc.) can be supplied.

Progress test 13

1. What are the costs involved in holding stocks?   **(3)**

2. What is meant by the concept of materials control?   **(2)**

3. List the main reasons why organizations hold stocks.   **(5)**

4. What are the key aims of materials control?   **(6)**

5. List the factors that affect the level of stock held.   **(7)**

Stock record systems

Purpose of stock records

1. Definition

Stock records are a formal set of records that contain information about the stock held within the stores system. The range of this information will depend upon the system employed and the scope of the operation. However, there are basic functions which every stock record system should aim to cover, the fundamental one being data on stock held at any given time. Stock records have been called the 'clerical memory' of stores, because of the wide range of information held within a good stock record system.

2. Basic functions of a stock record system

Stock records have several very important functions to perform, all of which are designed to provide information on which effective materials management and other operational decisions can be made. These functions include the following:

(a) To supply information as to the *calculated* level of stock for each item held in the store.

(b) To supply information for the *verification* of physical stock checking, via the process of comparison between stock as calculated by stock records and the physical count.

(c) To supply information for the formulation of *price lists* and the efficient carrying out of material costing activities (most stock record systems contain data relating to current prices of both stock for production and finished stock).

(d) To supply information for *financial control* of the stock by virtue of the process of stock valuation (balance of stock x price per unit).

(e) To supply information for the formulation of *production plans* and distribution plans, both of which require detailed information about the levels of stock, type, shelf-life, etc.

(f) To supply the clerical information on which the *stock control* system depends for effective operation.

(g) To supply information for the establishment and recording of *stock levels* for each item held in stock. These stock levels come under six basic headings:

  (*i*) lead time
  (*ii*) buffer stock
  (*iii*) reorder level
  (*iv*) order quantity
  (*v*) progress level
  (*vi*) maximum stock.

The formulation of these stock levels is fully explained in 15:3.

3. Perpetual inventory

This is the term used to describe the process of constantly updating the information held within the stock record system after each transaction is carried out, e.g. deliveries, issues, transfers, price changes, locations, etc., so that the information indicated in the stock record system is correct and accurate. This enables the stock records manager to supply information to the stores manager and other functional managers, as and when required.

Computer systems

4. Computer systems and stock records

Computers have the ability to store and recall information. This ability, coupled with that of calculation, means the computer has lent itself very well to the process of maintaining stock records. Many companies now use computers to hold and constantly update their stock records. The computer has to be programmed to perform the function of adjusting the stock records. The way in which the information is fed into the computer will depend upon the company and its operation. The basic means of data input into a computer system are as follows:

(a) *Direct input capture systems.* In these systems, the data required to update the stock record file is in a form that can be fed directly into the computer, without having to be processed first. Such systems are becoming very popular as they eliminate the need for input processing which means that the stock record system can be updated more efficiently and more quickly. The process of direct input capture is now widely used in the retail storage and distribution operations of many organizations. One common system employed is that of using the actual price tag-type label as a medium through which the stock record system can be directly updated. The tag is coded, usually in punch card form, and the section retained by the organization contains the relevant data relating to the item sold. Once the data has been fed into the stock record system, management has immediate access to that information.

(b) *Typewriter terminals.* These are specially designed typewriters which are connected directly to the main computer (this connection can be over any distance). As issues are made and deliveries received the storekeeper will 'type' the information on the keyboard, which will in turn feed the information into the computer system. This type of system is used a great deal when an organization has a large central warehouse and many outside units to service. (*See* 23:**9**.)

5. Advantages of a computerized stock record system

There are several advantages of an automatic stock record system, all of which would have to be fully utilized if the cost of operating a computer system were to be justified.

(a) *Increased quality* of the information produced, because of the computer's ability to update stock records immediately.

(b) *Improved access* to information stored in relation to stores management and related operations (i.e. production planning, purchasing, etc.). Because of the use of terminals and VDUs (visual display units), information is accessible to all sections of management.

(c) *Reduction in overall levels of stock.* This is because with the improved control derived from a computerized system, the need for high stock levels will be reduced and therefore overall levels of stock can be reduced.

(d) *Saving in space and storage facilities.* A very large organization holds thousands of different items and would need a great deal of valuable office space to operate and store a manual system, with bulky files and stock cards.

(e) *Reduction in labour costs.* A computerized stock record system will require less staff than a large manual system, which would employ dozens of clerks and supervisors constantly attempting to update the records.

(f) *Overall increase in management control* of the stores operation.

6.   Disadvantages of a computerized system
These include the following:

(a) Computer systems can be very expensive, which may prohibit the smaller companies from adopting this type of system.

(b) Computer control systems are only as good as the staff operating them and the data processed and fed into the computer. Badly trained staff or faulty documentation will not be solved by installing a computer.

(c) A major breakdown in the computer could cause chaos in the system and in the company's operational activities.

Stock record mechanism

7.   The basic stock record system mechanism
The logic on which stock records operate is really quite simple: it applies to the most complex computer system and the simplest manual system. For any given item held in stock, at any time, there is a 'balance of stock' held, which alters as stock is purchased and replaced and as it is issued for sale or production. The balance of stock is therefore constantly altering throughout the stores organization. Stores records are employed to alter the balance of stock, by adding stock in the case of deliveries and subtracting in the case of issues. The need for this type of clerical system is obvious, if one considers the alternative of counting each and every item held in a large store, every time it was necessary to know the level of stock held.

8.   Stock record and bin cards
The information produced by a stock record system has to be

stored on a suitable medium, i.e. a stock record card (*see* Fig. 14.1) which is designed to hold all the information required. Stock record cards are usually centralized and stored in the stock records manager's office. There are various forms in which these cards can be held, depending on the size and scope of the system employed:

STOCK RECORD CARD					
Description		Stock record			
Code number		Date	In	Out	Balance
Location					
Supplier					
Unit cost					
Delivery period					
Unit of issue					
Stock levels	Minimum				
	Maximum				
	Reorder				
Special handling and delivery instructions					

Figure 14.1 *Stock record card*

(a) index card system;
(b) Kalamazoo system;
(c) catalogue system.

9. Information stored

The scope and range of the information stored on a stock record card varies according to the needs of the organization and the resources that it can direct at stock records. However, taking a medium-sized manufacturing company, we could expect to see the following information on a typical stock record card:

(a) Balance of stock held for any given item, at any given time, on a calculated basis.

(b) Unit costs, in relation to goods supplied for production and goods held for distribution and sale.

(c) Supplier's name, company, addresses, telephone and telex numbers and contact (there is often more than one supplier).

(d) Standard delivery period (e.g. four weeks) as set by negotiations between the buyer and the supplier.

(e) Delivery times, in relation to the stores working time (e.g. deliveries of certain products may only be made in the morning).

(f) Unit of issue of the item recorded, e.g. kilograms, dozens, tens, metres.

(g) Method of delivery employed by supplier (e.g. lorry, train, air, sea — all of these may require different materials handling equipment). (*See* 15.1/14.)

(h) The item's code number and description, including specification details, recent alterations, design changes.

(i) Location of the item within the store, warehouse or stockyard.

(j) Special handling instructions that may be needed in relation to the item. This could include warnings about storage conditions (e.g. dampness, sunlight) or it could refer to protective clothing required by the storekeeper to handle certain goods (e.g. chemicals).

(k) The established stock levels (i.e. minimum, maximum and reorder) as set and agreed by purchasing and stores management. The use of this system of indicating the stock levels on each card ensures that as each transaction concerning the stock is carried out, a constant check on how that affects the overall stock position can be maintained. When the stock reaches any one of those predetermined levels, action is initiated immediately to correct the stock situation, e.g. if the stock falls to the reorder level, purchasing is informed and it reorders a new supply from the supplier.

10. Sources of stock record information

For any stock record system to operate effectively it has to receive a continuous flow of 'source information' about all the movements of and alterations to the stock held by the organization. This information is supplied by certain basic documents associated with the stores operation. These documents can be divided into two distinct groups, as follows:

(a) *Intake* (i.e. stock being fed into the store, e.g. deliveries, transfers, returns to stock). The documents involved will include the following:

    (*i*) suppliers' delivery notes
    (*ii*) internal transfer notes
    (*iii*) return to stock notes
    (*iv*) production to stock notes
    (*v*) consignment notes.

(b) *Outflow* (i.e. issues, transfers, damages, etc.). The documents involved will include the following:

    (*i*) issue notes
    (*ii*) allocated issue notes
    (*iii*) production plans
    (*iv*) internal transfer notes
    (*v*) goods damaged notes
    (*vi*) despatch notes.

All these documents hold information needed by the stock records manager to maintain the system as effectively as possible. It is vital that all these documents are passed to and analysed by stock records before being used for other purposes.

11. Problems associated with source documentation
As with any system of communication, there can be problems that will hold up or even stop the flow of information required by stock records.

(a) Source documents can be mislaid or filed before they are analysed by stock records.
(b) Basic source documents have other communications functions, e.g. delivery notes are needed by purchasing to check orders and invoices, so in some cases it might be that the document is used by one department which fails to pass it along the communication chain.
(c) Many of these source documents are completed in

unfavourable conditions, e.g. in workshops, inside lorries or in the stockyard, and this can lead to the information becoming illegible and possibly being misinterpreted by stock records.

12. Factors that have to be considered when formulating a stock record system

Obviously the needs and operations of individual organizations will be reflected in their stock record system and no general system could be designed to cover every need. However, there are some basic factors that any system would have to consider.

(a) *Overall size of the operation.* Obviously a large and complex organization would need a very sophisticated system.

(b) *The frequency of stock movements.* In a company where certain stocks are being 'turned over' at a very high rate (e.g. basic manufactured foods), a system of constant updating will be needed to maintain control.

(c) *Volume of stock and the range of items involved.* A very large stock of only a few lines will need a different system from a medium stock of numerous lines and types.

(d) *The level of training and expertise needed by the stock records staff.* A highly complex computerized system will need skilled staff to operate it.

(e) *Distribution system employed.* If the organization has a complex distribution network of depots and warehouses, the stock record system will have to be adapted to provide the necessary data for adequate control and distribution of stocks.

(f) *Obsolescence and deterioration.* The 'life' of the various items of stock can be recorded in the stock record system, which will allow accurate calculations to be made about the life of the stock held, thus reducing the levels of obsolete stock (*see* also **14**).

(g) *Source documents.* Are they acceptable in their present form for analysis by stock records? Are they used by other departments? Will they have to be redesigned?

(h) *Recording systems.* What kinds of mechanical or electronic recording systems are available? Could the system be converted to run on a 'direct input' basis? What would be the cost of such a system?

13. The role of the stock records manager

The stock records manager is a very important member of the materials management team. He has several vital roles to perform.

(a) To manage and coordinate the whole stock record operation. This will include analysis of information, control of staff and control of all devices associated with the control system.

(b) To communicate information to the other departments on which effective management decisions can be made. This information will also be provided in a form that can be easily interpreted and understood by the other departments.

(c) To develop the system and the service it provides to its full potential, thus ensuring that maximum use is made of the information collected.

(d) To ensure that the system is actually meeting the needs of the organization.

Deterioration and obsolescence

14. Dating of stocks

Because of the 'historical' nature of the information stored in a stock record system, it lends itself very well to the problem of controlling deterioration and obsolescence of stock, especially in relation to materials with a 'use-by date'.

All receipts and issues of stock are dated and recorded on the stock control card. This enables management to locate and date each item of stock held. Many organizations have their own system of dating all products either produced or stored by them. The following are the two main types of system:

(a) *Colour coding.* Different coloured stickers or marks are used to note different delivery dates and ages of stock.

(b) *Date marking.* This is where every item stored is stamped with a marking device, which usually shows the date at which the item will no longer be usable. In some cases this could be a matter of weeks, e.g. manufactured foods, chemicals, etc.

15. Control of deterioration and obsolescence

The following are two important ways in which stock records can control deterioration and obsolescence:

(a) All information concerning deterioration — time from production, purchasing, suppliers, quality control — will be channelled into the stock record system so that each aspect can be analysed and its effect upon the stock held calculated and fed back.

(b) All information concerning obsolescence, from production, design, engineering, maintenance, sales, etc., can also be analysed and acted upon.

Progress test 14

1. What are the basic functions of a stock record system? **(2)**

2. What are the advantages of a computerized stock record system? **(5)**

3. What kind of information could you expect to find on a typical stock record card? **(9)**

4. What are the problems associated with stock records source data? **(11)**

Stock control systems

1. Stock control systems
There are three basic stock control systems. These are as follows:

(a) *Fixed order point system* (fixed time and fixed quantity). A fixed order point system is based upon a reordering system that reacts when stock falls to a predetermined level of stock, the so-called reorder level.

(b) *Periodic review system* (fixed time and variable quantity). Periodic review is based upon the system of stocks being reordered at regular set intervals of time.

(c) *Programmed ordering system*. Gus Gillespie states that 'Different kinds of inventories require different stock management approaches' (*Modern Purchasing*, 1982). Examples are MRP (*see* **8–10**) and JIT (*see* **11–18**).

Fixed order point system

2. Introduction
The fixed order point system is used when the demand for stock is constant and known. The time and quantity to order is determined by a number of stock control levels.

3. Definitions
A stock control level is a predetermined quantity of stock to be held. When stock on hand falls to this predetermined quantity or stock level, certain action is taken. For example, when stock on hand falls to the reorder level a fresh order, for a fixed or variable quantity, is placed with the supplier.

(a) *Lead time*. This is the period of time taken from deciding an item needs reordering until the goods have been received and are ready for sale on the shelf.

(b) *Buffer stock*. This is a safety or policy stock to cover unforeseen delays during the lead time. Also known as minimum stock.

(c) *Reorder level*. The level of stock or predetermined quantity at which a fresh order should be placed.

(d) *Order quantity*. The amount of stock to order. This may be predetermined using mathematical formulae or based on personal judgment.

(e) *Progress level*. When stock on hand falls to this level a check should be made with the supplier as to the status of the outstanding orders.

(f) *Maximum stock*. This is the quantity of a stock item above which stock on hand should never rise.

4.   Formulae

(a) Lead time: The average delivery time, in weeks, during a period.

(b) Buffer stock: Policy stock in weeks multiplied by the usage per week.

(c) Reorder level: Lead time (in units) + Buffer stock (in units).

(d) Order quantity: The economic order quantity (*see* 5).
or
The year's usage, divided by the number of orders to place.

(e) Progress level: Buffer stock (in units) + ½ Lead time (in units).

(f) Maximum stock: Order quantity + Buffer stock.

Example – fixed order point system _____

Predetermining stock control levels under a fixed order point system.

Information: Code number 64
Usage 20 per week (constant demand)
Lead time 4 weeks
Buffer stock 1 week
Number of orders per year 6 (2 months stock per order)

Stock levels

1. Lead time (4 weeks × usage per week)   =   80
2. Buffer stock (1 week × usage per week)   =   20
3. Reorder level (sum of lead time
and buffer stock)   =   100
4. Order quantity (yearly usage
divided by 6) (52 weeks per year)   =   174
(rounded up)
5. Progress level (buffer stock +
half the lead time (in units)   =   60
6. Maximum stock (order quantity +
buffer stock)   =   194

Note:
When stocks fall to 100 units, an order for 174 units is sent to the supplier. When the level reaches 60 units the supplier is contacted to check if goods will be delivered as per schedule. If the goods are received on time the quantity in stock should rise to 194 (174 delivered and 20 buffer stock). If the quantity in stock rises above 194 (i.e. maximum stock) action should be taken to explain why this has happened.

Having established the levels of stock required to run the operation effectively and efficiently, stock control is also responsible for ensuring that the levels of stock are maintained throughout the whole stores system.

5. Economic ordering quantity (EOQ)

The EOQ is a mathematical formula used by many organizations to establish the most economic amount to order for any item held in stock. The formula is:

$$Q = \sqrt{\frac{2AX}{YZ}}$$

where:

Q   =   the value of the EOQ
2   =   the common multiplication factor
A   =   annual consumption
X   =   the administrative costs of ordering
Y   =   the cost of storage expressed as a decimal of
the average level of stock value
Z   =   cost per unit.

Example – economic order quantity _____
Information:

1. Annual usage   2,000
2. Costs of one order   £20
3. Costs of storage   0.25
4. Cost per unit   £2

Formula:

$$\frac{2 \times 2,000 \times 20}{2 \times 0.25} = 16,000$$

$$= 400 \text{ units}$$

The quantity to order is 400 units, when the reorder level is reached.

This formula tries to balance out in mathematical terms the advantages of low stocks and high ordering costs and high stocks and low ordering costs, and the costs of storage affected accordingly. In situations where bulk discounts are available, stock control must take these possible savings into account in their EOQ calculations.

6. Problems associated with EOQ based systems
    There are a number of problems that the stock controller must bear in mind when employing the EOQ method of stock control. These are as follows:

(a) *Accurately establishing the 'true' cost of ordering* and setting a standard to cover every type of order.
(b) *Establishing 'true' storage costs*, given that many organizations have a very wide range of stock, each requiring different forms of handling and storage.
(c) *How to cope with unexpected alterations* in the pattern of demand for stock.
(d) *How to cope with variations in lead time* — even though deliveries may be set at regular intervals, delays can still occur.

Periodic review system

7. Definition
    The periodic review system submits orders on a regular basis

but the quantity is different each time. A maximum stock is predetermined and a stock review period is set. When the review period arrives the stock on hand is counted and a quantity is ordered to bring the stock up to the predetermined maximum level (*see* Fig. 15.1)

Example

Predetermined maximum stock 2,000 units.
Review period every four weeks.

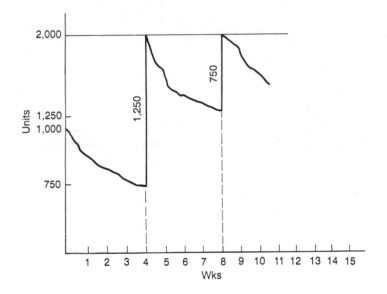

Figure 15.1 *Periodic review system*

Notes:
(a) Week 4 is the first review period. The stock on hand has fallen to 750 units. An order is sent for 1,250 units to bring the balance back to maximum stock of 2,000 units.
(b) Week 8 is the second period. The stock level has fallen to 1,250 units therefore an order for 750 units is sent to bring the stock on hand back to the maximum stock of 2,000.
(c) We have presumed in this example that there is no lead time and we hold no buffer stocks.

Dependent demand system (materials requirement planning)

8. Introduction

In both the fixed order point and periodic review systems we made assumptions that demand was constant and continuous. We also presumed that demand for individual stock items are independent from each other. In a manufacturing organization the demand for the majority of stock items is dependent on the quantity of the final products required. The time the finished product is needed is also known. This allows us to schedule the materials into production in the exact quantities at the required place and at the required time. This method of materials control is achieved by a computerized materials planning system called materials requirement planning, or MRP for short.

9. What is MRP?

Materials requirement planning is a computerized time-phased requirement planning system which aims to hold zero stocks of an item, unless it is required for current production.

10. How does MRP work?

The information for the material needs of the organization is taken from the master production schedule (MPS). The MPS is derived from either order books or sales forecasts. The MPS details the required outputs of the production system by periods (usually weekly or monthly). The MRP system converts the output needs into a time-phased report of materials requirements (RMR). The RMR is also called a bill of materials (BOM).

The BOM is a structured directory which lists all the materials or parts required to manufacture a finished product or sub-assembly. A BOM for a motor car would specify one complete engine, five wheels, one front windscreen, two wiper blades, etc. Items that are available ex stock will be allocated to the production run while the balance will be ordered. The MRP system calculates the total quantity of each item that needs to be ordered, their lead times and issues purchasing with the information to allow them to plan:

(a) Which materials or parts need to be ordered?

(b) How many to order?
(c) When to order?

The stages in materials requirement planning are illustrated in Fig. 15.2.

Sales Forecast

↓

Master Production Schedule

↓

Materials Requirement Planning

↓

Bill of Materials

↓

Stock Record File

↓

Purchase Request

Figure 15.2 *Stages in materials requirement planning*

Just-in-time materials controlled planning

11. Introduction
Traditional approaches to meeting production requirements rested heavily on holding safety stock just in case (JIC) something went wrong. The JIC idea resulted in high financial investment in stock. It also provided a buffer against inefficiencies in the production process which often caused unnecessary waste and delays. MRP has gone some way towards reducing inventory. The Japanese developed an approach that has been called Just-In-Time (JIT). JIT is more than a stock control concept. It sees stock as an evil and a waste. It seeks to eliminate it and anything else that does not add value to the product.

12. Definition
The JIT philosophy calls for gradual reduction of buffer stocks and for delivery of raw materials to production, and finished goods to the customer, just in time for use. Requirements are produced

just in time instead of the traditional approach that produced stocks just in case.

13. JIT and the supplier

JIT has also been called 'comakeship'. This highlights the importance of the supplier to the concept. Not only does the JIT system aim to reduce stocks, work in progress and finished goods within its own organization, but it insists on similar changes in the suppliers. Suppliers are seen as an extension of one's own plant and part of the production team. They receive daily requests (Kanbans) (*see* 15) and special containers. They are expected to make several deliveries per day. The materials are delivered directly to the point of production. The suppliers must guarantee the quality of their products so no inspection is carried out on the delivered goods. This has caused a rethink of the traditional relationship with suppliers and in most JIT systems there is a necessity for single source purchasing.

14. Choosing suppliers for a JIT system

(a) Usually on a long-term basis.
(b) To work successfully it must be seen as beneficial to both parties.
(c) They must be able to guarantee their product's quality with zero defects.
(d) Technical competence must be examined.
(e) Must be within a realistic geographical area.
(f) Price guarantees are essential.

15. JIT and the Kanban

The movement of materials from the suppliers to production and within different production processes is achieved by the use of a Kanban.

A Kanban is a sub-system of JIT. It consists of physical cards and containers. The Kanban or cards operate as a pull forward signal for parts or products. Kanban is both a method of production authorization and material movement in the system.

Example

Information:

(a) There are 8 containers in the system.
(b) Each container holds 40 items.
(c) Containers are used between production points A and B (Point A supplies point B).
(d) Maximum stock between the two points is 320 (8 containers and 40 units per container).
(e) Production at A will stop when all the containers are full and there are no more empty containers with production Kanbans.

Working of the system (containers numbered 1 to 8) as illustrated in Fig. 15.3:

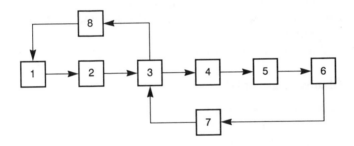

Figure 15.3 *Working of the Kanban system*

(a)	Container 1	–	Empty with production Kanban.
(b)	Container 2	–	Being filled by Process A.
(c)	Container 3	–	Full container waiting for movement Kanban from Process B.
(d)	Container 4	–	Full container in transit from Output A to Input Process B.
(e)	Container 5	–	Full container waiting in input section in Process B.
(f)	Container 6	–	Full container being used in Process B.
(g)	Container 7	–	Empty container in transit to Output A with movement Kanban from Process B.
(h)	Container 8	–	Empty container with production Kanban to input of Process A.

In this simple example the needs of the system required 320 items of stock and 8 containers. Reduction in stock could be achieved by:

(a) reduction of the transit times;
(b) less machine set-up times;
(c) more effective layout of the plant;
(d) the introduction of automatic equipment.

As we have seen, JIT is not just a concept for reducing inventory. It can have various other effects on the efficiency of the organization.

16. Advantages of JIT

(a) Reduction in stockholding.
(b) Better relationship with suppliers.
(c) Problems in production are highlighted.
(d) Less scrap or rework through zero defects in material received from suppliers.
(e) Multifunctional workforce.

17. Disadvantages of JIT

(a) Problems if orders are delivered late
(b) or not enough parts arrive
(c) or wrong parts arrive.
(d) Dangers associated with single sourcing.
(e) Shortage of skilled staff.

18. Differences between JIT and MRP
These are outlined in Table 15.1.

Management of stock control

19. Stock control and computers
Stock control is concerned with the processing of data into information on the basis of which major operational decisions affecting production, distribution, planning and engineering can be made. The computer's ability to process and store vast amounts of data and thus produce high quality management information

Table 15.1 *Differences between JIT and MRP*

	JIT	MRP
Stock	Seen as a liability	Seen as an asset
Quantity	Immediate needs only	As per EOQ
Suppliers	Seen as comakers of the product	Seen as an opponent
Quality	Zero defects	Some scrap expected and built into the purchases
Staff	Management by consensus	Management by dictate

at very high speed and low cost has had a major impact upon stock control operations in many organizations.

20. The role of the stock control manager

In most organizations the stock control element of materials management is controlled by a senior member of the stores operations staff. The stock control manager reports to the stores manager (*see* Fig. 15.4) and he has the following duties and responsibilities:

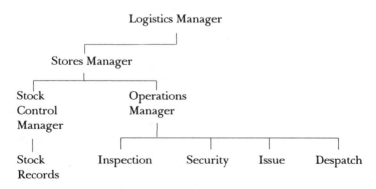

Figure 15.4 *Position of stock control within the stores function*

(a) To manage the organization's stocks and to ensure constant supply to the operation.

(b) To manage the stock control function as efficiently and economically as possible. This will include control of staff, organization of the office, and maintenance of files and records.

(c) To develop and improve the service provided by stock control to all the other sections involved, and thus aim to improve the overall stores operation.

(d) To communicate with other major departments within the organization to ensure that the information being supplied by stock control is accurate, usable and produced at the right time, and to ensure that decisions based on stock control are correct.

21. A stock controller's job description

The following is a typical controller's job description taken from a large UK retail organization:

Job title:	Stock Control Manager
Reports to:	Stores Director
Department:	Stock Control
Location:	Head Office
Date of evaluation:	1.1.90

Purpose: The job holder is responsible for preparing and gaining approval for a profitable trading plan for designated product groups and its successful implementation.

Dimensions:

Staff supervised	1	Clerical support
	2	Merchandisers
Product responsibility	£10–20 million p.a.	

Nature and scope: The stock control department has thirteen job holders at this level; each reports directly to a buying department manager and is supported by 1–2 merchandisers plus one clerical support person.

The stock control managers have a functional reporting relationship to a stock control merchandise executive in the stock control department. Each stock control merchandise executive is responsible for an assigned area of stock control with responsibility for a number of stock control managers.

Each stock control manager is assigned a specific product group and is responsible for ensuring that the level of stocks at depots/warehouses and stores is sufficient to meet the trading plan. The job holder's prime accountability is the maximization of profit by timing stock movement effectively. It is the encumbent's prime objective to hold stock levels within agreed parameters remembering at all times the effects of over- and under-stocked situations. To achieve this the stock control manager must liaise with the buying department manager, marketing department, depot/warehouse management and outside suppliers, balancing the requirements of each against that of the business in general. This provides the major challenge to the job holders, in that they must be aware of the consequence to cash flow and stock levels when deviation from the buying or selling plan occurs (i.e. moving one line early may mean that another has to be delayed, as the company only has limited storage space).

The stock control managers are involved in all aspects of stock control including preparation of the overall trading plan for the area under their control. From this detailed buying and selling plans are developed, setting of branch ordering levels for the automatic reordering system according to store classification, approval of contracts, agreeing and signing call-offs and advising the buying department manager of problem suppliers. In addition, the stock control managers are expected to make a contribution to the strategy and policies of the stock control department.

The job requires the stock control manager to interface with many levels of management up to director level. They will participate in discussions on issues outside their immediate control, during which they must ensure that the views of the Stock Control Department are clearly stated.

The stock control managers require in-depth knowledge of stock control and distribution systems and how they impinge upon the business as a whole.

Prime accountabilities: The prime responsibilities of the job holder are:

(a) To prepare a profitable trading plan for a designated range of products for submission to the trading committee for approval.
(b) To develop a trading model from the finalized trading plan, detailing by period the buying and selling pattern required for each product. In the case of clothing and certain hardware areas, the plan will have to contain data for manufacture and scheduling.
(c) To manage the supply of products from manufacturer to depot/warehouse and subsequent call-off to store in line with the trading model, taking into account the actual selling pattern of product groups.

(d) To monitor the call-off of stock to ensure that the correct display stocks are available to stores for all products and to take remedial action when the selling plan does not perform to standard.

(e) To monitor and maintain the computerized systems currently in use.

(f) To check that quantities delivered by suppliers fulfil contractual commitments.

(g) To manage in conjunction with the buying department manager and the marketing department the range of goods available against store classification.

(h) To dispose of slow moving stock and make recommendations for items to be promoted (9 promotions plus 2 sales per annum) for the product items under their control.

(i) To prepare variance reports by product detailing anomalous performance patterns.

(j) To manage merchandiser and clerical support, plus any other *ad hoc* duties.

22. Stock records and stock control

Stock records and stock control are two sections of stores management that have to work very closely together, because stock records provide stock control with much of the statistical information it requires to fulfil its aims and objectives, namely:

(a) information about previous levels of stock;

(b) information about past rates of consumption;

(c) information about stock distribution;

(d) information about suppliers' delivery periods and past performance;

(e) information about levels of stocks held at any given time, for any given item.

We can see from this the importance of good communications and relations between these two elements of the stores operation. In many organizations overall responsibility for both stock records and stock control is carried by the stock control manager and his staff, to ensure good communications.

Importance of an effective stock control system

23. Financial implications of stock control

Because the stock held by any organization represents money, the control of that stock has serious financial implications for the company. If the stock is controlled inefficiently it can cause high storage costs, obsolescence, and a reduction in working capital. Therefore stock control is very much concerned with ensuring that stock is controlled very carefully. In many situations, the actual level of profit earned by an organization will depend on the success of stock control.

24. Qualities of a good stock control system

From the points outlined previously, we can see just how vital good stock control is to any organization that holds stocks. Serious operational and financial breakdowns can result if a good stock control system is not operated by the stores.

Every stock control system must be designed to meet the particular needs of the organization. However, as a general rule, stock control systems should have the following qualities:

(a) Accuracy and speed of reaction to stock situations.
(b) Good channels of communication with the other major departments involved.
(c) Economy in its operation and in its demands upon capital and human resources.
(d) Centralization of overall control of the stock in the hands of the stock control manager to ensure good control and stock management.
(e) The ability to be run by various members of staff. All relevant information must be readily accessible, in order to reduce the risk of serious problems should the stock control manager be absent.
(f) Flexibility so that all items held within the store are controlled and any new additions will also be covered automatically.

25. ABC concept

Pareto's curve relating income to population can be used in the context of stock control. The stock controller must divide his total stockholding into three groups:

Group A: Items that account for 10 per cent of total volume, but account for 60 per cent of total stock value.
Group B: Items that account for 30 per cent of stock volume, and account for 30 per cent of stock value.

Group C: Items that account for 60 per cent of total stock volume, but only account for 10 per cent of total stock value.

This segregation of stock into volume/value groups enables the stock controller and the stores manager to allocate their resources in relation to control to groups A and B to maximize their impact on total costs.

26. Stock control and total control

Since stock control is such an important part of any organization's operations it has to be considered in terms of *total* control. This is because stock control affects so much of what the organization actually does, i.e. production, distribution, engineering, sales, etc.

Errors or miscalculations in stock control will affect each and every one of those major operations. Many organizations now realize the importance of stock control in terms of total control. It has been said that the reason why stock control is such a difficult task is that one miscalculation in any one of its basic aims (*see* 13:2) will render the rest useless! In other words, despite the time and effort employed, stock control has to be totally correct or it will be totally wrong.

27. Improving the control of stock

Because of the vital importance of stock control, even to the point of organizational survival, improvements in the control of stocks must constantly be sought. Laura Jamieson in *Modern Purchasing* (September 1982) put forward a large number of ideas to improve the control of stock:

(a) *Overall reduction of stocks.* The removal of obsolete stocks, avoidance of 'bargain buys', and general stock standardization — all of these assist in reducing the total stock held. The key to stock reduction is to be ruthless with non-working stocks. There is a tendency for stocks for which no immediate use can be found to accumulate.

(b) *Staff involvement.* It is vital that all members of the organization from the shopfloor to management understand and appreciate the implications of poor stock control.

(c) *Low cost computers.* The stores manager and stock controller must ensure that maximum use is being made of low cost computers in relation to stock control operations.

(d) *Stock levels.* The stock controller must ensure that stock levels are maintained at the lowest possible levels (*see* 13:**7**). Encouraging suppliers to hold stocks is one strategy for holding down stock levels.

(e) *Cooperation.* The stock controller, purchasing manager and supplier must cooperate to ensure effective control of stock. It is in the interest of the supplier that the organization has effective control of stocks, thus improving efficiency and growth.

(f) *Forecasting.* The use of modern forecasting techniques to accurately establish future stock levels.

(g) *Materials management.* A system of materials management could enable the whole materials system to be more tightly controlled, thus reducing overall stock levels (*see* 3:**9**).

Progress test 15

1. What are the two main types of stock control system? **(1)**

2. What is the EOQ formula? **(5)**

3. List the problems associated with EOQ-based systems. **(6)**

4. What do the initials MRP and BOM stand for? **(9–10)**

5. On what basis should an organization select a supplier for a JIT system? **(14)**

6. List the advantages and disadvantages of JIT. **(16–17)**

7. Identify the role of the stock control manager. **(20)**

Case study no. 5:

Delta Ltd

Delta Ltd is a large operating company based in the UK. The head of materials, John Smith, has recently had a visit from the sales representative of Elmore Engineering. Elmore produce consumable items which are used in the operating process.

John is very concerned about the issue of rising costs. Corporate headquarters of the company are constantly putting pressure upon the operating companies to reduce costs.

Against this background, the sales representative from Elmore has come with very good news. As a special concession to Delta, Elmore is willing to offer a unit cost reduction of up to 40 pence, compared with the normal cost of £6.00. This is based upon an order quantity of 4,000 or over (*see* Appendix below). This is convenient for Delta because by chance their annual consumption is 4,000 units. The sales representative from Elmore Ltd highlights the large saving the company will make in terms of reduced ordering costs. Ordering can be a very expensive business, clerical processes, computer time, authorization, postage, etc. Currently, Delta's ordering costs are estimated at £6.00 per order placed.

During the discussion, John raises the issue of storage costs, but the sales representative simply states 'What is the problem? You have got a huge storage capacity here, why not take advantage of this offer and reduce your unit costs?'

To help convince John, the sales representative makes the following calculation:

$$4,000 \times £6.00 \ = \ £24,000$$
$$4,000 \times £5.60 \ = \ £22,400$$

John is convinced and he places an order for 4,000 units.

Discussion question

1. Has John made the right decision?

Appendix 1

Discount schedule	
Cost per unit	Quantity ordered
£6.00	Less than 250
£5.90	250–799
£5.80	800–1,999
£5.70	2,000–3,999
£5.60	4,000 plus

Stockholding costs	
Insurance	25 pence
Storage costs	75 pence
Deterioration costs	10 pence
Opportunity cost	10 pence

Note: The EOQ has already been established at 250 units per order.

16
Stocktaking

Introduction

1. Purpose of stocktaking

The security of and accountability for all materials and equipment held within the stores system is the direct responsibility of the stores manager and his staff. Stock represents the organization's cash and must be controlled and accounted for as such. This responsibility for stock demands that the stores performs regular and complete physical checks of all the items held in stock and verifies that count in terms of the calculated stock figures contained within the stock record system.

2. Benefits of stocktaking

Stocktaking involves many valuable and expensive man-hours to arrange and carry out, plus a great deal of management time needed to investigate the almost inevitable list of stock discrepancies. However, the cost and effort are more than justified by the following benefits:

(a) Stock record and stock control systems will be tested. Verification by physical counts will act as a form of performance check on these systems and adjustments needed can be made.

(b) Computerized control systems can be verified. Computers are only as good as the data supplied to them, so the data being supplied from stock records and stock control must be accurate and relevant.

(c) Financial reports (including the balance sheet) produced by the organization's auditors will demand some form of physical stock verification to back up the value of stock shown within the balance sheet. Stock valuations which are not backed up by a physical count have little relevance to the critical auditors and the organization's accountants.

(d) The security aspect of stores management demands that regular and physical checks be made to ensure that any possible theft or fraud is quickly detected and investigations carried out.

(e) Stocktaking is an indicator of overall stores efficiency and management control. The number and size of stocktaking discrepancies is a good indication of efficiency. A high incidence of stock discrepancies usually warrants a close look at the personnel and system involved.

(f) Accurate stock levels shown within the stock records system, backed up by a regular physical count, will ensure that all requirements of the user departments are covered by existing stock levels and will be issued promptly and efficiently. This avoids the common situation of stock shown in the records system not being physically present.

Types of stocktaking operation

3. Introduction
There are several methods of carrying out stocktaking. The advantages and applications of the main recognized methods are described in **4–6** below.

4. Periodic stocktaking
This is where a complete stocktake is performed at regular intervals, usually at the end of each financial year or in some cases at quarterly intervals. It is the most common method of checking and counting the stock. This system has several advantages and disadvantages.

(a) *Advantages:*
  (*i*) The stocktake is usually carried out on a non-working day (as the store must be closed during a count) and therefore the stock checkers have time to count carefully and check discrepancies.
  (*ii*) A complete stocktake enables discrepancies which are brought to light to be investigated.
  (*iii*) Accurate stock evaluation figures can be provided for the annual balance sheet and accounts.

(b) *Disadvantages:*
- (*i*) The stores must be completely closed to ensure an accurate count. However, in a continuous process situation or a 24-hour, 7-day week shift system, the plant in theory never stops and neither does the stores operation.
- (*ii*) It is very costly and involves a great number of staff from both inside and outside the stores. Overtime for weekend working can be very expensive.

5. Continuous stocktaking
In this system a selection or section of items are checked every week. Throughout a twelve-month period every item in stock would therefore be physically counted and checked, without having to close the store.

(a) *Advantages:*
- (*i*) It enables the store to continue working.
- (*ii*) It spreads the disruption caused by stocktaking over a long period and therefore the disruption is reduced.
- (*iii*) It can act as a form of spot-checking (*see* **6**) if the schedule of stock to be checked is not disclosed.

(b) *Disadvantage:* Major discrepancies need a great deal of time to investigate properly, but because of the continuous nature of this type of checking, the time devoted to investigation will be limited.

6. Spot-checking
This is used in connection with the security and anti-theft aspects of stores management. Spot-checks are designed to verify the stock held, without a prior warning which could provide time for stock to be replaced illegally. The system also acts as a deterrent against those who may contemplate theft, knowing that a sudden check could herald an investigation.

(a) *Advantages:*
- (*i*) It acts as a strong deterrent to theft and fraud.
- (*ii*) It is simple to arrange and carry out on a limited scale.

(b) *Disadvantage:* It is limited in application in relation to a major stocktake and cannot really provide data for financial calculations.

Organization of stocktaking

7. Procedures

To ensure that stocktaking is an accurate and meaningful exercise, stores management must organize and control all stocktaking activities. Stocktaking demands a very high degree of care and attention to detail, if the physical count is to be effective. One of the biggest problems facing stocktakers is that if the count is due at a certain date (e.g. the end of the financial year) then any stock not counted on that day will have to be counted late and complex calculations regarding stock received and issued after that date will have to be made. Stores managers therefore need a stocktaking procedure to cover the following vital aspects of a complete stocktake:

(a) *A controller of stocktaking* should be appointed. Usually he is a senior member of the supply management team, and in some instances the stock control manager can take on this temporary role. This appointment means that one individual has full authority over all those involved in the stocktake, producing clear lines of authority and responsibility for those involved.

(b) *Stock areas should be allocated* to individual members of the stocktaking team. Each pair of stock checkers will be given a specific area of stock to check and count. It is good practice to have someone who normally works in the stock area as one of the pair, so as to have a degree of 'local' knowledge, but the other member of the team should *not* be familiar with the area allocated, to avoid possible fraud and to provide an outside view.

(c) *Adequate materials and equipment* must be available for the stocktakers, before the counting begins. Stocktakers will need pens, pencils, rubbers, stock counting sheets, calculators, clip boards, measuring equipment (*see* 18:22) and office space to calculate total stocks and make comparisons.

(d) *A comprehensive stocktaking meeting* should be held several days before the stocktake is due to commence. This gives the controller of stocktaking the opportunity to explain slowly and carefully to all those involved what is to be counted, how quantities are to be recorded, the assignment of stock location, the names of the pairs of staff taking part and also the actual timetables of events for the operation itself.

(e) *The stock to be actually counted* and recorded must be clearly explained. The stock to be counted should include all normal stocks, materials under inspection, scraps, packaging and items on loan. Stock to be counted but recorded on *separate stocktaking sheets* will include damaged stock, deteriorations and goods in transit.

(f) *A pre-stocktaking clear-up* of stockrooms, stockyard, warehouses and stores buildings will help to make the actual stock check more accurate and efficient.

(g) *There should be a complete closure of all store installations* and the stopping of all stores activities until the stocktake has been completed. A stocktake cannot take place while the materials being checked are being constantly issued and received.

(h) *All equipment and stock which does not belong to the organization* must be counted and recorded separately from the other stock classifications.

(i) *All items of stock which are in transit* (i.e. between the store and some other installation) or stock held in depots or warehouses must be accounted for at the same time as the main store stocktake, thus ensuring a complete picture of the organization's current stock. This may involve warehouse and depot managers attending the stocktaking meeting (*see* (d)).

(j) *All previously active stores documentation* (i.e. issue notes, delivery notes, quality control notes, etc.) should all have been documented and filed before the actual stocktake begins. This will ensure that calculated records are up to date.

8. Documentation

A complete and comprehensive stocktake involving large numbers of stock lines on several locations will demand a variety of stocktaking control documentation, including the following:

(a) *Stock counting sheets* (*see* Fig. 16.1). These sheets are produced especially for stocktaking purposes. They are designed to be used by each individual stocktaker for each type of item to be counted, and therefore every item in stock will have its own stock counting sheet. The sheets must be consecutively numbered so as to avoid the possibility of the same items being counted twice. The standard stock counting sheet will contain a great deal of useful reference data for the stocktaker, and will also aid the production of the final *master* stocktake document.

STOCK COUNTING SHEET		Date	
Description		Sheet ref. no.	
Code no.			
Physical count		Calculated stock	variance
Unit of issue			
Location			
Stocktakers (signature)			
Comments on stock condition			

Figure 16.1 *Stock counting sheet*

The following is the usual data contained on a stock counting sheet:

- (*i*) stock counting sheet reference number;
- (*ii*) quantity of stock physically counted;
- (*iii*) description and code number of the item;
- (*iv*) unit of issue;
- (*v*) date of stocktake;
- (*vi*) signature of stocktakers and general comments on stock condition.

(b) *Master stock sheet.* This document is produced by collating all the individual stock counting sheets from each of the various locations. Each contribution from the stock counting sheets is added and a total stock quantity for each item held in stock is produced. The production of the master stock sheet will be the responsibility of the controller of stocktaking, who must ensure that all the relevant stocktaking sheets are contained within the master stock sheet.

(c) *Stock certificate.* This is a formal document which indicates the value of total stock as at the date of the stocktaking. It is usually checked and signed by a member of the organization's senior management, in most cases a member of the financial management team.

(d) *Outside storage installations stock reports.* These are in fact a smaller version of the master stock sheet, produced by the individual warehouse, depot and outside storage unit managers and controllers. They are also included in the total stock calculations.

(e) *Internal transfer notes* These are needed to account for the stock which is in transit at the date of the stocktake.

9. Methods of performing the stocktake

The following are the main methods recognized for the actual physical process of checking and counting the stock:

(a) One person checking the whole store or warehouse, without assistance.

(b) A team of stocktakers working through large storage areas.

(c) Two stocktakers working independently of each other but counting the same stock. This method is the most accurate, as it provides an instant double-check for the stocktakers who can compare each section counted to verify each other's count.

The actual method employed will depend upon several important factors, including the size of the operation involved, the extent of stock variation (a single type of stock is quite easy to count), the size of the store, the staff and resources available, and the quality and reputation of the stocktakers involved.

Stock verification and discrepancies

10. Relationship between physical and calculated stock

Stocktaking involves the actual physical process of counting, checking and measuring all the materials, tools and other equipment held within the store. These figures are then compared with the calculated levels of stock indicated in the stock records system (*see* 14:7).

Because the stores manager has two individual sets of stock figures he can compare and verify the two sets, enabling him to report a final and agreed stock quantity. That does not mean that either stock records or stocktaking counts are always correct: it only provides an indication of how near or, indeed, how far out are the calculated and the physical counts.

11. Stock discrepancies

Every stores manager has experienced the problem of stock discrepancies, that is, a difference between the calculated and the physical stock quantity. Discrepancies are inevitable in a large and complex stores system and each must be investigated and corrected. There are two main types of discrepancy as follows:

(a) *Stock surplus or 'positive stock'*. This is a situation where more stock is physically counted than is indicated in the calculated stock.
(b) *Stock deficiencies or 'negative stock'*. This is a situation where less stock is physically counted than is indicated in the calculated stock.

12. Extent of discrepancies

There are three main classifications for stock discrepancies. Each classification denotes the amount of time and management energy spent in isolating the cause of the discrepancies and the steps needed to be taken to prevent a second incident.

(a) *Minor discrepancies*. This is where the variation between calculated and physical stock is very small, compared with the overall quantities involved. For example, if a stocktake of all the stores stock of lightbulbs produced a total of about 3,000 and a stock discrepancy of only two was found, then management would not waste time and resources on any attempt to investigate such a minor discrepancy.
(b) *Major discrepancies*. This is where a very large and valuable variation between calculated and physical stock is detected. Because of the stores' accountability and responsibility for all stock held, a complete investigation into the causes of the discrepancies must be carried out.
(c) *Operational discrepancies*. This is where, although the amount of variation involved is very small, the importance of the items involved in terms of the continued operation of the organization is so vital that a major investigation may have to be mounted to determine the fault and ensure that stocks of the vital material are secure and accurate.

13. Causes of stock discrepancies

A large percentage of all stock discrepancies are accounted for by one or more of the causes listed below. The stores manager must investigate each of the possible causes until the stock discrepancy is isolated.

(a) *Original incorrect stocktake.*

(b) *Mathematical errors* within the stock record card may produce an incorrect calculated stock for comparison.

(c) *Units of issue* in a large stocktake can become confused or changed without notification to the stocktakers, and therefore a miscount will occur.

(d) *Misplacement of stocks* into the wrong shelf, cupboard, bin, etc., can result in stock being counted but recorded against the wrong stock count sheet.

(e) *The basic stores documents* (e.g. issue notes, delivery notes, transfer notes, etc.) that carry the data needed to adjust stock records and stock control systems may become lost or incorrectly entered.

(f) *Stocktaking adjustments from previous stocktakes* can influence the accuracy of the current stocktake if the stock discrepancies were incorrectly written-off as lost, only to become a surplus in the current stocktake.

(g) *Stock taken from stores without proper documentation* or notification to the stores will result in stock deficiencies.

(h) *Unreported damage* to or deterioration of stock.

(i) *Theft or fraud* of the organization's stocks.

14. Management action to locate discrepancies

Stores management can take certain measures to locate and remedy stock discrepancies. These actions will include the following:

(a) *Check all stock record cards* and stock control calculations for errors in arithmetic.

(b) *Recheck the area of stock involved,* using a member of staff from outside the stores organization, and establish the actual physical count.

(c) *Check to ensure that units of issue are correct* for each item of stock taken. This will mean that all supplies details on packaging will have to be checked and the standard measurement of the material confirmed. (The recent changeover to EC metric measure has caused problems in relation to stocktaking in many organizations.)

(d) *Ensure that all rejected goods,* or those which have been damaged or have deteriorated, have been formally reported and the stock deduction made within the stock records system.

(e) *Investigate with the appropriate user departments* (as indicated by the type of material or item involved). For example, missing stock of electrical plugs would probably mean that the user was the maintenance department and that they had been removing stock without permission or notification. Once this has been established, an issue note can be made out to balance the stock record card and the costing department notified.

15. Discrepancy prevention

The location and correction of any major stocktaking discrepancy is a very costly and drawn-out process, often ending in stores management having to write-off stock as lost. It is therefore vital, once the cause of a discrepancy has been successfully isolated, that certain measures are taken to ensure prevention of a similar error at the next stocktake. These measures should include the following:

(a) *The existing system of control* should be closely studied to ensure that any faults can be eradicated.

(b) *Stores documentation* must be closely examined to ensure that all data needed to control the stock is provided, clearly, quickly and accurately.

(c) *Consultations* should be held between the stores and the other departments whose actions can affect the accuracy of stocktaking (i.e. transport, purchasing, distribution, production and other user departments) so as to ensure they realize and appreciate the role their actions play.

(d) *A complete review and overall check of security systems* should be carried out if theft or fraud is suspected.

16. Adjustment of stock records and stores accounts

Once a real discrepancy has been found and isolated then both stock record systems and the stores accounts have to be adjusted to balance the books. The adjustment of stock cannot be made without the authorization of the stores manager or a senior member of the management team. Obviously, only the most high ranking member of staff should be able to write off valuable stock, in order to avoid possible fraud.

17. Stock adjustment report

This document is used to list the items involved and the quantity and value of the materials concerned. It is an official document, and must be signed by the said senior member of staff. The stock adjustment report will contain all the relevant data needed by the stores accounts, stock records and stock control to enable them to write-off the amount of stock involved. That data will include the following:

(a) calculated stock (as per record card);
(b) full description and code number of the item;
(c) physical count of stock found;
(d) total discrepancy involved;
(e) value of discrepancy;
(f) unit of issue and unit price.

Progress test 16

1. What are the benefits of stocktaking? **(2)**

2. Describe the various types of stocktaking. **(4–6)**

3. How would you organize a typical stocktaking operation? **(7)**

4. Describe the procedures for investigating discrepancies. **(14)**

5. How are the records adjusted to account for the alterations produced by the stocktaking? **(16–17)**

Case study no. 6:

Chapman Ltd

Chapman Ltd is a small manufacturing company based in Scotland. The firm provides electrical motors for domestic and commercial use throughout the UK and EC. Stock represents an investment of £10,000 (*see* Appendix).

In recent times, the company has noticed a marked increase in stock investment. The current rises in the interest rates has begun to affect company profits to a significant degree.

The company recently took on Lee Turner as a Stock Controller, who has direct responsibility for stock management. At a meeting with Martin Chapman, the Managing Director of the company, he states: 'We have made significant reductions in stock items like code (5), (28) and (29). I spent many hours looking at these items and devising means to reduce our stock investment.' He goes on to state: 'If I had more staff we could really reduce the stock investment in the company!'

Discussion question

1. Comment upon his statement.

Appendix

Average value of stockholding per coded item

Code number	Value	Code number	Value
1	£300	17	£300
2	£300	18	£25,000
3	£2,000	19	£300
4	£3,000	20	£10,000
5	£300	21	£3,000
6	£3,000	22	£300
7	£300	23	£300
8	£300	24	£300
9	£300	25	£300
10	£2,000	26	£300
11	£300	27	£300
12	£300	28	£300
13	£20,000	29	£300
14	£300	30	£3,000
15	£300	31	£300
16	£300	32	£20,000

A classification of materials used in typical manufacturing operation

1	Abrasives	17	Machined parts
2	Adhesives	18	Machine tools
3	Bearings	19	Office supplies
4	Castings	20	Office furniture and
5	Chemicals		equipment
6	Coal	21	Packaging material
7	Containers	22	Paint
8	Electrical and	23	Plastic parts
	electronic components	24	Printed materials
9	Electrical and	25	Power sources
	electronic assemblies	26	Pumps
10	Electrical cable and	27	Rubber parts
	wire	28	Safety clothing
11	Fasteners	29	Sheet metal parts
12	Forgings	30	Shop supplies
13	Fuel oil	31	Stampings
14	Hardware	32	Tooling
15	Laboratory supplies		
16	Lubricants		

Part four

Modern materials handling

17

The materials handling system

1. Importance of materials handling

One of the most basic requirements of any organisation is to be able to transport materials, equipment, spares and plant from one designated point to another, as efficiently as possible. The importance of materials handling is indicated by the range and, in some cases, high cost of the equipment that has been designed and developed to tackle the numerous problems of materials handling that each organization has.

Materials handling is of vital importance to every organization in operational terms for the following reasons:

(a) *Materials flow* has to be maintained if output and distribution are to be maintained. Materials must be transported from the point of storage to the point of production, moved through the production process, returned to the stores and, finally, transported in, and often through, the distribution system (*see* Fig. 17.1).

(b) *The health and safety* of many members of the staff depend a great deal upon the type of materials handling system employed, the equipment operated and the level of training among the operators. A faulty system or a badly trained driver can lead to serious accidents.

(c) *The cost factor* is vital in terms of operational costs, profits and overall costs of production. Handling materials is very expensive in terms of materials handling equipment, plant, time and labour. Therefore, the more efficiently and quickly materials can be moved, the more the cost per unit moved will be reduced.

(d) *Material damage* can be a very expensive business and will undoubtedly reduce the stock-life of many materials. Poor materials handling can produce all the problems of premature stock deterioration and the costs that go with it.

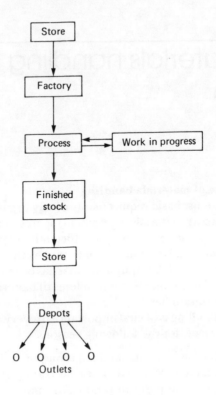

Figure 17.1 *Materials flow*

2. The three stages of materials handling

Materials handling is a process that involves three basic stages each of which is related to the other:

(a) selection of the materials from their place of storage;
(b) movement of the materials from A to B;
(c) placement of materials in the required place and position.

These three stages must always be borne in mind when dealing with any problem or project associated with materials handling.

3. Selecting the materials handling system

The selection of any materials handling system will involve the following departments:

(a) stores;
(b) production;
(c) distribution;
(d) senior management.

4. Factors to be considered

The following are some of the points that must be taken into account when selecting a materials handling system:

(a) *Location of material centres.* This relates to the relative positions of the store installations, production area and distribution areas. In many organizations the centres are separated by barriers (e.g. a road, rails or distance) which means that the flow of materials will have to be broken and various forms of materials handling devices and systems employed, for example fork-lift truck–gravity conveyor–tow truck–pallet truck.

(b) *The nature and characteristics* of the materials to be handled. Different materials will need different methods of handling. Large bulky materials, for example, tend to be handled best by a large number of small devices with a limited weight range, whereas very dense and heavy materials (e.g. steel) tend to be best handled by very large and powerful trucks, often crane powered. The following are some of the main categories of materials:

    (*i*) grains
    (*ii*) gases
    (*iii*) liquids
    (*iv*) pallets
    (*v*) small units
    (*vi*) construction materials
    (*vii*) plant and machinery
    (*viii*) metals.

Other factors affecting the materials handling system are the conditions under which the materials are stored (e.g. cold storage) and the potential for accidents (e.g. chemicals, explosives, acids).

(c) *Capital and resources* available with which to purchase the system. Limited funds will mean a limited system.

(d) *Future needs.* Whether there will be an expansion or contraction of operations. A flexible system has the advantage of being easily adjusted to the needs of the organization.

(e) *The total cost* of the operating system. This will have to include fuel, power, maintenance, labour, spares and depreciation.

(f) *Compatibility of the existing storage equipment* and facilities of the organization with the new system. For example, small shelf storage with mainly manual handling would be unsuitable for fork-lift trucks and palletized materials.

(g) *Materials handling devices* available on the market. The major producers of materials handling equipment have developed a wide range of devices for all types of situations. However, if the desired system does not exist, it cannot be purchased, unless the producers are willing to take on the problem and design a special device or attachment.

(h) *Forms of packaging* employed by both the organization itself and the suppliers and distributors. Table 17.1 shows how the various forms of packaging dictate the type of materials handling system to be employed.

Table 17.1 *Packaging and methods of handling*

Method of packaging	Method of handling
Palletized loads	Fork-lift truck
Sacks and bags	Conveyor system
Bulk grains	Conveyor system
Bulk liquids	Pipeline and tanker
Unit stores	Containers
Small units	Manual handling
Drums	Fork-lift truck

(i) *Method of final delivery* employed by suppliers and the organization itself. If materials are delivered in large bags or sacks, then a gravity conveyor system could be the most efficient. If goods are delivered by rail, then a side-loader is best suited.

Management and control of materials handling

5. Rule of materials management

Because of the importance of materials handling it obviously requires very careful and professional management if the full efficiency of any materials handling system is to be ensured.

Materials management should always be involved in the management or control of materials handling. Many organizations have adopted the system of appointing a member of the materials management team as materials handling manager, with overall responsibility and authority for all handling. This has the following advantages:

(a) Centralization of authority and control should mean better utilization of materials handling resources.
(b) A skilled and specialized person can be employed who will be able to recommend and employ the best and most efficient system in line with his own knowledge and experience.
(c) Central control will help to reduce the bottlenecks and hold-ups that plague many organizations.

6. Materials handling efficiency

The materials handling manager must bear in mind certain basic management procedures which can dramatically affect efficiency. For example, he should ensure the following:

(a) That only the correct equipment is employed for the task, never allowing materials handling devices to be misused, since this will only result in accidents and stock damage.
(b) That all materials handling operators are properly trained and tested in the use of the materials handling devices employed. Many of the larger producers of such equipment provide in-plant training schemes as part of the total service package.
(c) That, whatever system or systems are employed, it really meets the needs of the organization as far as it is practicable. In other words, a small company with a simple materials flow will require only a simple system. Management must resist the temptation to employ over-elaborate systems.
(d) That the other departments concerned with materials handling are fully aware of the problems and limitations of the system employed. This will help to ensure that the demands placed upon the system are not too great and also to avoid bottlenecks.

7. The problem of 'double handling'

This is probably the main management problem to be overcome. It refers to the situation where materials are being handled more times than is necessary, mainly because of inefficiency within the whole supply management system.

When materials are delivered to the store they should in theory make only a limited number of journeys in relation to materials flow, for example:

(a) delivery vehicle to the place of storage;
(b) selection from the place of storage;
(c) delivery to and through the process of production.

However, in many organizations this simple flow is not maintained and materials are often handled a great number of times. The real cost of handling, in terms of fuel, plant, labour, etc., is therefore greatly increased, along with the risk of accidents and stock damage.

8. Causes of double handling
The double handling of materials is usually caused by one or more of the following:

(a) *Lack of a good stores location system.* This means that materials are often stored in the wrong area and have to be moved again later.
(b) *Lack of good communications* between materials handling and the other departments involved, e.g. production. It is vital that materials are only supplied to production as and when they can accommodate them, otherwise the factory floor becomes clogged with materials.
(c) *Use of the wrong materials handling device* for the job. For example, a small capacity truck will need to make several journeys to unload a vehicle with very heavy units, whereas a large device could perform the task in one movement.
(d) *Lack of space.* This is the most common cause, especially in organizations that have developed and grown over a period of time. Because of this lack of space and the need to unload vehicles as quickly as possible, materials tend to be placed in the nearest space as a temporary measure.

9. Computer control of materials handling
Because of the expense and importance of materials handling in relation to the operation as a whole, many large companies have

developed complex computerized materials handling systems. Computers can be used to aid control of materials handling in the following ways:

(a) Central control boards displaying the position of every materials handling device can feed data into the computer which can then analyse the situation and direct the most efficient use of materials handling resources, in the total sense.

(b) Materials handling can become almost totally automated with the aid of computers. The large building societies have already developed systems using closed-circuit TV and automated selection and retrieval to enable them to select any documents or deeds from their vast vaults by the use of a coded signal on the computer input unit.

(c) Many organizations have their materials handling equipment radio-controlled, especially in situations where operations are spread over a wide area and a great deal of outdoor handling is being performed. This enables central control to be in constant touch with every truck.

Methods of materials handling

10. Role of manual handling

There are a great number of benefits associated with traditional manual handling such as hand-operated pallet trucks. Manual handling must always be seriously considered as an option for any materials handling system. The following are some of the advantages of hand trucks:

(a) Relatively cheap to purchase.

(b) Can be used in confined spaces and are often employed in the older stores that were built without the modern mechanical devices in mind.

(c) Efficient in relation to the loads that can be handled, especially when the hydraulic jack type is used.

(d) Relatively cheap and easy to maintain and repair.

11. The advantages of mechanical handling systems

Mechanical devices for materials handling are now commonplace in almost every organization dealing with the task of handling and storing stock. This growth of materials handling equipment and technology is a result of the following factors:

(a) Mechanical devices are able to handle extremely heavy loads, far in excess of man's capacity.

(b) Machines can be used in almost any environmental conditions and can be employed twenty-four hours per day. For example, many fork-lift trucks have several drivers working on a shift-system.

(c) Machines have been developed to cope with numerous dangerous and difficult handling problems safely.

(d) Machines are not only able to transport heavy loads, they can also be developed to lift and store them.

12. Disadvantages of mechanical handling systems

There are some inevitable disadvantages to employing mechanical devices. These should really be viewed as necessary evils, which must be reduced as far as possible.

(a) High cost of materials handling devices.

(b) High running costs in terms of fuel, power, maintenance and service.

(c) Cost of training and employing staff.

(d) Possibility of machine failure which can hold up many operations.

13. The problems of 'palletless' handling

Most materials handling devices are basically designed around the fork-lift truck, i.e. there are a wide range of devices that place mechanically operated forks under a load of materials placed upon a pallet (*see* 18). Pallets are usually made of wood and are a simple device designed to enable the forks to be placed under the load so that it can be raised and subsequently handled. However, there are packages that cannot be palletized and these can cause serious problems. Palletless packaging and materials will include the following:

(a) drums
(b) large rolls, e.g. carpets, textiles
(c) bricks
(d) concrete blocks

(e) tubs
(f) bottled goods
(g) soft loads, e.g. wool
(g) bulk grains and materials.

14. Devices to overcome palletless handling

The producers of materials handling equipment have looked very carefully at this problem and many have developed devices to overcome it. Lansing Bagnall, for example, have produced a range of attachments, designed for use with their large range of materials handling devices. The variety of equipment reflects the degree of variation in the handling of difficult materials.

Materials handling and unit loads

15. Definition of unit load

A 'unit load' can be defined as a quantity of material, either in full or individual items, assembled and if necessary restrained to permit handling as a single object. To get the greatest advantage from the unit load principle, it should be applied as far back in the manufacturing cycle as possible, even to the raw material and storage stage.

16. Advantages of unitization

There are several important advantages to employing a system of unitization.

(a) *Reduced handling* of individual items thus reducing the risk of damage or deterioration.
(b) *Load stability.* Because of the 'brick'-like structure of a layered pallet, the load will be more stable and thus safer to handle.
(c) *Reduced surface area* in that many of the items are enclosed within the outer layer of items and are thus protected.
(d) *More efficient use* of storage facilities.
(e) *Packaging costs* are reduced.

17. Methods of unit loads

The main methods of unit loads are pallets and containers.

Pallets

18. Function of pallets

The pallet is one of the most basic items of any materials handling system. In a mechanical handling system employing the principle of 'forks', pallets are vital. The main function of the pallet is to maintain a gap between the floor and the load to be handled.

19. Types of pallets

There are various types of pallets in use, each with a fairly specialized application.

(a) *Standard two-way wooden pallet* (0.914 X 0.914 m). This is one of the most common pallets and is often found in most organizations in some role or another. The two-way design of the pallet means that the fork-lift truck can approach the pallets from two sides.

(b) *Wood stillage.* These are not produced to a standard specification and are normally used in connection with small loads and pallet trucks or hand-operated trucks (*see* Fig. 18.1).

(c) *Box pallets.* These are usually standard size pallets with a box structure added. They can be used to handle or store goods. In some situations they are used as a form of 'immediate access' storage for certain items that may be required in the factory and are on 'free-issue'. (*See* Fig. 18.12.)

(d) *Post pallets.* These are pallets that have a framework around them based on various sized posts. This enables the pallet to handle goods which would not normally be suitable for palletized handling. (*See* Fig. 18.16.)

(e) *Universal steel pallets* (1.106 X 1.219 m). These large pallets are made of steel and are able therefore to cope with extremely heavy loads without damage. Steel pallets are often employed in heavy industrial environments such as steelworks, engineering works, and shipyards, etc.

20. Advantages of wooden pallets

Wooden pallets do have several advantages in relation to both materials handling and costs:

(a) inexpensive and cheap to maintain;
(b) relatively long life;

(c) have a degree of 'friction' that can improve the stability of loads and handling;
(d) can be stored in the stockyard.

21. Disadvantages of wooden pallets
These are as follows:

(a) tend to get damaged and need repair;
(b) difficult to keep clean (this can be very important when dealing with foodstuffs).

22. Problems common to all types of pallets
All pallet systems suffer from the following problems:

(a) *Loss*. In most systems, organizations deliver on pallets, and therefore they should expect to collect the relevant number of pallets from the customer's 'pool'. If, however, these pallets are not collected then, eventually, the stock of pallets will be reduced and new ones will have to be purchased from the producers. A strict control system is therefore required.
(b) *Misuse*. Pallets may be used for purposes other than those for which they have been designed. Such misuses can range from a supply of timber to a device used to separate areas of stock, all of which deny materials handling the use of pallets and therefore hinder and reduce the efficiency of the materials handling system.

Modern handling and storage systems for unit loads

23. Adjustable pallet racking
Adjustable pallet racking is the most widely used system for storing unit loads and pallets in such a way that effective use is made of the building height and every individual load is accessible. The system consists of vertical frames and horizontal beams and the beams are adjustable in height to accommodate changes in the height of the goods. This is illustrated in Fig. 17.2 and Table 17.2.

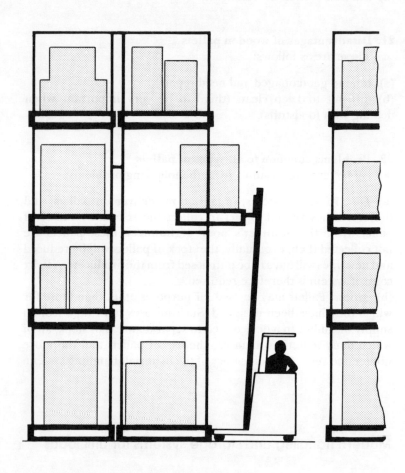

Figure 17.2   *Adjustable pallet racking*

Table 17.2 *Key features of adjustable pallet racking*

Floor space utilization	Good — around 30%
Speed of throughput	Very good, more than one truck can serve racks at one time
Stock rotation	Easily achieved
Selection and order picking	Very good — all individual loads accessible
Stock variability	All pallets can hold different goods if required
Safety of goods	Very good. All pallets individually supported in rack
Handling equipment	Any conventional truck
Typical applications	Palletized consumer goods, beverages and food products, all types of cartoned goods, carpets, coils, drums and large cans, electrical goods and consumer durable products, spares and automotive components, bulk raw materials in sacks or drums.

24. Narrow aisle racking

Narrow aisle pallet racking allows more pallets to be stored than adjustable pallet racking. This is because the aisles are narrower, and the trucks can lift higher. Placement and packing of the goods is also faster. Narrow aisle racking is served by specially designed trucks which do not need to turn through 90 degrees but run on a fixed path between the racks and pick up and set down on either side as required. As a result, the aisle is only marginally wider than the handling equipment which operates within the confines of the system. Goods are taken to and from the system by general purpose handling equipment which uses a pick and deposit station (P & D) located at the ends of the narrow aisle system. This is illustrated in Fig. 17.3 and Table 17.3.

Table 17.3 *Key features of narrow aisle racking*

Floor space utilization	Very good
Speed of throughput	Excellent. Forks can elevate while truck is traversing
Stock rotation	Easily achieved
Selection and order-picking	Excellent. All pallets accessible
Stock variability	Every pallet can hold different goods if needed
Safety of goods	Very good. Every pallet individually supported in rack

Handling equipment   Racking can be designed around any specialist narrow aisle machines

Typical applications   Tall buildings, which are frequently underemployed as storage, can be cost-effectively transformed into safe, high density warehousing with narrow aisle racking.

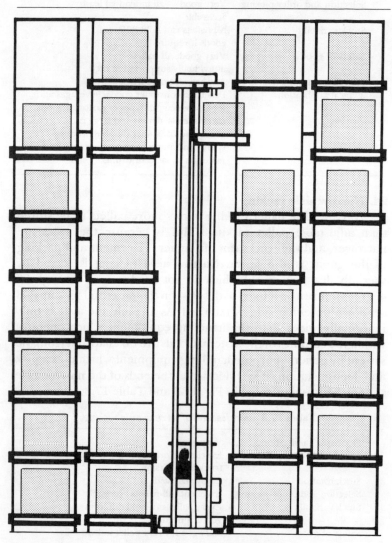

Figure 17.3 *Narrow aisle racking*

25. Drive-in racking

Drive-in racking provides storage for pallets whilst using a minimum of floor space. It offers the same goods protection and preservation as other rack applications but without 100 per cent selectivity.

Drive-in racking is widely used in cold store conditions where cost of space is paramount and refrigeration costs are reduced by keeping products blocked together.

Racking can be designed to be drive-through or drive-in, providing high density low cost storage with the benefit of improved housekeeping and safety.

In most cases, existing fork lift trucks will be completely compatible with drive-in or drive-through racking.

This system is illustrated in Fig. 17.4 and Table 17.4.

Table 17.4 *Key features of drive-in racking*

Floor space utilization	Excellent, up to 85%
Speed of throughput	Good with bulk movements of pallets
Stock rotation	Easily achieved with drive through. Can be achieved with drive-in by complete lane but not by individual pallet
Selection and order picking	Condensed picking face means reduced travels between picks, with drive-through providing two picking faces
Stock variability	Drive-in would generally restrict each lane to one product
Safety to goods	Excellent. Every pallet is individually stored and supported and most are 'inside' the cube and protected
Handling equipment	No special handling equipment required, but trucks may need minor modifications
Typical applications	Cold stores, bulk food stores, distribution. Drive-in is fundamentally block stacking with added safety, increased stock control and reduced product damage.

26. Powered mobile pallet racking

Powered mobile pallet racking in its simplest form comprises units of conventional pallet racking mounted on a steel framed

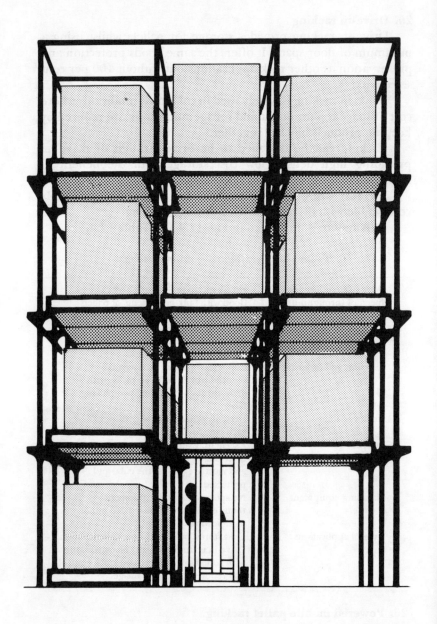

Figure 17.4 *Drive-in racking*

base, fitted with electrically driven wheels which run on a track set into the floor. This system enables a run of racking to be 'closed-up' against an adjacent run. By moving the runs the position of a single aisle can be set to give access to the required rack face.

Up to 80 per cent of the floor area can be occupied for storage, compared with 30 per cent for conventional pallet racking whilst still retaining total access to individual pallets.

Controls may be mounted at the bay-ends or centralized at a console. Alternatively manpower requirements can be reduced by installing radio control equipment on the fork-lift truck. A wide range of safety and warning systems prevents an aisle being closed while still in use.

The increased storage density effectively reduces the building and servicing costs, or releases floor space for other activities, possibly eliminating the need to expand the warehouse or move to larger premises.

The system is illustrated in Fig. 17.5 and Table 17.5.

Table 17.5 *Key features of powered mobile pallet racking*

Floor space utilization	Excellent, up to 80%
Speed of throughput	Fairly good. A picking programme can be used to collate all the requirements from the open aisle before progressing to the next
Stock rotation	Easily achieved
Selection and order picking	Very good. All locations are readily accessible
Stock variability	Very good. All locations can hold differing products
Safety to goods	Very good. All pallets are individually supported in the racking. Most pallets will also be enclosed within the system therefore reducing pilfering
Handling equipment	Any conventional fork-lift truck can be used
Typical applications	Cold storage, high rental premises, bulky multi-product applications, palletized consumer goods, food products.

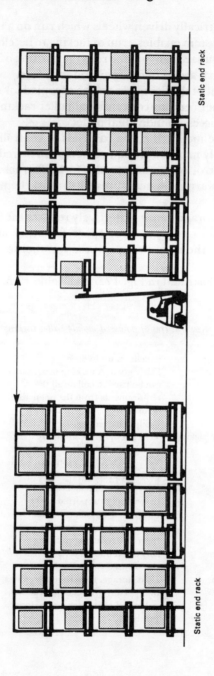

Figure 17.5 *Powered mobile pallet racking*

27. Live storage

Live storage systems are designed to handle successfully either cartons or pallets and in both cases the load is supported on inclined roller or gravity wheel tracks so that the goods travel automatically from the loading side of the installation to the unloading side.

Live storage systems for both pallets and cartoned goods can give high space utilization by reducing the number of aisles necessary to load and access the goods, and live storage ensures that stock rotation is automatic.

Each lane of the system requires to be filled with the same kind of stock, however, so that live storage systems generally provide the most efficient solution when there are at least ten or more identical pallet loads or cartons to be stored for a wide range of items.

This system is illustrated in Fig. 17.6 and Table 17.6.

Table 17.6 *Key features of live storage*

Floor space utilization	Very good. At least 70% of the floor area should be occupied with racking
Speed of throughput	Excellent. A condensed picking face reduces travel distances and should result in time savings of 30–70%
Stock rotation	Excellent. By loading at the back and picking from the front, automatic 'FIFO' is ensured
Selection and order picking	Excellent. Easy access for each product variant, which may be totally or partially unloaded
Stock variability	This system is suitable only when a lane can be kept occupied by a single product variant
Safety to goods	Excellent. Most units are shielded away from access faces
Handling equipment	No special handling equipment needed
Typical applications	Perishable goods requiring failsafe stock rotation, component storage, pre-assembly, pharmaceuticals distribution, speciality foods, stationery, any unpalletized goods, drums, cardboard cartons, plastic trays, fast-moving multi-product ranges, particularly where small quantities of different items must be collated at speed.

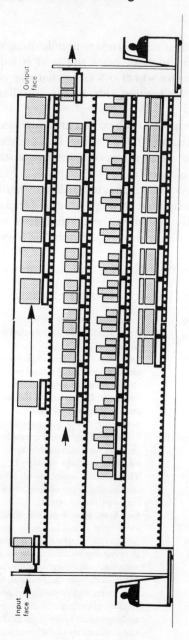

Figure 17.6 *Live storage*

28. Crane systems

The use of stacker cranes within a unit load storage system can provide significant advantages compared with rack systems which are designed for fork-lift truck operation.

The height of the installation can be increased substantially — rack heights in excess of 30 metres are commonplace — whilst space utilization is also enhanced since the crane needs less aisle width and can function with much reduced operating clearances. In addition, the precise tracking of the crane enables higher speeds of movement of the crane and the forks (which can safely move simultaneously), achieving a much faster cycle time when loading or unloading the racks.

Crane systems can also be fully automated since most stacker cranes do not require a driver. With the addition of conveyors or AGVs to move pallets into or out of the storage area, the entire warehouse operation can be computer-controlled.

Crane systems are further described in Table 17.7.

Table 17.7   *Key features of crane systems*

Floor space utilization	Very good. The crane aisle width will normally be only 150–200mm greater than the pallet depth. Utilization of at least 60% of the floor area should be achieved. Double-depth racking gives even better utilization of the floor area
Speed of throughput	Excellent, provided that the crane does not have to make frequent use of the aisle transfer carriage
Stock rotation	Can be simply achieved
Selection and order picking	All locations are individually accessible
Stock variability	No problem — all locations available for any product
Safety to goods	All pallets are individually supported. Security fencing for personnel safety in crane aisles also prevents unauthorized access for pilfering
Handling equipment	Always tailored to the particular requirement of the system

Typical applications	Large capacity warehousing projects where long-term operating economics are more important factors. In general, applications are similar to those of adjustable pallet racking (*see* Table 17.2).

Containerization

29. Introduction

Containers are being regarded more and more as a *mode of transport* rather than as a packaging. Containers are large unit loads which reduce the number of handlings to which materials within the container will be subjected. Containers are now being transported by the following:

(a) road;
(b) rail;
(c) ferry;
(d) deep sea vessel;
(e) aircraft.

30. Integration

Containerization has led to a high degree of *integration* between transport systems. For example, a standard 40 ft container is loaded at the factory with finished goods, a lorry then transports the container to the docks. The container is stored on the dockside until the ship is ready to be loaded. Once the ship has reached its destination, the container can be loaded on to a vehicle and delivered to the customer.

31. Advantages of containerization

The speed at which this system has been adopted indicates its cost-effectiveness but there are several other important advantages.

(a) *Minimization of handling of materials* thus reducing damage, deterioration and theft.
(b) *Improved turnaround time for vehicles* given that containers can be 'handled' at the docks by specialized materials handling equipment.

(c) *Greatly improved efficiency* and time saving in relation to the loading of vessels, thus reducing freight tariffs.

(d) *Lower insurance rates* due to reduced risk of theft, damage and deterioration.

(e) *Transport mode integration.*

32. Disadvantages of containerization

There are several problems associated with containerization which are as follows:

(a) *Deterioration of containers* causing damage to materials.

(b) *Condensation and rust damage* due to a lack of ventilation.

(c) *Lack of handling facilities* in less developed countries.

33. Container systems

There are several container-based systems currently employed in the field of transport.

(a) *Containers by road.* The standard 40 ft long container is a very popular means of handling unit loads in the UK. The majority of UK transport organizations have some proportion of containerized transport.

(b) *Rail-borne container systems.* The UK Freightliner network is a very successful system — containers are transported by rail to and from strategic locations in the UK. The system also deals with overseas handling, ships being loaded with containers to be transported across the English Channel to Europe.

(c) *Containers by ferry.* This system is termed RORO (roll-on/roll-off) services to Europe. The vehicle and its container are driven on to the ferry, and taken across the Channel or North Sea to Europe. The vehicle then drives off the ferry and continues on its journey.

(d) *Containers by deep sea vessel.* The basic concept of containerization is that to load a ship with a number of similar sized units enables loads to be taken on and off the ferry quickly and efficiently. It has been estimated that before containerization ships spent up to 60 per cent of their working lives tied up at a dockside. This percentage has been greatly reduced; ships now spend a far greater proportion of their time at sea actually transporting goods.

(e) *Containers by air.* Air freight is becoming more popular and is an expanding mode of transport. The use of containers is an expanding mode of materials handling (*see* **3(d)**). The use of containers to handle materials is still developing in relation to air transport. The 'igloo' container is designed to fit into the aircraft, and thus maximise space usage. These containers tend to be very light (obviously given the restrictions of load imposed by air transport) and are usually semi-disposable.

34. Types of container

There are a number of types of containers, each designed and developed to deal with the various materials being transported and the various modes of transport involved. The main variations are as follows:

(a) *Standard 40 ft box (end-door loading) container*. This is the most common type of container, employed by both road, rail and sea systems.

(b) *Box 40 ft (side-door loading) container*.

(c) *Soft-top containers*. These have a removable waterproof top to facilitate loading by overhead crane.

(d) *Tilt containers*. These have a soft-top and drop sides, thus enabling side-loading by fork-lift truck and top loading by overhead crane.

(e) *Half containers*. These are small containers (20 ft long) and are normally used to handle heavy loads.

(f) *Bulk liquid containers*. These are liquid tanks set in the framework of a standard container, so as to facilitate handling.

(g) *Refrigerated units*. A refrigeration unit is built into the container, the power being supplied by the transporting mode.

35. Problems associated with 'specialized' containers

There are several reasons why the vast majority of containers are standard 40 ft end loading types. These are as follows:

(a) *Strength of construction*. The basic end loading type is the strongest configuration.

(b) *Reduced risk of damage to materials*. Soft-top and side systems can leak causing damage.

(c) *Flexibility of application*. A large number of different loads can be handled by the standard 40 ft end loading container.

Progress test 17

1. What is the importance of effective materials handling systems? **(1)**

2. List the factors that need to be considered when selecting a materials handling system. **(4)**

3. Outline the role of materials management in effective materials handling systems. **(5)**

4. List the main causes of double handling. **(8)**

5. What are the advantages of mechanical handling systems? **(11)**

6. Define a unit load. **(15)**

7. What are the key features of narrow aisle racking systems? **(Table 17.3)**

8. List the main advantages of containerization. **(31)**

Case study no. 7:

Across Ltd

Across Ltd is a medium sized warehouse. The main business of the company is handling, packing and distributing a wide range of computer-based educational games. The companies are normally software houses who design the games and then produce a given number of copies. The goods are then sent to Across Ltd. Once the tapes have been received from the customer, the process of packing and distribution can begin quite quickly or the tapes may lay in stock for some months.

The goods arrive on strapped pallets by lorry. The goods then have to be moved from the unloading area through the packing area to the main store. The throughput of pallets is normally above 20 every hour. The main store has a system of ASPR, up to 12 metres high. Space is very tight in the warehouse and the company has a system of narrow aisles. Once the goods are required for packing they have to be located in the stock, lifted and placed beside the appropriate packing station. The finished product then has to be moved from the station to the loading bay. This is some distance away. Once at the bay, the goods are packed into a 40 foot container for shipment to the EC.

Discussion question

1. Describe the types of MHE required by this company.

Materials handling and storage equipment

Introduction

1. Development
The store and its associated installations are becoming more and more places of high capital investment and automation of handling and storage of stock. The desire to increase efficiency has led to the development of a wide range of equipment, far too wide to be covered completely in a book of this nature. However, this chapter tries to present as broad a view as possible of the equipment currently employed in many stores.

2. Functions of storage and handling equipment
The functions of materials and storage equipment can be classified under four headings, each of which will be dealt with in the following section:

(a) *movement of materials* (e.g. trucks, fork-lifts, cranes, conveyors, etc.);
(b) *storage of materials* (e.g. racks, shelves, bins, open stores);
(c) *measurement of materials* (e.g. scales);
(d) *selection of materials*.

Description of equipment

3. Movement of materials
Materials handling equipment has been developed to tackle a great number of materials handling problems. Each device has its own specialized area of operation. The equipment available includes those listed in **4–19** below.

4. Hand pallet trucks (*see* Fig 18.1)

These are manually operated devices, relatively cheap to buy and maintain. They are robustly constructed and the hydraulic-jack system enables quite heavy loads to be moved in confined spaces. They have a lifting capacity of 2,000 kg.

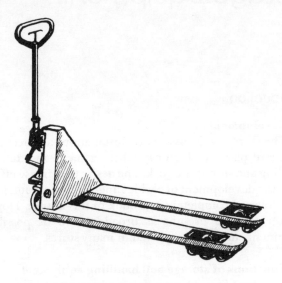

Figure 18.1 *Hand pallet truck*

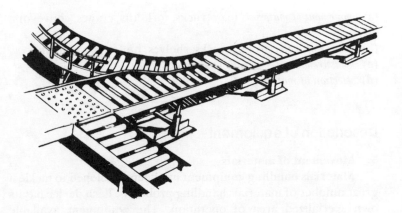

Figure 18.2 *Gravity conveyors*

5. Gravity conveyors (*see* **Fig. 18.2**)

These use the force of gravity and a series of low friction rollers. They enable small units of stock to be moved more cheaply and more quickly, provided the material flow is arranged to enhance the force of gravity. Gravity conveyors can be easily constructed and are totally flexible.

6. Powered conveyors

These are powered usually by electric motors and are widely used in many organizations. There are the following variations:

(a) *Belt conveyors* used when loads have to be elevated, lowered or moved at a constant speed.

(b) *Overhead conveyors* employed in situations where space is limited.

(c) *Chain slat conveyors* for the transportation of heavy materials.

(d) *Powered roller conveyors* used in the movement of unit loads.

(e) *Telescopic conveyors* which can be extended to reach into the rear of vehicles to facilitate efficient loading and unloading.

7. Electric fork-lift truck (*see* **Fig. 18.3**)

This is the basic materials handling device employed in a wide number of situations. The truck is driven by an operator and has the ability to use its forks to lift heavy loads (when on pallets).

The heavy duty batteries have to be regularly recharged to ensure continual service. This type of truck usually has a capacity of around 1,500 kg, and is employed mainly indoors, owing to the pollution-free characteristics of electric power.

Figure 18.3 *Electric counterbalance fork-lift truck*

8. Electric pallet truck

These are driven by operators and are designed to move palletized goods without having to raise the forks more than enough to clear the load off the floor. They cannot therefore be used for any kind of stacking, as can the fork-lift truck. The capacity of these pallet trucks is around 2,000 kg.

9. Pedestrian electric pallet stacker (*see* **Fig. 18.4**)

This device is designed to be used by various members of staff as and when required, rather than by a full-time sole operator. It can be used in place of the traditional hand pallet truck, where the stacking of pallets is required. These devices normally have a capacity of around 1,000 kg.

Figure 18.4 *Pedestrian electric reach pallet stacker*

10. Tow tractor

This is a small, electrically powered, man-operated tractor, designed to pull a trailer train. It is very powerful and can be used in a wide variety of roles in relation to materials handling. It can be employed in moving bulk materials and stock items. Because it is electrically powered, it needs to be recharged at given intervals.

11. Electrically powered stand-on reach truck

This is a development of the standard fork-lift truck, which has been given the facility to extend the forks above the normal height (by means of a system of telescopic units) so that it can reach the highest shelves of many stores installations. It has been especially developed to operate in narrow aisles and gangways. The forks when fully raised will reach a height of 3.5 m and can handle a load of over 1,300 kg.

12. Electric turret reach trucks (*see* **Fig. 18.5**)

These devices are designed for work in very confined storage areas. They have the ability to reach high levels (like the reach truck described above) but with the added capability of being able to select and place items by a moveable 'turret' arrangement attached to the forks. This enables the forks to be moved from side to side, without having to manoeuvre the whole truck, making it ideal for high density storage areas with restricted access. These devices normally have a capacity of around 2,000 kg.

Figure 18.5   *Electric turret reach truck*

13. Basic engine-powered fork-lift trucks (*see* **Fig. 18.6**)

The use of diesel-powered trucks is normally associated with heavy materials in an outdoor environment. The trucks have the same basic abilities as the electric fork-lift, but they are far more powerful and robust, being able to operate on rough and uneven surfaces, and in all weather conditions. These types of devices are often used in industrial stockyards. The average capacity of this type of fork-lift is around 7,000 kg.

Figure 18.6 *Engine-powered fork-lift truck*

14. Electric container loader fork-lift truck
This device has been especially developed to deal with the problems of loading and unloading palletized containers, which are fast becoming the most common method of transporting materials. The device has a high degree of accuracy of placement and is able to fill containers using every last inch to capacity.

15. Engine-powered container handler (*see* **Fig. 18.7**)
This is probably the largest and most powerful of all the materials handling devices in use today. It has been developed to handle, stack and transport the large containers which now dominate shipping and road transport. These devices have a capacity of over 30 tonnes.

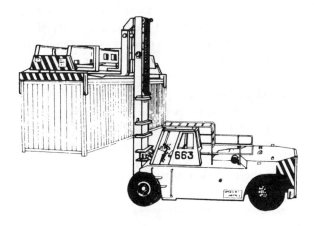

Figure 18.7 *Engine-powered container handler*

16. Engine-powered side-loaders (*see* Fig. 18.8)

As the name suggests, these are powerful materials handling devices designed to enable the forks to be placed under the load from a side-on position. Side-loaders have been developed mainly to deal with the handling of materials transported by rail.

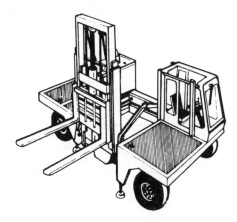

Figure 18.8 *Engine-powered side-loader*

17. Engine-powered mobile cranes

These devices are mainly used in stockyards and are extremely useful for handling heavy and awkward materials — large piping, steel girders, etc. The common type has a capacity of 3,000 kg. It is operated by a trained member of stores staff and it is completely mobile around the store.

18. Motorized pulley block

This is an electrically powered mobile device, designed to operate on a monorail system controlled by the stores staff via a remote control unit which is attached to a long flex. It provides for quick and efficient lifting and transportation of materials around the store and the factory or warehouse.

19. Electric overhead travelling crane (*see* Fig. 18.9)

This is a device similar to the motorized pulley block, but it is designed to cope with much heavier units, and as the title suggests the crane travels the length of the factory and storage areas on a system of rails. This type of device is used a great deal in the more traditional heavy industries, e.g. shipbuilding.

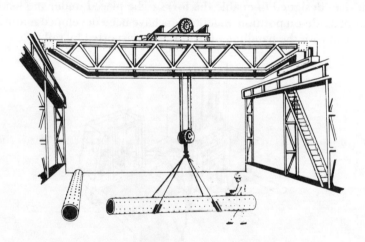

Figure 18.9 *Electric overhead travelling crane*

20. Storage of materials

It would be impossible to describe every piece of stores

equipment in this book, but those illustrated in Figs. 18.10 to 18.18 are the most common, as used in a wide spectrum of situations.

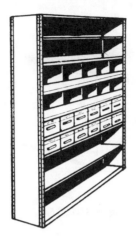

Figure 18.10 *Closed shelving*

Figure 18.11 *Pallet racking system. This allows vertical storage of pallets thus substantially increasing the capacity of the storage area*

Figure 18.12   *Box pallet*

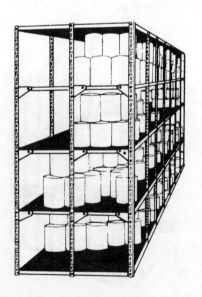

Figure 18.13   *Open shelving*

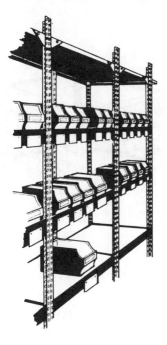

Figure 18.14 *Storage trays. Usually used in conjunction with open and closed shelving for storing small items*

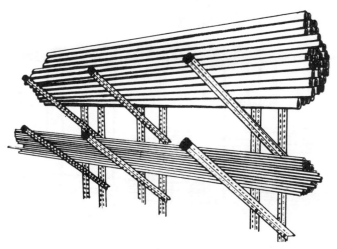

Figure 18.15 *Bar-racks. Usually custom-built, this equipment is used for storing bars, rods and awkwardly shaped material that would otherwise 'shift'*

Figure 18.16   *Post pallet*

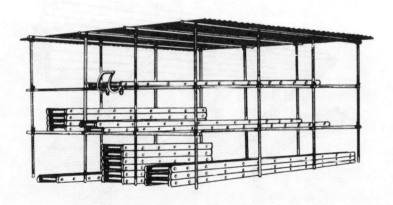

Figure 18.17   *Stockyard open-racking shed. This is used for storing metal rods, ladders, scaffolding, piping, etc.*

Figure 18.18 *Mezzanine platform. Its function is to increase
storage capacity and utility; it may be used to segregate certain stores.
The stores office may be part of the mezzanine*

21. Measurement of materials

It has been seen that one of the basic functions of stores is to
receive and issue stock. To enable stores management to do this
task efficiently and accurately it needs certain pieces of equipment,
designed to measure the materials involved. The units or method
of measurement will depend upon the nature of the materials. The
main classifications are as follows:

(a) weight (tonnes, kilograms and grams);
(b) dimensions (length, breadth, height, clearances, specifications);
(c) density;
(d) liquid measures (litres).

22. Types of equipment

The equipment to perform these measurements could include
a weighbridge (*see* Fig. 18.19), scales, dipsticks and a hydrometer
for measuring liquids, rule tapes and rules, micrometers, and so
on.

Figure 18.19 *Weighbridge. Used to ascertain the weight of stores loaded on a vehicle without unloading it. Vehicle and load are weighed together. The 'tare' weight is deducted from the total load giving the net weight of the load*

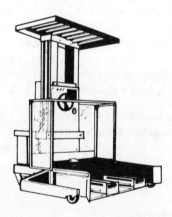

Figure 18.20 *Electric order picker*

23. Selection of materials

The stores employs various devices to assist in the process of selection of materials. In situations where the stock is stored in a system of open shelving and narrow gangways, an electric order-picker (*see* Fig. 18.20) is used. This allows staff to be lifted up to the level of the materials, while still controlling the movement of the truck.

The manual trolley system (*see* Fig. 18.21) employs a simple trolley, manually operated to collect the materials required for individual orders.

Figure 18.21 *Manual trolley*

Progress test 18

1. What are the four main categories of storage equipment? **(2)**

2. What are the differences between a typical electric fork-lift truck and an engine-powered fork-lift truck? **(7, 13)**

3. What is an electric turret reach truck used for? **(12)**

4. List some common pieces of equipment used for the storage of materials. **(20)**

5. What are the main categories of measurement for typical materials? Name one piece of equipment used for each category. **(21, 22)**

6. Describe two types of system used in the selection of materials. **(23)**

Case study no. 8:

Increased productivity in Atlas Copco warehouse

Reproduced with the kind permission of the Institute of Materials Management

Two very narrow aisle trucks comprise the only mobile handling equipment in a computerized distribution warehouse in Hemel Hempstead. The new Atlas Copco centre has achieved a 75 per cent increase in productivity.

Commenting on the improvement, Mike English, distribution manager of Atlas Copco, the Swedish owned manufacturer of compressors and air-driven equipment, says 'We had to change our storage system because continued growth was putting pressure on the warehouse operation. After a series of acquisitions it was decided to consolidate all warehousing in Hemel Hempstead. This presented Atlas with a 30 per cent increase in inventory and 40 per cent more stock lines. At the same time we needed to be able to process 53 per cent more orders, including a 120 per cent increase in export orders.'

'The need to store more in less space while speeding materials flow around the warehouse was recognized immediately. It was achieved by installing very narrow aisle (VNA) storage areas for medium to large size items and a carousel for small storage — an efficient and flexible system given that each of the 23,000 items stocked is a different size. By linking each area with a conveyor system and controlling the entire operation by computer, we attained the required throughput.'

Atlas Copco assembles orders in small tote bins, in a sequence dictated by a picking list generated by the company's warehouse computer. Small parts are picked first from the carousels and the tote bins then pass to the VNA high density storage area along a conveyor which deposits the bins at a P & D adjacent to the VNA area.

The Boss WK 'man aloft' order picker was selected for this VNA high density storage area. Four rows of storage bins, ten rows high, give over 1,200 locations for thousands of small parts. The computer-generated picking list identifies the part number required, the quantity and the location. Fast operation and 'diagonal lift', where the truck lifts as it travels, means minimum time is spent reaching each location and in completing the job.

The investment required to install this efficient operation is summarized by Mike English: 'We estimate the savings in storage space achieved and the increased productivity will mean repayment on total investment in three years or less.'

Part five

Aspects of materials management

Materials management and production planning

Purpose and scope of production planning

1. Aims

The function of production planning is to ensure that the orders placed for the goods and services produced by the organization for its customers are dealt with by the most efficient utilization of the organization's resources.

Production planning is, therefore, basically concerned with tactical planning, that is to say, practical implementation of corporate strategy in relation to production, distribution and stocks.

The actual aims of the department can be listed as follows:

(a) Meet customer demands.
(b) Minimize overall costs.
(c) Maximize utilization of resources.

2. Detailed objectives

Within the above general aims are the following more specific objectives:

(a) To maximize labour utilization and ensure that staffing levels are always in balance in relation to overall sales trend.
(b) To maximize the use of plant and equipment, therefore reducing unit cost by ensuring as large a production run as possible.
(c) To ensure supply of materials, parts and components against a predetermined production programme.
(d) To liaise with marketing in the production of its sales forecasts

and distribution plans and thereby to incorporate marketing needs into tactical planning.

(e) To provide a databank of information relating to output levels, stock levels, quality control, labour situation, etc.

3.   Production planning activities

Production planning covers a wide spectrum of activities because of its tactical role and its need, therefore, to coordinate the actions of other departments. The activities of the production planning department could include the following:

(a) *Long-term planning* involving the analysis and interpretation of sales forecasts, production forecasts, investment programmes and the labour market to assist the organization in developing a long-term strategy.

(b) *Short-term planning* involving the translation of the organization's long-term planning into workable time periods of activity.

(c) *Formulation of an actual production plan* which will dictate what is to be produced, the quantity, the time and all other important factors.

(d) *Monitoring* of production plans both long and short term in terms of accuracy and effectiveness.

(e) *Updating* production plans to ensure constant control over the whole operation.

Formulation of production plans

4.   Introduction

This is one of the most important aspects of production planning. The efficiency of the whole productive operation will be directly affected by the skills and judgment of production planning in relation to their efforts to fulfil the aims of the production plan.

5.   Information required for the formulation of production plans

The aim of a production plan is to coordinate the actions of other departments towards a common goal. A whole range of information therefore needs to be fed into the production planning system to ensure effective planning. The volume and quality of that information will directly affect the planners' ability to plan. The data required would be as follows:

(a) *Outstanding orders.* All demands of a short-term nature need to be recorded and included in the production plan.

(b) *Long-term stock requirements.* This information will cover stock reduction or stock building against long-term market plans and the storage capacity of the organization and its distribution network.

(c) *Labour availability.* This information should cover not only the actual numbers available, but also their skill and functions. For example, the loss of several highly skilled operators will have far more effect upon the production plan than, say, the same number of junior packers. This information is usually supplied by the personnel department which keeps the staff records and controls training and recruitment.

(d) *Plant availability.* The capacity of the organization's plant and its distribution among the product range will affect what is produced and how much. Data regarding the availability of plant comes from the production department itself and from the engineering department, which may have altered the plant available owing to maintenance or repairs.

6. Method of formulating the plan

The method employed to plan production will depend upon several factors, all of which are related to the size of the operation and its complexity. These factors include the following:

(a) training and skill of the production planners;
(b) whether it is a computerized or manual planning system;
(c) whether the organization uses batch or flow production methods.

Bearing in mind these factors, we can produce a typical method of formulating production plans and relating the data required on a production planning control sheet (*see* Table 19.1). The production planning control sheet shows how the planner can relate some of the basic demands and restraints upon the system. This data must now be translated into a workable production plan, which will be produced by the production planner.

Table 19.1 *Production planning control sheet*

Item	*Stock*	*Average sales per week*	*Stock (weeks)*	*Materials stock*	*Plant capacity*	*Prodn*
1	2,000	1,000	2.0	3,000 max	25,000	Yes
2	500	100	5.0	2,000 max	10,000	No
3	3,000	1,000	3.0	3,000 max	10,000	No

7. Production plan layout

Obviously the actual layout of a production plan will depend upon the needs of the organization, but a typical layout could be as illustrated in Fig. 19.1. The plan indicates what is to be produced, the amount and the sequence.

Plant 1	*Monday*	*Tuesday*	*Wednes-day*	*Thursday*	*Friday*
Shift Day Eve Ngt	2,000 Item A		2,000 Item A		2,000 Item A
Plant 2					
Shift Day Eve Ngt		3,000 Item B		3,000 Item B	
Plant 3					
Shift Day Eve Ngt			2,000 Item C		

Figure 19.1 *Production plan layout*

Production programme

8. Functions of a typical production programme

The basic aim of the production programme is to communicate the tactical plan of the organization to those departments concerned with production, storage and distribution. The information contained in the programme should be comprehensive and practical, and should cover the aspects outlined in **9–13** below.

9. Specification of the items to be produced
It is vital that the programme gives clear details of exactly what is to be produced, along with full details of any special requirements regarding such factors as:

(a) quality;
(b) performance;
(c) packaging;
(d) colour;
(e) types.

Production planning must ensure that any abbreviations, signs or marks used when producing the programme are fully understood by the departments that will need to interpret the programme.

10. Quantities to be produced
Both production and stores need to have data on the exact requirements of the programme. Production will need this data to enable it to plan its utilization of labour and plant to ensure that the output required is produced. Stores will need this information so that it can calculate the amount of stock needed to produce the finished items listed. A simple example could be:

Planned output:	500 saloon cars	
Stock needed:	Wheels	4 × 500 = 2,000
	Seats	4 × 500 = 2,000
	Tyres	4 × 500 = 2,000
	Headlights	2 × 500 = 1,000
	Steering wheels	1 × 500 = 500

11. Sequence or order of production
Most programmes relate to a period of time (one week or one month), so the output required is set in sequence. This sequence may bear a relationship to the needs of sales and marketing, e.g. a special order which needs to be produced and despatched during the early part of the programme's life will be produced as soon as

the programme commences. The sequence of production is of vital importance to stores management, bearing in mind that its primary objective is to supply the goods and services needed for production as and when required. Obviously, stores must be fully aware of the sequence set by planning, so that it can supply the materials required.

12. Indication of the overall product 'mix' required by the organization
This will assist production in allocating plant capacity and stores in estimating its material and stock needs for the future.

13. Output of finished goods
Distribution and sales will be able to calculate from the production programme the forthcoming levels of output and availability of finished goods. The distribution department (*see* 24:**1**) is responsible for ensuring that goods are transported to the point of consumption. Knowledge of what is being produced, and when it will be available, will assist it in utilizing its transport as efficiently as possible.

Materials management and production planning

14. Relationship between management and production planning
The relationship between these two departments is a very important one. It must be a practical and working relationship. The materials function is committed to ensuring a continuity of supply in terms of materials and services to the organization as a whole, planning is committed to ensuring that output meets the needs of the organization in terms of sales, production and stocks. The relationship between these two departments depends a great deal upon the quality of communications and the level of mutual confidence that exists between them.

15. Duties and responsibilities of production planning
Production planning has a wide and complex range of duties and responsibilities towards its counterparts in materials management, including the following:

(a) *Advance warning of large increases in demand* and stock requirements must be given. Planning will have data concerning the long- and short-term stock requirements of the organization. A degree of notice will enable stores to make provision for the excess demand efficiently.

(b) *Production trends* as formulated by the planning department are of special interest to materials management. Such trends should give an indication of future demands and the expected range of goods to be produced, or the effects upon the levels of stock and stock distribution throughout the organization.

(c) *Notification of alterations* in the production must be given. In most productive situations unforeseen circumstances (e.g. machine breakdown) will suddenly make current production plans obsolete, and a new plan will have to be instituted to account for the alterations. Planning must ensure that materials management is notified as soon as possible of these alterations, the effects in terms of materials required and the time period involved. This will enable materials management to supply the materials needed and avoid the situation of production demanding materials and materials management being unaware of any problems or changes.

16. Duties and responsibilities of materials management
    Materials management must be aware of its duties and responsibilities towards the production planning department, many of which will directly affect the overall efficiency of that department.

(a) *Accurate and up-to-date information* must be available on the current level of stocks held and their location. When planning is formulating its production programme it must have information concerning the stocks available and their distribution. There is no logic in planning production of a product if the materials needed to produce it are not in stock.

(b) *Stock condition.* Production planning can only plan to utilize stocks which are in an acceptable condition, in terms of quality and the level of deterioration and the estimated shelf-life required of the finished product. For example, in the case of an organization producing manufactured foods, the finished product may be designed to last several weeks on the shelf. If, however, one of the ingredients has a shorter life than the whole product's life then the whole product's life is reduced accordingly. Planning must therefore be kept fully informed of the condition of all stocks.

(c) *Continuity of supplies* to the point of consumption (factory floor, workshop, depots, etc.) must be maintained. The stores must ensure that the goods and services required by the production planning programme are available and allocated as instructed in the programme. The production planning programme will involve the employment of labour, man-hours and time. All of these are very expensive resources and if the stock required is not provided these resources will be unable to combine to produce the goods required by the organization and therefore they will be wasted.

(d) *Control of work in progress*. In any productive situation at some time in the process there will be a degree of work-in-progress. The materials management must ensure that this stock is stored and recorded, and that production planning is made aware of the range and amount of work in progress held. Planning will make provision on its production programme for this stock to be fed into the overall production process. Materials management must ensure that it monitors carefully these times and supplies the work in progress to the shopfloor.

(e) *Distribution of stocks*. The materials management must ensure that the materials required for production are in the right location at the right time. Production planning relies on materials management to ensure that at each stage of the production process (which may not all be on the same site) the materials required by production are available. Failure to do this will inevitably lead to loss of output and production.

(f) *Production specifications* produced by planning must be completely adhered to in terms of the materials supplied by materials management for production. Planning will have to incorporate all the detailed requirements in terms of designs, types, packaging and performance in relation to the market for which the goods are being produced in accordance with the information received from the sales and marketing departments. Materials management has the responsibility of ensuring that the materials indicated on the programme are those supplied. In situations where these specific items are not in stock, then materials management must:

(*i*) inform production planning immediately of the shortage;

(*ii*) suggest a suitable alternative for the given item involved.

(**g**) *Following the production programme* is a vital responsibility of materials management in relation to production planning. The production programme is produced, bearing in mind the capacity of the organization in terms of plant, space and labour. It is also designed to reflect the needs of the organization in terms of sales and stock building. The production programme is a detailed tactical plan and requires a great deal of time and skill to produce and issue. Materials management must therefore ensure that it strictly follows the instructions contained within the programme. It is vital that changes are not made by materials management to the programme, so that materials unsuitable or not required might be issued to production, thereby forcing an operational change in the programme.

(**h**) *Reaction to alterations* in the production programme must be quick and efficient on the part of materials management. Materials management must react to any alterations as soon as official confirmation has been received from the production planning manager. In many instances these changes will be a result of some unforeseen circumstances and therefore tend to be of an emergency nature. Plant and labour already committed to a certain production run may be idle for long periods if the reaction to production programme changes is not swift and efficient.

(**i**) *Feedback of information* to production planning relating to the efficiency and workability of the programmes devised is also vital. In many situations materials management is the first direct contact that production has with purchasing, stores, planning and distribution. Materials management responsibility is therefore to ensure that all relevant information concerning production programmes is fed back to production planning so that action may be taken to improve the programmes produced.

17. Ways of improving materials management and production planning relationships

There are several practical ways in which the relations and cooperation between these two vital departments can be achieved. Some of them are listed below.

(**a**) *Sound and practical production programmes* are essential if materials management and planning are to cooperate fully. Production programmes which are not practical, or requests for stocks that do not exist, or timetables that are not practical in terms of distribution etc. will only create problems between the departments. It is vital that production programmes are carefully produced and issued in advance of production commencing, to allow materials management time to select and assemble the materials required.

(b) *Established channels of communication* both formal and informal between the departments are also vital. A system of regular meetings should be introduced and maintained. These should be held before the preparation of any production programmes, enabling all the interested parties (i.e. production, planning, sales, stores and purchasing) to have an opportunity to put forward their comments and constraints in relation to the proposed programme. This should help to avoid impractical programmes being produced and circulated. Each of these departments can put considerable demands and constraints upon any production programme, as follows:

(*i*) Purchasing — lack of stocks;
(*ii*) Stores — stock control;
(*iii*) Sales — promotional demands;
(*iv*) Production — labour shortages.

It is essential that these channels of communication are constantly employed, that materials management and production planning have regular meetings, and that a constant exchange of information takes place.

(c) *Adherence to production programmes* is very important in relation to the materials management/planning relationship. A typical cause of friction between materials management and planning is materials management failing to follow the instructions contained within the programme. This can include factors such as:

(*i*) incorrect quantities of materials;
(*ii*) variations in packaging;
(*iii*) alterations in timetables;
(*iv*) variations in actual output.

Such deviation from the standard production programme is usually brought about by the fact that the original programme has subsequently become impractical (e.g. stock allocated for production may have deteriorated and so now cannot be used).

However, materials management must inform production planning immediately of such problems, and should refrain from making any alternative arrangements without full consultation with that department.

(d) *Professional and well-trained production planning staff* will make a major contribution to the relationship between planning and materials management. Production planning is a highly skilled and involved profession and the influence that this section has over the rest of the organization's efficiency is such that it must be practised only by those with the qualifications and experience to do so. An efficient and well-organized planning section will create fewer of the problems that can affect the very important relationship between materials management and planning in their day-to-day contacts.

18. Advantages of a sound materials management and production planning relationship
There are obviously several very important benefits that the organization can derive from a sound relationship between materials management and production planning. Many of these benefits have substantial financial advantages for the organization as a whole. They can be listed under the following headings:

(a) *Continuity of output* is maintained by the efforts of materials management to supply the goods and services required by the production programme. Failure to follow the programme could result in a costly loss of output.

(b) *Mutual exchange of information* between materials management and planning will help to reduce the risk of major problems and faults in the system from becoming damaging to the whole organization. The constant exchange of data between these two sections will improve the efficiency of both.

(c) *Lower levels of stocks* may be possible because of this sound relationship. If materials management has confidence in the abilities of the production planning section, then stocks of certain items may be reduced, in view of the fact that the production programme is likely to be practical and based upon the information supplied by materials management in relation to the levels of stock. Provided planning does not exceed the limitations imposed by materials management then the level of stock can be reduced.

(d) *Links between production planning and purchasing* will be improved via planning's relationship with stores management. As will be noted materials management and purchasing work very closely together, and therefore a great deal of the information needed by both planning and purchasing is communicated via stores management.

Progress test 19

1. What are the aims and detailed objectives of the production planning department? **(1–2)**

2. Outline some of production planning's main activities. **(3)**

3. What information is required for the formulation of a production plan? **(5)**

4. What aspects should be covered by a production programme? **(8–13)**

5. Describe the relationship between materials management and production planning. **(14)**

6. What are the main advantages of a sound materials management and production planning relationship? **(18)**

20
Materials management and purchasing

Objectives

1. Introduction

Purchasing is the department within materials management which is concerned with the process of ascertaining the organization's material and service needs, selecting suppliers, agreeing terms, placing orders and receiving goods and services. It is by nature a 'service' function, orientated to providing a complete supply-function service for users within the organization.

In 1980 the British Institute of Management carried out a survey into purchasing management in the UK. From this study a job description for the head of purchasing was produced.

(a) To formulate purchasing policies, approve material strategies and ensure implementation through efficient and flexible organization and administration.

(b) To contribute as an executive director to the policies and administration of the organization.

(c) To procure raw, packaging and stores materials to the current specifications at the most economic value, to meet the constantly changing deadlines imposed by the production plan as scheduled and amended, irrespective of market conditions and events.

(d) To maintain a programme of value improvements in materials through the continuous exercise of purchasing techniques and expertise. To locate and develop new sources of supply, materials, processes and methods, in order to facilitate innovation, product improvement and new products.

(e) To control the delivery of materials and the negotiation of credit in order to minimize working assets tied up in materials and to improve cash flow.

(f) To maintain good supplier relationships so as to increase purchasing negotiation effectiveness and secure preferential treatment in terms of information, development and help, particularly in times of shortage.

(g) To forecast material availability and prices for eighteen months ahead, or more, for inclusion in costings, sales and financial forecasts.

(h) To develop, train and provide opportunities to managers and staff so that they are able to meet objectives set within the overall policy.

Sir Terence Beckett, Director-General of the CBI, said in relation to purchasing in March 1984: 'You are on the edge of your companies' activities. You should know what's going on in the outside world. You should be aware of the best practices and the latest developments, buying for your company's best advantage but also prodding and stimulating your own company's performance.'

The objectives of the purchasing department will of course vary a great deal, depending upon the organization's policy, complexity, size, operations, etc. However, some of the more common objectives can be identified and are outlined in **2–5** below.

2.   Cost reduction

The purchasing department is one of the few sections within any organization that is actually involved in spending the organization's cash resources. It therefore has a unique opportunity to reduce some of the organization's costs and thereby increase profits. The organization can become more profitable by the introduction of efficient and professional purchasing practices and techniques. Savings in terms of agreements, quality, delivery, price, performance, etc., are all the rewards of effective purchasing.

3.   Continuity of supplies

The statement that any purchasing department will be judged

by its ability to ensure that goods and services required by the organization are always available is a true one. The user departments will use the efficiency of this part of the operation as a yardstick of overall departmental performance.

The purchasing department must ensure that the goods and services required by all sections of the operation are constantly available, provided that this can be achieved at an economical cost in relation to the cost of storage. Here we have the concept of a balance between the level of service and the cost of storage. The purchasing manager must balance these two factors very carefully.

4. Contribution to the organization's corporate plans

It must be remembered that the purchasing department is also a member of the organization's management structure and that decisions taken about the corporate plans of the organization must involve the purchasing manager. It is an objective of the purchasing department to be able to contribute effectively to the organization's overall corporate strategy. Changes in policy must be communicated to the purchasing department, and alterations, costs, quality, prices, stockholding, etc., can then be effectively managed to meet the overall policy of the organization.

5. Control of negotiations

Another primary objective of the purchasing department relates to negotiation with all the suppliers of the organization. The purchasing department must ensure that the best possible terms (prices, delivery, quality, service, etc.) are achieved in every contract and agreement. The skill and experience of the buyer will, to a great extent, affect the terms of the contract between the buyer and the vendor. The buyer's approach towards the supplier will, of course, vary according to the relative positions of the two parties, as follows:

(a) *Monopoly buyer*. This is where the buyer has a great deal of power, by virtue of the fact that he is the only major source of income for the supplier and the supplier is obliged to bear that fact in mind.

(b) *Monopoly supplier*. This is where the supplier has the only source of supply and has great power in terms of distribution and prices. This situation sometimes occurs in times of shortage or greatly increased demand.

(c) *Competitive environment*. This is a situation in which both the supplier and the buyer are in positions of competition amongst their peers. In most cases the supplier faces the most competition and relies on the quality and price of his product to secure orders.

Functions

6.   Introduction

The purchasing department has a wide range of functions in terms of the overall purchasing operation within the organization. The scope of these functions will, of course, depend upon the structure of the organization and the relative role of other departments, such as stores, distribution, planning, etc. The more common functions are outlined in **7–16** below.

7.   Supplier selection

One of the most important functions of the purchasing department is that of selecting suppliers. The benefits of accurate supplier selection can include such factors as reliability, quality, delivery, performance, reputation and continuity of supplies.

Great care must be taken over the selection of every supplier: short-cuts in this area will lead to inefficiency and loss of profitability in the long run. The supplier selection decision is based on the following factors, all of which must be carefully researched and analysed by the purchasing department:

(a) *Relative prices* of goods and services supplied by the supplier, compared with his competitors.

(b) *Delivery dates, methods and cost of delivery*. In many instances the delivery element is more important than price, provided the prices are within the boundaries of the main competitors.

(c) *Reliability* in terms of performance of materials, delivery dates and prices. The term 'reliable supplier' is not often used in the practical world of purchasing, but once a really reliable supplier has been selected, tried and approved, then the relationship between buyer and supplier will remain a close working one. Many buyers regard the selection of reliable suppliers as of paramount importance.

(d) *Reputation* of the supplier within the industry or trade. Information about the relative performance of suppliers can be obtained from various sources, e.g. trade journals, the press, other companies, word of mouth and past experience of the buyers concerned.

(e) *Quality.* More and more the concept of quality is becoming a predominant factor in the selection of suppliers. The growth in recent years of quality control as a specialism (*see* 8:6) and the realization of the primacy of consumers' demands in relation to consistency of quality and performance of all goods and services, has meant that the importance of quality has greatly increased.

8. Quality control

The purchasing department has a very important role to play in quality control, mainly in relation to the quality and performance of the goods and services purchased on behalf of the organization. The purchasing manager must be involved at every stage of the process of establishing acceptable levels of quality (*see* 8:11–15). The purchasing department's function is to enforce the quality policy of the organization and to monitor the performance of suppliers, and yet at the same time keep purchasing costs within the limits set by the organization's budgets.

9. Maintaining records

The purchasing department is obliged to maintain a complete set of records regarding the operations and activities of the department. The information stored will include details of the following:

(a) *Suppliers' past performances* and evaluations of them.
(b) *Current prices* of the goods and services required by the organization.
(c) *Copies of orders,* contracts and current agreements.
(d) *Progressing data* for outstanding orders.
(e) *Specifications* and standards as set by the user departments.

10. Progressing activities

The purchasing department will often have a wide range of

outstanding orders at any given time, orders which are in the process of being produced or obtained by the supplier. All these orders will be at various stages of completion. The purchasing manager must maintain a degree of control over this area of the purchasing operation. To enable this control to be effective, a system of *progressing* has to be introduced and monitored.

As each order is issued, the date of completion is noted (usually on a wall chart system) and at a given date the progressing section will contact the suppliers for a progress report on each particular order. Progress should not commence until a reasonable period of time has elapsed: constant progressing can become counter-productive and sour supplier relationships.

Progressing has the following advantages:

(a) The supplier is aware of the purchasing department's interest and control.

(b) Possible late deliveries or delays will be identified via the early warning system and therefore alternative suppliers can be secured or alterations of production programmes can be made, without loss of output.

(c) The purchasing manager has a complete and updated visual picture of the purchasing department's position in terms of ordering and suppliers.

11. Production of orders

The purchasing department has to complete a standard order form for every transaction entered into with the supplier. The purchasing department is acting as an *agent*, in legal terms, on behalf of the organization. The standard order therefore represents a binding contract between buyer and vendor. Because of the binding relationship of the order, great care must be taken to ensure that the details of each order are correct and accurate. In cases of error, situations could arise when unwanted goods would be supplied and the organization would be liable for payment to the supplier, provided the supplier was acting upon the instructions contained within the order. In view of this, many purchasing managers apply the concept of the '20/80 rule', that is to say, the orders which are the largest in terms of value (the 20 per cent of total orders) are given the closest scrutiny and inspection, thus affording the greatest coverage in terms of the organization's capital. (In other words, it is more economical for the purchasing manager to spend, say, thirty minutes checking the details of an order for £5,000 than to spend that time checking five small orders for £25.)

12. Stock control overview
   The purchasing department may not be directly responsible for stock control within the organization (*see* 13:2), but it does maintain a close working relationship with stores management and therefore has a stock control overview, bearing in mind that it has information affecting the supply and demand for stocks not always available to stores management. The purchasing department must therefore maintain that close working relationship with the stores, to ensure that the aims and objectives of the two functions are in tune.

13. Supplier relationships
   The purchasing department must ensure that relationships between the organization and its suppliers are sound. The problems associated with relationships that have not been professionally conducted are many and costly. In many instances, the relationship between buyer and supplier has a direct effect upon the continuity of supplies and the continuation of output. The advantages to be gained from a sound supplier relationship can be listed as follows:

(a) *Improved reliability* of supplier in relation to agreed prices and delivery dates.
(b) *Action in emergency situations* of overall shortages by preferential treatment on the part of the supplier.
(c) *Cooperation* in relation to alterations in specifications and designs of products purchased.
(d) *Involvement in future developments* and investment schemes as envisaged by the supplier for the coming period.

14. Monitoring of technical developments
   The purchasing department must be fully aware of all developments affecting the operations of the organization. Innovations that could improve output or reduce costs must be

fully investigated and researched by the purchasing department. Demonstrations and displays should be researched by the purchasing department. Demonstrations and displays should be arranged, along with supplies of samples wherever possible. These innovations can affect any of the goods or services purchased by the organization. Some large organizations have purchasing research sections within their overall materials system. A typical job description for the head of purchasing research would read as follows:

(a) To determine (and regularly update) the requirements of major materials used by the organization world-wide and to ensure that all companies in the organization are in possession of this information, together with information on common related materials or suppliers.

(b) To improve and maintain communications in purchasing throughout the organization so as to promote awareness of important market trends, developments or opportunities.

(c) To encourage combined or coordinated purchasing action within the organization by ascertaining and bringing to the attention of all companies and directors opportunities to take advantage of the organization's total purchasing power, expertise and information.

(d) To plan and direct, as chairman of the quarterly UK group purchasing coordination meeting, UK purchasing strategies.

(e) To coordinate negotiations for the supply of common materials within the UK and overseas.

(f) To control value improvement programmes through value analysis, rationalization or standardization exercises.

(g) To undertake special projects or investigations as requested by the UK Group Director.

(h) To advise and assist companies in the UK and overseas on purchasing problems of any kind.

(i) To conduct purchasing research investigations as requested by purchasing departments world-wide.

15. Specialization
The scope of the purchasing department in relation to the range of goods and services purchased will depend upon the size

and complexity of the organization, but the following list gives an indication of the wide range possible in a typical manufacturing environment:

(a) raw materials;
(b) equipment and spares;
(c) packaging;
(d) services;
(e) capital items;
(f) maintenance materials.

All of these types of stock will require a degree of specialization in terms of the purchasing staff responsible for the procurement. In the organization of the purchasing function, overall control will lie with the purchasing director, while individual buyers deal with a certain category of stock.

16. Advantages of specialization
This system has the following advantages:

(a) *Skill and knowledge* of experts in the given fields of purchasing activities.
(b) *Centralization of data* in terms of records, files, assessments, etc., of suppliers and their service record.
(c) *Improved supplier relationships,* since the buyer will have a body of knowledge concerning the range of items involved and will therefore be aware of problems facing the supplier and will also be able to detect inferior service.
(d) *Advantages of bulk discounts.*
(e) *The use of computer based systems.*

The integrated role of stores and purchasing management within the materials management organization and stores management

17. Purchasing as a related operation
Purchasing is an operation or activity which is directly and closely related to that of stores management. Both are vital parts of materials management and their common objective is effective

control of the goods and services purchased by the organization. The relationship between stores and purchasing involves both parties in having a series of duties to each other, in terms of their respective roles within materials management.

18. Duties of stores in relation to the purchasing operation
    The following is a list of the possible duties and responsibilities of a typical stores department to its counterparts within the purchasing department:

(a) *Communication of current stock levels.* The stores must ensure that purchasing is kept completely informed regarding the current levels of stock for all the items held within the stores system. Stores is able to perform this duty using the stock record system.

(b) *Provision of data for establishing stock levels.* The stores must ensure that information regarding the amount of working stock required at any given time is supplied to purchasing. This may include factors such as deterioration rates, handling problems and bottlenecks, all of which can affect the amount of stock required and are of such a nature that purchasing may not be aware of the problems.

(c) *Accurate stock records.* These are a vital element in the stores/purchasing relationship. Purchasing will use the data stored on stock record cards to make management decisions regarding the ordering and provision of stocks, as well as using the trends outlined in the stock records to forecast future stock levels and demand for items.

(d) *Security.* This is also a very important duty performed by the stores in relation to the purchasing operation. Stores management is responsible for stores security. Failure to maintain security will obviously lead to a lack of confidence on the part of the purchasing manager in the stock figures produced by stores. Added to this must be the objective of purchasing in relation to maximization of profits and its need to reduce losses via theft and deterioration to maintain cost reductions.

(e) *Stock checking.* The stores must ensure that the physical stocks are checked and counted at the periods of time laid down by the organization. Stores must inform purchasing of any shortages, damages, deterioration or losses of stock that are discovered during stock checking. This will enable purchasing to amend its purchasing programme to ensure continuity of supply.

(f) *Flow of documents*. Stores must ensure that all the documents handled by stores which are also needed by purchasing are processed as soon as possible and then passed on to purchasing for further processing. The most common of these documents are:

 (*i*) delivery notes;
 (*ii*) advice notes;
 (*iii*) invoices;
 (*iv*) issue notes;
 (*v*) costing allocation sheets;
 (*vi*) quality control documents.

All are required by purchasing and they are still so-called 'active' documents until all the sections concerned have analysed the data they contain.

(g) *Data on deterioration*. The stores must ensure that a continuous flow of information regarding the condition of stock is maintained. Deterioration must be avoided at all costs by stores management, but in cases of stock-loss purchasing must be informed, not only because of the implications of a reduced stock, but also because of the possibility that the materials could be at fault and therefore a claim against the supplier may have to be considered. It must also be noted that storage conditions as recommended by the supplier could also be incorrect or unsuitable for the type of storage environment maintained by the organization. Both of these have serious implications for future orders and supplies.

(h) *Requisition of stocks*. The stores must ensure that when stocks reach the established reorder level (*see* 15:**3**), the information is communicated to purchasing as soon as possible for checking and reordering. The purchasing department will react to this information and contact the supplier for a fresh delivery. Obviously any delays in this process could result in the deliveries being delayed and therefore a nil-stock situation could arise with all its implications of loss of output and sales.

(i) *Quality control*. The stores is responsible for inspection of all goods and services delivered to the store. In many cases the stores is the first line of defence against faulty materials being introduced into the organization's system (*see* 8:**14(f)**). Stores must contact purchasing immediately suspect goods are detected and quality control has been contacted. Stores must also ensure that all suspect and rejected goods are isolated from the rest of the stock and recorded accurately and that this information is passed on to purchasing as soon as possible.

(j) *Information feedback*. This comes from the shopfloor, or wherever the goods and services supplied are being employed in their designated roles within the organization. Feedback concerns the performance of the materials supplied in terms of output efficiency, the reliability and suitability of the materials supplied and suggestions for possible improvements. All of these can contribute towards effective value analysis by the purchasing manager.

(k) *Stock control activities*. Although it has been stated that purchasing has an overall stock control role within the organization, stores has the responsibility for the tactical or day-to-day operation of the stock control system. Stores must ensure that data produced by the system has the following characteristics, so that it can be used as a basis for sound management decisions:

    (i) *On time*. Information which is communicated late is of little use to the purchasing manager, if he has already placed the order incorrectly.

   (ii) *Accurate*. Information which is inaccurate is positively counterproductive and can lead to serious errors and waste.

  (iii) *Comprehensible*. The information must be in a form which is easily under stood by the purchasing manager. Masses of meaningless statistics are useless. Clear and obvious 'indicators' are needed to illustrate a point (e.g. charts, graphs, etc.).

  (iv) *Relevant*. The information must be relevant to the needs of the purchasing manager. He is not really concerned with data that does not directly affect his decision-making processes.

   (v) *Cost-effective*. Management information of any classification is expensive to produce in terms of labour, time and resources. The information produced must therefore be of advantage to the manager and the organization to justify the costs involved.

19. Duties of purchasing in relation to materials management

The purchasing department has several operational duties and responsibilities in relation to materials management, including the following:

(a) *Establishment of stock levels.* In all decisions and discussions relating to the establishment of stock levels, the purchasing department must ensure that materials management is fully aware of factors that influence the level of stock, e.g. budgets, long-term planning, organization policies, etc., so that materials management is in a position to make a worthwhile contribution to the decision-making process.

(b) *Commitment to stock levels.* Once stock levels have been established, purchasing has a responsibility to materials management to ensure that the levels are maintained as agreed, until a firm decision to adjust them is made.

(c) *Reaction to information received.* Purchasing must take note of, and if necessary act upon, all information passed through by the stores manager. Information requiring action will include that relating to low levels of stock, deterioration, damages and shortages, and poor performance. If purchasing does not react to information supplied by materials management, this will have the following serious implications:

  (*i*) the flow of information will decline and finally stop;

  (*ii*) breakdowns and loss of output will eventually occur.

(d) *Communications.* The purchasing department must ensure that the channels of communication between purchasing and materials management are fully employed. Because purchasing has direct contact with senior management and supplies it tends to receive information that directly affects materials management operations. It is therefore vital that such information is passed to materials management as soon as possible. This information could include the following:

  (*i*) Alterations in delivery schedules. Materials management may have to arrange labour, equipment and storage space at a given time.

  (*ii*) Special handling of certain materials. The equipment required may need to be allocated in advance.

(*iii*) Alterations in the organization's policies regarding stock levels, quality control, staffing levels, etc.

(*iv*) Shortages or non-deliveries by suppliers, along with revised delivery dates and quantities.

(e) Future plans (*see* 21:1) for the stores operation in terms of staffing levels, stock range, stock levels, distribution, and the role of stores within supply management are an area that purchasing will have information and views upon. Materials management must be kept fully informed and given an opportunity to contribute ideas, comments and suggestions.

(f) *Stock trends*. Long-term stock levels and trends are also very important to materials management and the implications of these must be fully discussed between materials management and purchasing.

(g) *Staff development*. In an organization where purchasing has overall responsibility and control over the stores operation, the purchasing department must be aware of the need for development of stores staff in relation to positions and opportunities within the purchasing section. Staff development is vital if the motivation and efficiency of the stores is to be maintained and improved.

(h) *Management support by purchasing of the stores operation*. This can be in terms of support for resources at senior management levels, or management services such as work study or organization and methods. The purchasing department has a responsibility to assist stores at every opportunity.

20. Aims of the stores/purchasing relationship

It can be seen from **18** and **19** that the relationship between stores and purchasing is preoccupied with the following:

(a) sound two-way communications;
(b) total involvement and participation;
(c) mutual aid and support.

21. Improvement of stores/purchasing relationship

There can be little doubt that the relationship between these operations is vital to both their efficiencies and the overall efficiency of supply management. It is also an obvious fact that in many organizations this relationship is not as sound or productive as it should be. Some of the steps which can be taken to improve the relationship are outlined below.

(a) *Improvement of channels of communication,* both formal, i.e. memos, letters, meetings and interviews, and informal, i.e. telephone conversations, discussions and expression of views.

(b) *Complete understanding* of the problems and difficulties facing both parties and a degree of insight into the problems created for each other by inefficiencies on both sides. This should help to avoid major problems.

(c) *The relative roles* of both departments must be clearly defined and outlined, thus helping to prevent the two operations clashing on points of authority and responsibility. For example, in most instances stores should not become involved in direct contacts with the supplier. That is the responsibility of the purchasing department.

(d) *Professional management* on both sides will help a great deal. Stores and purchasing managers who are well trained and qualified will have a better understanding of the concept of supply management and the implications for their relationships with each other. They will also be aware of the latest management techniques and developments in the field of stores and purchasing.

(e) *Supply management,* by which we mean stores and purchasing combined in the operation of supply management, will tend to improve communications and the working relationship between these two operations.

(f) *Standardization of documentation and procedures* will also aid the relationship between these two functions. Documents which should be standardized include:

    (*i*) issue notes;
    (*ii*) rejection notes;
    (*iii*) orders;
    (*iv*) stock record cards.

22. Advantages of a sound stores/purchasing relationship

These advantages are many and varied. Some have a clearly quantifiable advantage to the organization in terms of reduced costs. Others are not so easy to calculate and yet are of major importance (e.g. high motivation). The advantages listed below contain both quantifiable and non-quantifiable elements.

(a) *Reduced stock levels*. Since information concerning the levels of stock will be quickly analysed and acted upon by both sides, less buffer stock will be needed, thus reducing overall stock levels.

(b) *Effective utilization* of resources in the most cost-conscious manner. Resources include materials handling equipment, storage space and management time and skills.

(c) *Industrial relations* will also be assisted by the participation and involvement needed to sustain the relationship.

(d) *Organizational objectives* and corporate strategy will be easier to implement when both purchasing and stores managements are aware of mutual problems.

Progress test 20

1. Outline the objectives of the purchasing department within the organization. **(1)**

2. What are the main functions of the purchasing operation? **(7–16)**

3. What are the duties and responsibilities of stores management to the purchasing operation? **(18)**

4. What are the duties and responsibilities of purchasing to the stores operation? **(19)**

5. How can the relationship between stores and purchasing management be improved? **(21)**

Case study no. 9:

Importance of partnership sourcing — the CBI view

By Sir Derek Hornby, Director-General, Partnership Sourcing Ltd

By promoting partnership sourcing throughout industry it is hoped that many more manufacturers and other businesses can be encouraged to work closely with their suppliers to drive down costs and at the same time improve quality to the benefit of customers as well as their own companies.

To illustrate my point, I will take two companies, one quite small, the other very large.

The small company (company A) is a supplier of plastic components and the owner described tendering to two major companies for a large order. The first reviewed his production capabilities and finished product and said that they were satisfied with quality and capability but he would have to meet their price if he wanted the job.

The second company went through exactly the same process. They were satisfied with company A's quality and capability, accepted his tender right away and would then propose that they work together to help meet their target cost. Company A was not at all keen on the thought of the purchaser's production engineers coming into his shop but, as it turned out, they were helpful with suggestions on raw material sourcing and other improvements and over the next few months he was able to lower his prices without affecting his margins. He now has a highly satisfactory long-term contract with the customer.

The second example is of a large company (company B) fighting to maintain market share and profitability against fierce competition. They decided on a total quality programme as the main focus of their efforts. As the programme was introduced into the manufacturing process, the management appreciated, of course, that 40 per cent of the product components were sourced from outside suppliers and a total quality programme for 60 per cent of that product did not make a lot of sense. So they decided to meet with their suppliers who immediately told them that they (company B) were lousy people to do business with. They were told that order sizes were based on sales forecasts which were invariably optimistic and had to be cut back. Design and specification were constantly altered and 'by the way you are late payers'. The suppliers asked 'Why not let us in at the development stage — and we can help with cost reductions?' Eventually, agreements were reached between Company B and its suppliers on optimizing manufacturing cycles, reducing the length of the supply chain, longer term contracts, payment on time and quality standards. In turn, this led to satisfactory long-term relationships and other cost benefits, for example reduction in progress chasing through delivery on time, goods being neither early nor late, and the abolition of goods inwards inspection through working towards zero defects.

These are two examples of what is becoming known as Partnership Sourcing. It can be practised under a variety of names — proactive purchasing, added value purchasing, supply chain management. Because most people involved in this area are now familiar with the term, let us stick with Partnership Sourcing. But I do stress that I use the term to embrace all aspects of modern professional purchasing policies, notably quality programmes, just-in-time methods, simultaneous engineering, logistics and sophisticated computer and electronic developments such as electronic data interchange (EDI).

Closer relationships

I would define Partnership Sourcing as the adoption of a deeper and more cooperative relationship between a company as a purchaser and those businesses supplying its goods and services. A long-term relationship of this type can result in significant improvements in performance. In addition to direct cost savings, effective partnership sourcing can benefit almost all other functions in a company including in particular quality and production, corporate strategy, research and development and marketing and design.

Rather than concentrating on price reductions — the traditional 'adversarial' approach — the essence of partnership sourcing is that purchasers and suppliers work together to drive down costs and improve quality, at the same time preserving margins for both parties. In other words, instead of products being 'price driven' they become 'cost driven' and instead of raising prices automatically, partnership sourcing provides an opportunity for driving costs down.

Indeed, some time ago a small group led by Sir Keith Joseph came to the conclusion that partnership sourcing could be a significant step forward for the competitiveness of British Industry and received very practical support from the DTI and the Bank of England and, of course, the CBI. As a result, we have established Partnership Sourcing Ltd, a non-profit-making company with a three-year funding from the DTI and an office promoted by the CBI at Centrepoint.

Our objective is to promote the concepts of partnership sourcing as widely as possible, using meetings, seminars, articles and supporting publicity.

We are not starry-eyed and naive about this. There are some super stories of great success in this area with both sides of the purchasing link delighted with the improvement that they have achieved. But, we are well aware that there are pitfalls and obstacles, not least the effort and cost involved in meeting the certification standards usually required and the concerns about being too dependent on one customer or, indeed, one supplier. There is naturally some cynicism from some small suppliers. They are suspicious that long-term relationships are only for as long as it suits the large company and that the openness is to do with getting access to their costs in order to shave margins.

But, the potential benefits to us all are immense. To the purchasers, quality components going direct to the manufacturing process without inspection costs, deliveries on time, and shortening the length of the supply chain. The supplier often gains through larger orders with the security and ability to plan ahead because of longer contracts, and with agreed payment terms. The quest for quality and overall cost management means that price becomes less important, thus reducing the risks to suppliers and purchasers from low price, low quality competitors.

Successful suppliers find that their achievements provide a very effective marketing tool for attracting other customers.

Perhaps the biggest change of all needs to be a change in attitude. This will not work under the old adversarial relationships and the most necessary ingredients, complete openness and trust, do not come overnight.

Part six

Strategic considerations for materials management

Strategic considerations for potential management

Materials management and forward planning

Purpose and scope of planning

1. Definition

Forward planning is the process of looking at trends and expectations and producing some kind of picture of what will happen in the future regarding the operations of the organization and its effects upon management. The materials system has often been neglected when it comes to involvement in forward planning discussions and meetings and many companies have found to their cost the error of leaving out a major part of the organization so directly involved with operations.

2. Corporate planning

The process of corporate planning within an organization is the responsibility of senior management and is strategic in nature rather than functional. R.C. Eyre defines corporate planning as 'A systematic and comprehensive process of long-range planning.' Part of the corporate planning process involves evaluating the organization's strengths and weaknesses. Materials management should be involved in this audit so as to ensure that data from the materials aspect of the business is considered when corporate plans are devised. Corporate planning has in recent times come under attack, in the sense that many organizations feel that the cost of preparing complex corporate plans is not worthwhile, bearing in mind the rapid rate of change. Many plans became unworkable within a few months of being published; organizations were being constrained by unrealistic corporate plans. However, corporate planning still has a contribution to make to overall strategic management. Here are the main reasons:

(a) Building into corporate plans a degree of flexibility, companies can take into account technological, environmental, social and political influences on the organization's long-term plans.

(b) Formal planning enables the organization to examine and evaluate a number of possible strategic options.

(c) Communication between managers and departments is improved; managers have to discuss the corporate plan.

(d) Aids integration between functions. The use of common objectives motivate and direct all the resources within the organization.

3. Benefits of corporate planning in materials management

Planning of any nature is very difficult, time-consuming and costly. However, the efforts and costs involved are worthwhile since it enables materials management to do the following:

(a) To plan its capital expenditure over a long period of time.

(b) To recruit and train suitable staff for the future demands of the organization in relation to the stores operations.

(c) To put forward its own views and predictions as to the future effect of change and the situation it envisages in the future.

(d) To prepare and plan for change in advance. This is far more efficient and professional than waiting for the predictions to become reality and then having to cope with the situation and take hasty and often incorrect action.

(e) To ensure maximum utilization of the stores resource and potential.

(f) To plan for redundancies (if that is the prediction) by means of natural wastage, thus avoiding unpleasant redundancies when the time comes for implementation.

4. Who should be involved in corporate planning?

As far as the whole organization is concerned, every member of the management team, marketing, production, finance, engineers and purchasing, should be involved at some stage of the planning process. If we look only at materials management, the list consists of:

(a) Stores managers;

(b) Stock control and stock record managers;

(c) Materials handling managers;
(d) General administration;
(e) Transport;
(f) Purchasing;
(g) Distribution;
(h) Production control.

All these people will be affected by alterations in the organization's activities and therefore need notice of any changes so that plans can be made to accommodate the new situation as efficiently as possible.

5. External factors that affect planning

There are external factors that can affect the organization's operations and activities; some are more fundamental than others. The materials operation reflects directly the activities of the whole organization (e.g. more output means more stock), therefore external factors will indirectly affect stores management. Such external factors include the following:

(a) *The level of demand* for goods and services produced by the organization. High levels of output could mean higher stocks and a need for more storage capacity in the future.

(b) *The general economic climate* will influence the decisions of the organization in relation to possible expansion or contraction of output.

(c) *Energy policies* of central government can affect certain industries dramatically (e.g. petrol, chemicals and their ability to stockpile).

(d) *Government legislation* may affect the organization's policy on output (e.g. tax cuts, VAT).

(e) *Local conditions* in terms of demand and employment prospects and the development of communications and industry.

(f) *Supply markets* — the state of the commodity markets in relation to supplies, prices, delivery period and market trends.

6. Internal factors that affect planning

The following are some of the factors that can affect the future plans of any organization:

(a) *The organization's general policy* in relation to investment, development and future direction.

(b) *Capital available* for investment and improvement projects.

(c) *Management awareness* of the need for long-term planning. In some organizations this need is not seen and planning tends to be of a very short-term nature.

(d) *Labour* — numbers of qualified staff required.

(e) *Capital equipment* — the capital equipment of the organization in relation to storage and materials handling, transport and computers.

The planning process

7. Organization of planning meetings

For any form of planning to be effective it must be organized and have specific objectives. The group of managers will discuss future plans and will exchange ideas and views on the most appropriate means of tackling the problems that might lie ahead. When organizing a forward planning meeting, the following points must be borne in mind:

(a) *An agenda* should be prepared for the meeting, listing specific aspects to be discussed.

(b) *Interested parties* must be given adequate time to prepare data and formulate questions.

(c) *A complete record* of what has been decided must be kept on file for future reference.

(d) *Relevant data* and statistics must be available, along with the organization's corporate plans for the coming period.

8. Forward planning cycle

In organizations where forward planning is undertaken, the forward planning cycle is often used by management. The cycle relates the collection and analysis of data and the decisions made based upon that data. The actual stages are as follows:

(a) *Collection of all relevant data*, statistics and forecasts available in relation to the area of the operation under investigation.

(b) *Injection of management experience*, expertise and judgment and an outline of personal predictions and trends for the future.

(c) *Analysis* of all data collected and management contribution using computers, network analysis (*see* **11(d)**) etc. to formulate forecasts and trends.

(d) *Predictions* of what the needs of the organization will be in relation to each area of the operation involved (e.g. increase stores capacity by 30 per cent).

(e) *Actions* to ensure that the organization is prepared for these predicted changes in advance. Projects must be established and work started towards achieving these aims.

(f) *Feedback* as to the accuracy and success of project predictions once the reality of the situation becomes apparent. This will aid management to evaluate the planning techniques employed and promote improvements.

9. Planning cycle and materials management

In the context of the materials operation the planning cycle stages would reflect the current situation and the forthcoming facts that could affect the stores. The following is a typical planning cycle relating to the question of future storage requirements:

(a) *Collection stage.* Materials management would collect data from production and sales regarding the predicted level of activities in the next two years. It would also collect information on the organization's general policy towards stockholding and the level of capital likely to be allocated for new buildings or other projects.

(b) *Injection stage.* The materials management team, including stores management, stock control, stock records and materials handling, would meet to discuss their ideas and predictions. Discussions would cover the advantages of outside warehouse space, the feasibility of building a new store, and the possibility of converting existing installations to increase storage capacity.

(c) *Analysis stage.* Statistics and calculations produced at the collection stage regarding levels of output, activity, purchasing policy, stock levels, etc., would be added to the management predictions and an overall prediction as to the storage capacity required would be formulated.

(d) *Prediction stage.* The ideas and statistics produced at the analysis stage must be turned into workable and implementable predictions. The analysis of simple sales forecasts and production plans may produce a prediction about an overall increase in stock, but this will not in itself indicate the operational increase in storage space required. This is where the materials management expertise and experience comes into play. A given increase in stock will not only require space for itself; it will also mean an increase in administration, materials handling capacity, storage facilities, equipment, etc. All these need extra space.

(e) *Action stage.* The need for extra storage space of whatever amount will require the hiring of outside warehouse space, new buildings or conversions. Each of these possibilities has to be examined and investigated and work commenced to increase the capacity of the organization, as soon as possible, to be able to cope with the future expected stock increases.

(f) *Feedback stage.* In this example the feedback of information would be only too easy. If the extra space provided is seen to be fully utilized, that will indicate accurate predictions. The quality of the prediction will be directly quantifiable with the under- or over-utilization of the storage capacity.

10. Information required for forward planning

To enable materials management to plan effectively and accurately for the future, a great deal of detailed information is required, relating to both the present and the future as seen by the rest of the organization (e.g. production, purchasing, marketing). The range of data would include the following:

(a) *The level of stock presently held* by the organization and its future expectations and output plans. This information enables materials management to plan in relation to capacity, materials handling and administrative functions.

(b) *Nature of stocks* at present and in the future. This is needed by materials management to plan for special storage facilities, materials handling equipment and staff training.

(c) *Future role of materials management* within the context of the whole organization. If materials management is seen as taking a more active role in, for example, quality control (*see* 8:6–10) the staff will need to be trained and new procedures introduced.

(d) *Administrative facilities needed* for the future in relation to stock control, stock records, inspection, etc. The proposed introduction of a computer-based system could mean a dramatic reduction in staff requirements and the development of a whole new generation of documents and control systems.

(e) *The outside warehouse market* needs to be closely watched as sudden changes in demand within the whole industry can result in all the spare warehouse space being taken. The hiring rates and charges may well change with alterations in supply and demand. If extra space is needed, therefore, careful planning could save the organization a great deal in terms of hiring contracts and agreement rates.

(f) *The materials handling system's capacity* and its ability to be flexible to deal with changes in the demands placed upon it. Materials management will need to have up-to-date data on the latest materials handling devices and developments, so as to be aware of the full range of products on the market and their ability to meet the needs of the organization in terms of price, performance and running costs.

(g) *The purchasing policy* of the organization is vital in relation to any planning carried out by the materials management department. The rate at which materials are to be purchased, order frequency and quantities involved will all affect materials planning.

(h) *Staff efficiency* and expertise required of materials management in the future by the rest of the organization. A more active role within the operations of the organization and a more technically advanced system of working will require the recruitment of new staff and the introduction of training for existing staff resources. Training takes time to develop and produce the results required.

(i) *Organization policy and corporate strategy* in relation to the future role of the materials management and the operations that affect materials management operations.

(j) *Capital and resources available* for the development of the materials management operation in the future, in relation to new buildings, equipment and staff. Plans that do not have the capital to back them up are a waste of valuable management staff and time.

11. Techniques to aid materials management

There are many techniques that can be employed to aid management in its forward planning, including the following:

(a) *Cybernetics*. This is the technique associated with the study of communications and control. A vital element of physical materials management is directly affected by these aspects.

(b) *Operational research*. This is the application of scientific analysis to provide a quantitative basis for predictions and forecasts. It can be used for the establishment of stock levels.

(c) *Ergonomics*. This is the study of human physical and mental ability in relation to the working environment. The ability to obtain more from the workforce in relation to materials handling could have an important impact on the future plans of management.

(d) *Network analysis*. This is a technique which involves the timing and planning of major projects (e.g. a transfer into a new storehouse). It explains and indicates visually the interrelationship between numerous activities that must be performed at given stages of the project, if it is to be properly planned and carried out.

12. Characteristics of management information

The information produced by forward planning is management information, that is, information which materials management will use to make both long and short-term decisions. To ensure that these decisions are correct, management information has to have the following qualities:

(a) *Timing*. It is vital that any management information produced is received by the management in time to effect the relevant decisions.

(b) *Accuracy*. It is vital that the information produced is accurate and correct. False information will lead to false decisions.

(c) *Intelligibility*. Information should be produced in a suitable form for all materials management to be able to comprehend and assimilate quickly. This can be achieved with the use of graphs and charts.

(d) *Relevance*. Management information must be relevant and useful.

Progress test 21

1. What are the benefits of forward planning in materials management? **(3)**

2. List the internal and external factors that will affect planning. **(5–6)**

3. What are the main stages of the forward planning cycle? **(8)**

4. What information is required by materials management for planning? **(10)**

5. Describe some of the techniques that can aid materials management. **(11)**

Case study no. 10:

SWOT analysis

1. *Task 1*: Consider your own organization's inventory management system and attempt to analyse it against the SWOT classification.

2. *Task 2*: Prepare a set of objectives for the system.

3. *Task 3*: The next step is to then produce a strategy to achieve the objectives stated.

Training and development of materials management staff

The importance of training and staff development

1. Training as an investment

Training of staff is vital if full use is to be made of their abilities and talents. Labour is a very expensive commodity and therefore it makes good economic sense to make full utilization of this resource.

Training must be seen as an investment in terms of time, money and energy on the part of the organization and its management. The rewards for this investment could develop into major operational cost savings if only more organizations would examine their own operations and the potential that exists for improvement via training.

Unfortunately, however, in many organizations, training is not seen in its investment light, rather just as another cost which reduces profits. This negative attitude is very common in relation to materials and is a symptom of the neglect by many managers of materials as an important element of the total operation.

2. The benefits of training

Although managers have long accepted the benefits of training for production workers, many still question whether expensive training for the materials operation is worthwhile. However, the returns to be expected by the organization from investing in well-trained staff can be considerable and cover a wide spectrum of activities, as follows:

(a) *Increased efficiency* in relation to all the operations of materials management — physical, clerical and managerial. The materials operation costs a great deal and increased efficiency will result in a reduction in real costs.

(b) *Improved health and safety.* Health and safety are important in any section of the organization, but particularly so in stores because of the working conditions under which the staff operate and the numerous potential hazards. Dangers arise from badly stacked stock, hazardous materials, heavy duty equipment, mechanical handling equipment, etc. Accidents can cost a great deal, but training should help to reduce the risk of accidents and therefore save the organization money.

(c) *Materials handling.* This is one of the most important roles of materials management involving staff, equipment, energy and space, all of which are very expensive commodities. The proper training of staff connected with this function will reduce double handling and increase the output of the equipment and, therefore, capital employed, as well as improving safety.

(d) *Prevention of deterioration of stock* as a result of incorrect ordering and storage. Many organizations lose millions of pounds each year in lost stock and even more in terms of lost production and sales. It is important to note the development of liability laws in relation to goods produced by the organization, which may lead to heavy law suits for damages if materials used in a product are faulty. Great savings can be made if staff are trained to prevent stock deterioration and to spot potential problems. Not only the materials department but the organization as a whole will benefit.

(e) *Training for the future.* Development of skilled and professional staff will enable a great deal of on the job training to be carried out and staff development and promotion from within can be encouraged, to improve motivation and incentives among the staff. Sound basic training will help to provide the managers of the future.

(f) *Motivation* is vital in any section. Training helps to foster motivation and organizational loyalty on the part of the employee, who will feel valued and have a sense of obligation to stay and develop within the organization that trained him, thus reducing the cost of staff turnover and maintaining the continuity which is so vital if personal relations are to be formed (*see* 1:**20**).

3. Personnel problems in materials management
It has been said that the stores is the section of the operation

that is regarded of least importance and staff who cannot be accommodated elsewhere for various reasons often find themselves 'dumped' there. This raises a wide range of problems for materials management, including the following specifically in stores management:

(a) Frustrated and unhappy staff tend to be inefficient and reduce the overall efficiency of the stores.

(b) Lack of well-trained and motivated staff tends to mean that promotion for the higher level posts within the stores is given to staff from outside, thus increasing the frustration.

(c) Lack of quality staff tends to mean that the introduction of new methods, techniques, equipment and attitudes is very slow and difficult.

4.   Staff development
It has become an accepted fact that staff development is vital if a section is to remain dynamic and efficient in its working. Materials management is no exception to this rule. Materials management should make every effort to impress upon the rest of the organization the importance of their operation and the need to develop well-trained and motivated staff. Staff development can be encouraged in the following ways:

(a) *Rewards for the attainment of skills,* e.g. passing examinations, attending college courses or improving in practical efficiency. This would encourage staff to take part-time courses and improve their knowledge and skills. Such rewards could include increases in pay, promotions and improved prospects. Here we see the importance of real motivation.

(b) *Internal promotion policy* (where possible) is also a very sound means of staff development. Many materials management staff feel that, regardless of their efforts, the 'top' jobs in stores and also in related operations, e.g. purchasing, tend to be allocated to others from outside. This is bad for morale and efficiency. Staff must be given goals to strive for.

5.   Role of materials management in training and staff development
Materials management has a vital role to play in these

activities, in a number of ways, each of which is very important and should not be overlooked.

(a) *Organization of training schemes within its functional areas* in ways which best suit the needs of the staff and the materials management operation.
(b) *Ensuring that the rest of the organization is aware* of the need for training within materials management.
(c) *Ensuring that time and resources are available* wherever possible to assist the training of staff, e.g. practice of materials handling techniques on 'dummy' stocks.

Planning and organization of training

6. Scope of training within materials management
Because of the wide range of activities and tasks performed by the materials management department, training needs to cover a broad spectrum. The activities that demand training could include the following:

(a) *physical activities* (e.g. materials handling);
(b) *clerical activities* (e.g. stock records);
(c) *management and supervisory tasks*;
(d) *judgmental tasks* (e.g. quality control inspection).

7. Approaches to training
There are several methods that can be employed to train staff. The method used will depend a great deal upon the attitude of management and the resources available for training. The two main approaches to training are 'trial and error' and a planned programme.

8. Trial and error
This is usually operated on the job. The trainee observes the actions of a skilled operator and attempts to follow his steps to perform the task. As the name suggests a great deal of error can take place during this period, although this method is still very popular. Trial and error learning has several basic disadvantages as a method of training.

(a) It is slow in terms of the time it takes to train staff to perform tasks.

(b) Frustration can develop on the part of both the trainer and the trainee. The trainer will find himself having to answer questions and repeat tasks and therefore may lose financially in terms of bonus or productivity payments. The trainee may feel that he is not being properly trained or that he could contribute more, but is being held back.

(c) Bad practices can be passed from the operator to the trainee and will result in a badly trained operative.

(d) Skilled and useful employees do not necessarily make good instructors or trainers.

9.   Planned programme

This approach is based on the logic of a properly planned and coordinated programme, leading step by step to a fully trained operative. Setting up training programmes involves a great deal of thought and effort if the programme is to be effective and provide the stores with the kind of staff required. However, the efforts are usually justified by the returns, namely a properly trained working team.

10. Who would be involved in planning the programme?

Before any programme can be introduced, discussions between the following must take place to ensure that all views and needs are reflected in the programme:

(a) *Trade unions* are already interested in training and often feel that one of their major functions is to promote, and to be constructively involved in, all training within the organization.

(b) *Materials management* must obviously be involved in planning the objectives of the programme, what is to be taught and how. The support of senior management is vital if the programme is to be workable and successful.

(c) *The training section* will need to be involved in preliminary discussions, as they will have the experience and skills needed to estimate the time needed to train staff for certain types of tasks and the resources required.

11. The training plan

The following points will need to be considered when formulating the training plan:

(a) *The objectives of the plan.* It is vital that both the trainers and the trainees understand what is being taught and its application to their new job or position within the materials organization. Without clear objectives, management of training becomes very difficult and ineffective.

(b) *Allocation of resources.* This needs to be known by all those concerned with training so that they are aware of the equipment, money and time they have. If the training is to be carried out 'in house', the materials manager must ensure that adequate materials and resources are available, including visual aids, stationery, photocopying equipment and suitable accommodation.

(c) *Organization.* The training needs to be organized and coordinated. Arrangements have to be made concerning the source of the training (*see* **12**), the dates, and the areas to be covered.

(d) *Methods of instruction* (*see* **13**). Decisions will need to be made as to which methods are most appropriate to the various areas to be covered by the training.

(e) *Progress reports.* These must be established so that a full evaluation of the trainee and the training can be made and used later for the purposes of staff development.

12. Sources of training for materials management

The sources of training for materials management come under the following three headings:

(a) *In-service training.* This is where the organization sets aside resources to train all staff including those destined to work in materials management.

(b) *Colleges and training centres.* Many colleges operate part-time training and education in materials management and related operations.

(c) *Specialist trainers and professional institutes* also provide tailor-made training in materials management.

These courses provide excellent training for staff at every

level. Many organizations use such courses as a major element of their own in-house training.

13. The method of instruction

This will depend a great deal upon the task to be learned by the trainee. For example, training in deterioration of stock and quality control tends to need a change in the trainee's basic awareness of the problems involved. In this situation the discussion method has proved to be more effective than traditional straight instruction. The other main methods of instruction are as follows:

(a) lectures;
(b) handouts;
(c) visual/audio techniques of programmed learning;
(d) examples;
(e) demonstrations;
(f) practice;
(g) distance learning systems.

14. Analytical method

This method of training makes full use of the psychology of training and education developed over the last twenty years. The analytical method involves the following:

(a) *Analysis of the task* to be performed and a breaking down of the task into a series of small steps or stages, each of which must be completed successfully before the next step can be attempted.
(b) *Demonstration* of each step by a skilled operator, with continuous reference to the previous steps covered and the role of future steps in the total task.
(c) *Practice* on the part of the trainee. This allows the trainee to feel totally involved and it will also give him an opportunity to isolate his own strengths and weaknesses.
(d) *Verbal guidance* by the instructors throughout the practice stage to help reinforce positive skill development.
(e) *Knowledge* of the results of the efforts of the trainee, which is vital to maintain his interest and motivation, or as a means of evaluating the training programme as a whole.

15. Data overload

This is a term used to describe the problem of too much training in a small space of time. We know that the human brain has a limited capacity to take in and hold new data, so all training must be at a pace at which the trainee can accept and digest the information being supplied. Beyond this point the data is not retained by the trainee and is therefore wasted and will have to be repeated.

Materials management operations manual

16. Introduction

A development of training within the materials management department is the operations manual. This is designed to provide the trainee or operative with a precise and complete step-by-step guide to the working of the materials function and its activities, from stock control to materials handling. These manuals are usually kept within the department and are originally written by the materials manager in conjunction with the heads of the various sections within the materials operation.

17. Problems of compiling manuals

There are several basic problems facing the compilers of manuals.

(a) Decisions have to be made as to what to include in the manual, i.e. the amount of detail that may or may not be needed. Manuals have to be complete, but they also have to be capable of being read quickly so that they can be used while the operative is actually working on the job.

(b) The manual must also be understandable to the many different types of trainees and staff that will be using it at some stage or another, from the manager to the raw recruit. The text must therefore be clear and logical.

(c) The time spent on compiling and updating the operating manual can lead to problems if a clash between established duties comes about. Often, because of this reason, manuals tend to become out of date quickly as procedures change but the time cannot be found to update the manuals.

18. Advantages of operations manuals

Despite these problems manuals have some definite advantages and play a key role in the whole stores training area. These advantages are as follows:

(a) It is a reference book of all procedures for both the trainee and the established staff. If problems arise then the manual can always be consulted for guidance. This has the advantage of enabling a new member of staff to read the manual and therefore gain some idea of the working of the department before he becomes actively involved.

(b) Standardization of all procedures will enable stationery, computer inputs and staff training schemes to be made standard and therefore less expensive and complex.

(c) Staff mobility from one part of the materials operation to another will be improved, because once trained in one part of the system, the trainee will be able to work in others, regardless of their location.

(d) Comparison of efficiency is made much easier if all procedures and methods of working (as established by a manual) follow the same guidelines. This will allow senior management to compare departments and isolate the efficient and the inefficient accordingly.

(e) A complete and comprehensive manual can form the basis of the whole materials training scheme and may also be incorporated into the total training scheme of the organization.

19. Disadvantages of operations manuals

There are several disadvantages of manuals, although in reality these are more faults of the system itself, than of the manuals.

(a) They restrict individual actions, as the circumstances dictate. Often the man on the spot at the time of a crisis or problem has a very clear view of what needs to be done to correct the situation. If his actions are too closely dictated by the manual, then he may be forced to take action that he knows will not succeed. In all things a degree of flexibility and judgment is vital.

(b) Variety in the types and sizes of warehouses, stockyards, etc., often within the same organization, will make complete standardization of procedures and systems very difficult, if not impossible.

(c) Manuals are very expensive to compile and update, requiring a great deal of management time and effort.

Progress test 22

1. What are the benefits of training stores personnel?   **(2)**

2. Why is there a need for staff development?   **(4)**

3. Outline the scope of training within the stores.   **(6)**

4. What are the two main approaches to training?   **(7)**

5. What factors need to be considered when formulating the training plan?   **(11)**

6. Describe the analytical method of training.   **(14)**

7. What is meant by the term 'data overload'?   **(15)**

8. Describe the role of stores manuals in training programmes. **(18)**

Materials management and information technology

Information technology

1. Introduction

Information is the life blood of all organizations. Materials management needs information if it is to successfully manage. Every decision managers make involves risk, and decisions are important to the survival and growth of the business. Having good information can reduce the risk; it does not eliminate it altogether but it means your decisions have a better chance of success. The modern materials manager has access to a vast amount of information compiled from a variety of business data.

This revolution in the availability of data is a direct result of what is described as information technology (IT).

2. Definitions of IT

The term information technology is defined by Johannsen and Page in their 1990 *International Dictionary of Management* as 'the umbrella term for acquiring, processing, storing and disseminating information whether in textual, numeric or graphical form, and using computers and telecommunications'. The basic disciplines of information technology are computing, communications, control and instrumentation, and micro-electronics.

3. Information and data

Data are facts acquired by research or observations and can be defined as groups of non-random symbols (words, values, figures) which represent things that have happened. Information is data that has been received and understood by the recipient of the message. Accurate data is a key element of effective materials management.

4. Materials management and data processing

Data processing is concerned with the transformation of data into up-to-date, accurate and understandable information — for our purposes, information that will benefit management. Data processing employs electronic *computers* to assist the processing of data. A computer system is a collection of electronic devices which can receive, process, store and produce information from data.

5. Components of a data processing system (*see* **Fig. 23.1**)

All data processing systems are made up of the basic elements listed below. Obviously, the more complex the work involved, the more sophisticated the hardware (*see* **3**) required.

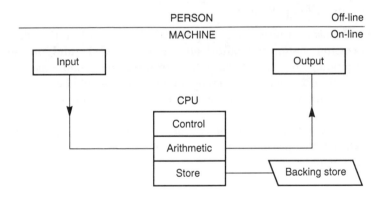

Figure 23.1 *Elements of a data processing system*

(a) *Input*. This is the device that converts human language into a form that can be processed within the computer itself.

(b) *The central processing unit (CPU)*. This is the real heart of a computer system, which performs the following three major functions:

    (*i*) The arithmetic unit performs all the calculations required upon the data.

(*ii*) The control unit directs and controls the whole system. It brings into the system the circuits required to perform all the actions.

(*iii*) The store holds the data in a magnetic form so that the computer can call in facts and figures that it requires at any time.

(c) *Output.* This is a device that converts the machine-language of the computer back into a form that users can understand.

(d) *Backing store.* This is the part of the system that is used to store data away from the actual data processing system. The CPU has a limited storage capacity so larger amounts of data are stored in various forms (*see* 8) and held in the backing store to be loaded into the CPU when needed.

6. Hardware and software

These are two terms that are constantly used in relation to computers and data processing systems. In fact to a large extent they are self-explanatory.

(a) *Hardware* refers to any physical device within the data processing system including all the input, CPU and output equipment. The type of computer hardware one would expect to find within the materials management system would be either a microcomputer configuration or a traditional terminal (*see* Fig. 23.5)

(b) *Software* describes all the computer programs (*see* 8) that are produced by the manufacturer for a specific data processing function and system.

7. Computer programs

These are detailed lists of 'instructions' coded in the language of the computer. When the computer works its way through a given program, data is processed accordingly. Programs can be purchased as software (*see* 3) or they can be produced by the organization itself, so long as it has systems analysts and programmers on its staff.

8. Types of software

Within any data processing system, various types of software are required to enable the system to function. Each type of software has a part to play in the total data processing system. The types of software are as follows:

(a) *Service programs.* These are written by the computer manufacturer and are supplied with the system. The role of these programs is to perform some of the common tasks of the system, for example:

    (*i*) storing records;

    (*ii*) file copying;

    (*iii*) dumping;

    (*iv*) file maintenance.

(b) *Sub-routines.* Within a data processing system a similar function may be repeated on numerous occasions. To save programming time, this part of the program is written and stored under the heading of a sub-routine. It can therefore be brought in when the programmer requires that series of actions in a program.

(c) *Translation programs.* It must be remembered that all computer manufacturers design their systems based upon a unique computer language. In other words, before other software can be used on the system, a means by which programs can be translated into that language has to be employed. There are two main types of software under this heading:

    (*i*) *Assemblers.* These are designed to translate low level programs.

    (*ii*) *Compilers.* These are designed to translate high level programs.

(d) *Operating systems.* It had been found that many systems were operating less than efficiently mainly due to the fact that the CPU was not being used to its maximum because setting-up jobs and corrective actions were being performed manually. To overcome this waste of data processing resources, a series of programs was developed, designed to take over many of the manual functions.

(e) *Applications packages.* These are programs written in high level language (COBOL, BASIC, etc.) and are designed to operate within common business applications, i.e. stock control, stores accounting, distribution planning. This type of software can be purchased from a software house, or it can be written by the organization's data processing department.

(f) *Programming languages.* There are basically three levels of computer language:

(*i*) *Machine code.* In this type, every instruction to the computer has to be expressed in a numeric form. This makes programming very difficult indeed.

(*ii*) *Low level.* Here language symbols can be used to instruct the computer. However, to facilitate CPU understanding of the instructions a translating program is required.

(*iii*) *High level.* This type of language has a large vocabulary of words and programs can be written to solve specific problems. The advent of high level languages like COBOL and BASIC was a major step forward in data processing. An example of the simplicity of programming with a high level language (BASIC) is illustrated thus: If we require the computer to add a series of numbers together it could be expressed as 'PRINT X & Y X Z'. From that simple instruction the computer would be able to add together any three random numbers entered into the system.

Collection, storage, processing and transmission of data

9. Data collection

The collection of data required by materials management in connection with the data processing system will depend upon the following important considerations:

(a) *The main clerical methods* employed by the organization.

(b) *Quality and design of source documents.*

(c) *The system design* within the organization.

(d) *The capital available* for the data processing system.

(e) *Operational needs* of materials management and the rest of the organization. The main methods are as follows:

10. Methods of data collection

It must be remembered that the majority of data collected by any organization is not in a machine sensible form. Therefore a process of translating the data into a form that the computer can understand is required. Whichever system is employed will have to meet the needs of the organization. The main methods are as follows:

(a) *Keyboard to magnetic tape system.* Data is fed into the computer system via a keyboard and the magnetic tape encoder.

(b) *Keyboard to magnetic disc system.* The data is encoded on to the disc via a keyboard.

(c) *Direct-input captive system.* This is a system whereby data collected in 'raw' form is fed directly into the computer system via a terminal which is linked via a data transmission system (*see* 17) to the mainframe computer.

(e) *Data tag system.* This is becoming very common in wholesale and retail storage. Attached to each product is a small tag which states the sale price but is also punched with a series of holes. These holes identify the item and the tags are fed into the computer system which is able to update both the stock record and stock control systems.

(f) *Optical character recognition (OCR) systems.* The use of special printing enables the computer to read the data on the source document and the data can also be understood by the users of the system. The source documents used with this system will produce these special typefaced forms, the user will complete the required sections, i.e. stock used, and will then return the document to the CPU where it can be fed directly into the system.

(g) *Magnetic ink character recognition (MICR) systems.* These employ a special ink that has magnetic characteristics. The system enables source documents to read directly into the CPU at very high speed by means of a MICR reader, thus updating the records instantly. This system was developed for UK banks and is mainly used by them for the clearing house cheque system.

(h) *Embossed plastic cards.* This system is based on the idea of a precoded plastic card. The data contained on the card could relate to authorization to request materials from the store. Each withdrawal of stock from the stores requires the requisitioner to input his 'card'. Materials used by certain departments can then be directly costed to that particular operation.

(i) *Bar-coding.* This system employs a light-pen and a series of printed 'bars' displayed on the materials involved. The storekeeper will run the light-pen across the barcode displayed on the item concerned, the bar code representing that item (usually its stores vocabulary number). Once the pen has 'read' the bar code the data can be fed into the computer and records can be updated.

11. Methods of data storage

There are various methods by which data can be stored. The main point to bear in mind is that computers cannot understand human language in written or verbal form, so all data storage has to be in a form that can be read by the computer. The main methods of data storage are as follows:

(a) *Magnetic tapes*. These are plastic tapes with an oxide coating. The principle is similar to that employed in standard audio tape, but more sophisticated. The data is stored in magnetic form on the tape as a series of dots that cannot be seen by humans, but can be read by the computer.

(b) *Magnetic discs*. These operate on the same principle as magnetic tape, but the data is stored on a disc. This has the advantage of allowing information to be taken from the disc without having to run through a whole magnetic tape to the spot required. This ability is called 'random access'.

(c) *Punched paper tape*. Paper tape operates on the principle employed with punch cards, except that the tape is a continuous piece of stationery similar to the magnetic tape.

(d) *Floppy discs*. These are similar to magnetic discs and have been especially developed for use with the earlier generation of microcomputers (*see* 37).

More modern systems use a new disc that is only 3 or 3.5 inches in diameter. These smaller discs come in solid plastic packages and are capable of holding a megabyte or so of information.

12. Computer files

Computer-based files are made up of a collection of records. The records hold data which is required to produce management information. These files are stored on magnetic media, i.e. tape or disc (*see* 11) and are accessed by the use of specially developed programs. The basis of any data processing system is its files. There are three main types of file that make up a typical data processing system.

(a) *Master files*. These are files that are regularly updated and the data stored is required for continuous processing. A stock control file would be a good example of a master file. The stock control file would be updated at the end of each working period and would be used to provide information for reordering stock.

(b) *Transaction file*. This is used to record all the daily transactions carried out by the system. All stock movements would be recorded during a specific period of time and at the end of that time the transaction file data would be used to update the master file. The transaction file is then wiped clean and a new batch of transactions is then recorded.

(c) *Reference file*. This contains data that may be needed by various parts of the system and which are of a fairly permanent nature, i.e. stores vocabulary numbers, price lists, names and addresses of employees, etc.

13. Computer records

A computer file is made up of a number of individual records. These records contain the same kind of data that traditional clerical records would contain. A typical stock record would need to contain the following:

(a) the product's stores vocabulary number;
(b) rate of usage;
(c) stores location number;
(d) product description;
(e) supplier details;
(f) storage instructions;
(g) handling instructions.

The records for each product are combined to form a stock record file. In computer terms each file is made up from the following elements:

(a) *Records* made up of related fields.
(b) *Fields* made up of related characters.
(c) *Characters* are the individual letters and numbers used to make up the fields.
(d) *Key field*. These are unique numbers or names by which the computer can locate the record required by the operator (*see* Fig. 23.2).

Vocabulary number	Stock issues	Stock receipts	Stores location	Handling instructions
001	12346 kilos	20000 kilos	Bay no. 5	Dangerous material Do not expose to air

Note that: 001 = Key field
Stock issues = Field
12346 = Characters

Figure 23.2 *Stock record*

14. Computer files in materials management

The materials management department will need to create a number of computer-based files. These will be entered into the computer system so that the files can be maintained. There are a number of computer files that could be found in a typical materials management department:

(a) *Stock files* contain data recording stock movements, locations, suppliers and storage information.

(b) *Depot stock files* provide data on stocks held within the organization's depot network.

(c) *Stores vocabulary files* contain a complete vocabulary, each record relating to a particular line of stock.

(d) *Transport files* contain data relating to the movement of stocks and the availability of transport for stores use.

(e) *Stock control files* contain data regarding stock levels and stock reordering.

15. Updating stock files

The materials management department will be processing data regarding movements of materials within the organization. The updating of stock files will require the following data processing activities, as illustrated by a systems flow chart (*see* Fig. 23.3)

(a) *Input of stock issues* and stock receipts into the computer system, via a method of data collection, e.g. punch cards.

(b) *Validation of data* via a validation program to ensure that all inputs are correct and should therefore be processed. Data which

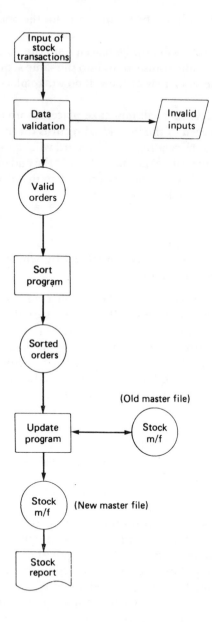

Figure 23.3 *A systems flow chart*

is not valid will be rejected by the program for the operator to deal with.

(c) *Valid transactions* will now be placed onto the magnetic tape.

(d) *Sorting* of the valid transactions into the same sequence as they are stored on the stock master file will now take place using a sort program.

(e) *Update of master files* will now take place. An update program will go through each of the individual records on the master file, and any transactions relating to that record will be used to update and amend that record on the master file. At the end of this process the master file will be completely up-to-date in relation to stock transactions that have been processed.

16. Methods of data processing

The following are the two methods by which data can be processed through a system:

(a) *Batch processing.* This is when data is collected together in large quantities before it is processed. The data is sorted into groups of similar data and fed into the computer system *en masse.*

(b) *Real-time processing system.* This is where the data is fed directly into the computer system and the response is immediate. Decisions that require up-to-date information can be made using a real-time system to keep them constantly up to date.

17. Data transmission systems

In situations where the storehouse is at a different location from the main out office, data can be transmitted along British Telecom's datel telephone lines to the mainframe computer at head office. This allows data to be passed to and from the stores building and materials control immediately, thereby improving communications and materials management. The system comprises an intelligent terminal the output of which is converted into electronic impulses that can be transmitted along the British Telecom datel line by a device called a *modem*. At head office the message is received by another modem and converted back into its original form and then passed into the mainframe computer for processing and reply along the same link.

18. Time-sharing systems

Organizations that cannot afford their own computer can rent computer processing time from a time-sharing company which owns a large and powerful mainframe system. The organization can employ British Telecom's datel system to transmit and receive the data it requires.

Applications of computers in materials management

19. Introduction

The computer has always played a part in materials management, traditionally in terms of stock records systems. However, its application is far more diverse than just stock records. Computers are being used not only as recorders and storers of data, but also as aids to operational decision-making. The following are some of the current and future applications of data processing systems within the stores.

20. Materials handling systems

These are some of the most important aspects of materials management and by application of computerized control systems they are becoming more sophisticated.

Because of the workflow found in a modern materials handling environment, the computer can be employed to form a network of the system and the movement involved, thus ensuring that the materials handling system is constantly employed to capacity, so reducing costs. Many organizations that have large and complex warehouse systems have almost totally automated the selection, marshalling and loading of goods (e.g. Halfords warehouse complex in the Midlands). Once the program is introduced into the computer the system follows the instructions laid in the program.

21. Decision-making process

The process of making any decision is based upon a combination of factors: skill, judgment and information. The ability to refer to up-to-date information via the data processing system will greatly improve the quality of the management information employed, and therefore the quality of the decisions made will be far greater in terms of accuracy, utility and cost. The database system (*see* Fig. 23.4) enables the materials manager to 'tap into' all the information held by all the departments within the organization and therefore improves interdepartmental communications and thus decisions.

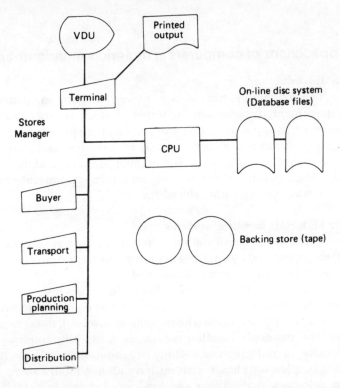

Figure 23.4 *Database system (materials)*

22. Stock rotation systems

The stores must ensure that stock is used in the correct order or rotation, so that materials are used before they can deteriorate and become unusable. In a large and complex stores system with a great variety of materials held in stock, each with its own particular rotation code or 'sell-by' date, the computer's ability to store a vast amount of data will be of great assistance to stores management. Each item is identified by its code number and the computer will have the current rotation codes and dates in its memory. A simple comparison between the codes will enable the computer to print out a list of all materials and state at what stage of the rotation process they have reached. A task that could take a team of stock controllers a week will be done in a few minutes by the computer system. This ability to keep track of all 'sell-by' dates will reduce stock losses and greatly increase stock control.

23. Issue of stock
As has been previously stated, the ability to issue the correct stock to the user as and when required is often the yardstick used to judge the overall materials department's performance. The use of a computer can greatly improve the issue function. In many situations the issue counter may have its own terminal linked directly to the organization's mainframe computer. As materials are required the stores staff can use the terminal to do the following:

(a) Instantly verify the authorization. The computer will have a constantly updated list of all staff able to request stock.
(b) Instantly check stock records to establish that sufficient stocks are held to cover the user's requirements.
(c) Instantly establish the exact location of the materials required.
(d) In a fully automated system, automatically have the item required selected and delivered.

24. Linear programming
This is a mathematical method of tackling problems related to limited resources and combinations of output, the idea being to enable managers to calculate how to optimize the use of the resources at their disposal. These resources can include labour, plant and materials engaged in transportation, production and storage. Computer programs have been developed to tackle many of these allocation problems. They are supplied in software packaging (*see* 8) by computer manufacturers and are very popular indeed.

25. Forward planning
Materials management is involved in the overall long-term

plans of the organization and therefore it needs to be able to express its requirements and its role in the future plans of the organization. A computer system will enable complex forecasts to be prepared, giving full details of long-term trends in stock levels, space requirements, labour needs, equipment needs and stock rotation. The ability of computers to construct such forecasts is very useful indeed to materials management.

Electronic data interchange (EDI)

26. EDI

This is the integration of computerized information systems and the automatic transfer of documents between the materials management department and their suppliers. It can also be used to transfer and receive information from the organization's customers.

EDI has also been described as 'paperless trading'.

The main benefits from EDI are savings in the cost of paper handling, less errors in the transmission of information, shorter lead times and the benefits of clear links with the supplier. Many organizations see EDI as essential to successful just-in-time implementation.

27. Stock-recording systems

It has been stated that computers began their relationship with materials management via their ability to store and update data regarding the level of stock, and this is still the most common application of data processing within the stores. Stock record systems are usually real-time processing systems so that materials management can obtain data regarding the stocks at any time or place (where a terminal has been installed). A typical computerized stock record system is shown in Fig. 23.5.

28. Marshalling systems

Part of materials management is to ensure that materials required for distribution are made ready as and when required by the transportation section for loading onto transport and delivery to customers, warehouses and depots. A computer system enables the distribution to feed into the data processing system its needs in terms of stock types, code numbers, quantities and destinations.

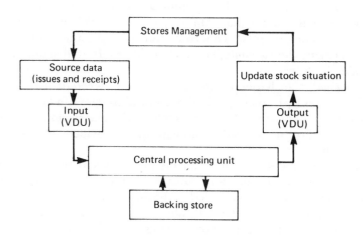

Figure 23.5 *Computerized record system*

All this data can be used by materials management, via its own link with the database, so enabling loads to be made up quickly and efficiently.

29. Stores accounting

In organizations calculations relating to the value of stock held and the costing of operations via the cost of materials used, the computer can be of great service. There are many standard software packages designed to deal with this task. The materials manager need only feed in the variables (i.e. quantities, costs, applications, dates, etc.) to calculate all materials accounting problems.

30. Computers and stock control

It was stated previously that stock control is one of the most important aspects of materials management and the area that required the greatest organization and management to succeed in its task. The added dimension of computer power to stock control is therefore very important. Stock control is where the maximum effect of computers could be felt in the whole materials operation. The role of computers in materials control is as follows:

(a) *Quantity.* The computer can assist materials management in its efforts to calculate the optimum amount of stock to hold and despatch, in order to maintain adequate stock levels and satisfy the user's requirements. The computer can do this simply by comparing the variables, i.e. stocks held, levels of demand, dates of delivery, etc.

(b) *Quality*. Each user department has its own levels of quality that it requires by its own standards system. This data can be fed into the computer so that all materials selected by that section will have the quality demanded, automatically, provided stocks are available.

(c) *Time*. Stocks must be available as and when required. The computer, with its 'memory' function, is able to be programmed to react to instructions related to the allocation of stocks at given times and dates. It will also be able to update these time periods so as to enable a constantly moving timetable of issues to be maintained, a task that could take a great many man-hours to achieve without the application of computers.

(d) *Location*. It is vital that stocks are in the correct location so that they can be consumed by the user departments for whatever task they have been allocated. The computer, with its links to distribution and transportation, will be able to ensure that materials management is kept up-to-date with transportation movements, and the needs of depots and warehouses can be fed directly into the data processing system via the data transmission system to the main computer. Thus the materials manager will have knowledge of what is required, when and where it is required, and the availability of transport to deliver the materials.

(e) *Costs*. The computer is able to calculate the total cost of stock control for each given option. Materials management is therefore able to select the best method, based on cost. It also assists the stock controller to ensure that stock control is being performed as efficiently and as cheaply as possible.

31. Word processing

The use of computers has led to the increased use of word processing systems with the materials operation. A word processor is a highly sophisticated 'typewriter' with a number of extremely useful functions which assists in the required text. If at any time words need to be deleted, altered or in some way changed, the word processor is able to make these changes automatically. Errors and alterations do not require the whole text to be retyped as with traditional typewriter systems.

(a) *Data storage.* The word processor employs a floppy disc system to store permanent text. If the materials manager has, for example, the operator's manual stored in this way, the operator only has to locate the correct disc and then instruct the word processor to 'print'. A complete copy of the manual will be reproduced in a few seconds by the high speed printer, which is part of the word processing system.

(b) *High quality reproduction.* Because the copies produced by a word processor come via a high speed printer, all copies are first or 'top' copies. Therefore regardless of how many other managers in the organization require a copy of the current stocks, each will receive a high quality first copy.

(c) *Structure of text.* Text can be automatically laid out, the word processor following instructions as to spacing, margins and paragraphs. This will enable the operator to type text continually into the system with no regard to style.

32. Application of word processing in materials management

The materials manager, as a member of the organization's management team, has responsibilities in relation to the production of management information for the organization. Coupled with this are the day-to-day operations of the materials flow that require production of printed material. There are a number of useful applications of word processing within stores management.

(a) *Production and storage of management reports and projects.* The ability of the word processor to reduce production time of lengthy documents like reports and its ability to store such information on compact floppy discs aids the materials manager's role as a member of the management team.

(b) *Materials documents.* Issue notes, stock receipts, training manuals, authorization of issue lists and the stores vocabulary can all be produced from text stored on a floppy disc via a high speed printer.

(c) *Improves the quality and range of secretarial services* available to the materials department. Traditionally materials management is not an area that is allocated high quality secretarial services.

33. Databases

The 'term' relates to a collection of related files. The database is a complex piece of computer software designed to integrate the data held on a number of different computer files.

34. Data processing and standardization

The process of standardization involves reducing the variety of stock held. This task is made simple by the application of a logical coding system and the computer's ability to store and compare data. Similar codes can thus be quickly located and the standardization of stock can be carried out as a continuous process, with all the savings that standardization can produce for the organization.

Computer costs

35. Introduction

Data processing has great advantages for the materials operation, as can be seen from the long list of applications (*see* **19**). However, it does also involve costs, as outlined in **36–39** below. Although these costs do not relate only to the materials operation, since the computer would be used by the whole organization, nevertheless they are costs that have to be recognised.

36. Hardware and software

The devices needed for a complete data processing system, e.g. terminals, VDUs, etc. are very expensive to purchase and expensive to rent. It must be noted, however, that the trend is for the cost of hardware to be reduced as the effects of silicon chips make themselves felt (*see* **40**).

The manufacturers who produce software packages obviously do not do so without profit.

37. Storage media

Storage media such as magnetic tapes, discs and floppy discs are expensive and have to be replaced when they become worn. This is therefore a continuing cost.

38. Space

If the organization has a large mainframe computer, it will need space to locate the computer and the associated equipment.

39. Staff and training

Data processing staff need to be highly trained and experienced if full use is to be made of the computer's resources. Therefore salaries need to be paid that will attract suitable staff.

Apart from those directly connected with the computer, training is needed for those who have to use the VDUs, terminals, etc., as part of their duties.

Microcomputers

40. Materials operations and the microcomputer

The development of microprocessors (silicon chips) has enabled computer manufacturers to develop a whole new generation of small, high capacity computers, easy to operate and cheap to maintain. This technical innovation, which dramatically reduces the cost of computer technology, has encouraged many organizations to purchase microcomputer systems for use in connection with the materials management operation. Standard programs for dealing with certain aspects of materials management can be purchased in software packages, covering such operations as:

(a) stock control;
(b) stock records;
(c) stores accounts;
(d) materials handling;
(e) distribution of stocks;
(f) word processing.

The full impact of microcomputers is yet to be fully realized. Estimates for the 1990s indicate that, within a few years, any section or organization that has more than ten members of staff will have access to microcomputers.

41. Advantages of microcomputers

The microcomputer has the following basic advantages over

traditional computer technology, especially in relation to stores management:

(a) *Very inexpensive.* In relative terms microtechnology is very inexpensive and is becoming even more so. This factor will enable even a low-budget company to obtain and employ a data processing system. At the present time, a microcomputer system, including VDUs, keyboard and CPUs, can be purchased for around £1,000.

(b) *Environmental conditions.* Microcomputers do not need to be kept in specially created and controlled environments as do traditional mainframe systems. This means that the materials department can be given microcomputers without any environmental problems or costs.

(c) *Simple to operate.* The operation of microcomputers is very simple and they are designed to enable training to be quick and easy. This again suits the stores section and will encourage all members of the stores team to use the system.

42. Future developments
The huge growth in micro- and mainframe computers and their ability to tackle numerous tasks, coupled with the price and ease of use, will mean a rapid growth of computer technology through the whole organization and therefore the stores. Many of the costs related to traditional mainframe computers (e.g. space, hardware and training) do not affect the microcomputer revolution.

Progress test 23

1. What are the basic elements of a data processing system? **(5)**

2. Describe the main methods of data storage. **(11)**

3. What are the main methods of processing data? **(16)**

4. What is meant by a data transmission system? **(17)**

5. What is meant by time-sharing? **(18)**

6. List some of the ways in which a computer can assist stores management. **(20–25)**

7. Outline the role of computers in stock control. **(30)**

Case study no. 11:

Coca Cola

By David Malpas, Operations Director, Synergy Logistics Ltd

Total control of stock rotation and age profile is essential in any food and drink company. The new £60 million Coca Cola and Schweppes Beverage's (CC&SB) canning and bottling plant at Wakefield, Europe's most advanced factory of its type, is no exception. It will run 24 hours a day, seven days a week producing up to six million soft drinks a day.

CC&SB has installed a £250,000 version of the warehouse management system, Locator, to control the entire production and stock flow throughout the 40 acre site.

Working closely with CC&SB, Synergy modified the standard Locator package to cover the company's exact needs. The software will handle the cases of soft drinks leaving the production line every hour, control their flow to 36 fork-lift trucks replenishing 22,000 pallet locations within the warehouse and manage 300 HGV movements on and off the site every day (*see* Fig. 23.6).

Stock movements

All vehicle and stock movements are actioned with a minimum of management time. For an incoming lorry, Locator decides where it parks, when it should be pulled forward to the bays and coordinates the fork-lift trucks to load or unload the vehicle as required.

Stock management is vital in the active environment of a production warehouse with very little space available for the new pallets continually arriving from the production lines. All warehouse movements are timed to the requirements of individual tasks.

Fork-lift trucks are controlled via radio data terminals which directs the location of goods and where they should be placed.

The system ensures minimum redundant travel time and actions tasks based on the ability of both the vehicle and the driver. If after a user defined period the task has not been completed, it becomes a critical task and is actioned immediately.

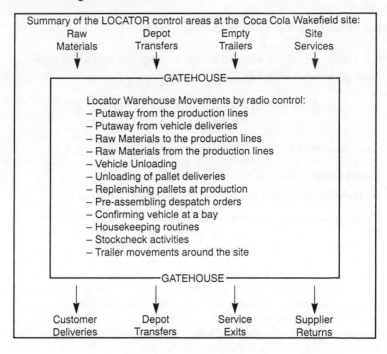

Summary of the LOCATOR control areas at the Coca Cola Wakefield site:

Raw Materials	Depot Transfers	Empty Trailers	Site Services

GATEHOUSE

Locator Warehouse Movements by radio control:
- Putaway from the production lines
- Putaway from vehicle deliveries
- Raw Materials to the production lines
- Raw Materials from the production lines
- Vehicle Unloading
- Unloading of pallet deliveries
- Replenishing pallets at production
- Pre-assembling despatch orders
- Confirming vehicle at a bay
- Housekeeping routines
- Stockcheck activities
- Trailer movements around the site

GATEHOUSE

Customer Deliveries	Depot Transfers	Service Exits	Supplier Returns

Figure 23.6 *Summary of the Locator control areas at the Coca Cola Wakefield site*

A large pool of labour is required to operate up to 36 fork-lift trucks per shift over 24 hours. The software has been designed to manage every task an individual is given based on that person's experience and training. Using specially designed logic and algorithmic techniques, the system ensures a novice driver is not given tasks requiring special skills and that they are not driving a truck for which they have not passed the required training course.

Locator also controls raw material flow and the number of pallets at the palletiser to ensure production lines are fully supplied, and the movement of trailers around the complex by a vehicle shunter and stock checking.

All the paperwork necessary to keep a busy warehouse running including goods receipt notes, despatch notes and special reports is produced automatically.

Integrated system

Locator has been integrated with the company's other corporate systems at a high level to avoid the possibility of transcription errors and improve the speed and effectiveness of information flow.

Vehicle schedules are entered at the company's Nottingham offices with order information processed and entered at a number of regional sales offices. All this information is automatically downloaded to Locator.

If any changes are entered at source then a screen enquiry and printed report is produced automatically at the warehouse office in Wakefield. This allows supervisors to manage and keep complete control over their operation at the production plant.

Information about the quantity of stock from the production lines per shift is interfaced to the main computer at Birmingham and from there to the company's head office at Uxbridge. Similarly the use of raw materials is also monitored and interfaced with the purchase order system.

Meeting CC&SB requirements

The software package has been expanded since its installation in October 1989. One important development — a sub-system called Tracer — enables CC&SB to trace the full history of stock at pallet level from production to end user.

To ensure that the system met the company's requirements, Synergy worked closely with CC&SB to establish the exact needs of the Wakefield plant.

The initial hardware at the CC&SB plant was a dual cluster of DECVax 3400s with full system data shadowing. Locator currently operates on a dual cluster of DECVax 6310s.

Part seven

Physical distribution management

Aims and scope of physical distribution management

1. Definition

Physical distribution management (PDM) is the task of ensuring that the goods and services produced by the organization are transported from the place of production to the point of consumption, as efficiently and as economically as possible. Physical distribution involves the following aspects:

(a) packaging
(b) despatch
(c) finished goods
(d) warehousing
(e) transport
(f) marshalling and loading.

Physical distribution is a vital element of the whole organization. Many experts believe that distribution is a sector of modern business that has the most to offer in terms of reduced costs via investigation and reorganization. Research has shown that from 1972 to 1982 the cost of operating a typical delivery van has risen by 75 per cent more than the RPI. Another developing role of physical distribution management is its relationship with marketing to maximize customer service.

2. Objectives of physical distribution

Distribution is essentially a service function, and it has the following objectives, each of which is related to other elements within the organization:

(a) *Transportation*. To manage and coordinate the transportation of goods and services produced by the organization from the point of production (i.e. factory, farm, mine, etc.) to the point of consumption (shop, warehouse, cash and carry store, supermarket, etc.). (*See* 26:**1**.)

(**b**) *Cost reduction.* To ensure that the system is used to capacity and therefore reduce the unit cost of distribution.

(**c**) *Organization's needs.* To ensure that the system employed meets the needs of the organization in terms of method of transport, cost, delivery period, labour usage, etc.

(**d**) *Corporate plan.* To ensure that distribution acts within the overall corporate plan of the organization and that it is constantly aware of the distribution needs of the other major departments within the organization (e.g. stores, sales, production and transportation).

(**e**) *Customer service.* To ensure that the distribution system meets the needs and requirements of customers to an individually agreed standard.

Channels of physical distribution

3. Introduction

A distribution channel is the path a product follows from producer to user. Manufacturers can choose from many channels for their products. There is no such thing as a 'best' channel, and instead of searching for the best channel for all products at all times, they should consider a range of alternatives and then select one that reflects the specific needs of the customer over a given period.

4. Physical distribution channels

Channels for consumer and industrial products are summarized in Table 24.1

Table 24.1 *Physical distribution channels*

Consumer products	Industrial products
Manufacturer	Manufacturer
Wholesaler	Wholesaler
Retailer	Industrial user
Consumer/user	

In servicing these distribution channels manufacturers often rely on the activities of intermediaries, or middlemen, to deliver products to customers. Because of their experience, specialization, contacts and scale, middlemen can offer producers a service superior to any they can offer on their own.

5. Using more than one channel

It is becoming increasingly common for a manufacturer to use more than one channel for similar products, for example beer sales through public houses, supermarkets and — increasingly — private clubs. Likewise, Michelin tyres are distributed not only to car accessory shops and garages but as a fabricated part of new Citroen cars. Each channel enables the manufacturer to serve a different market.

6. Consumer wholesalers and physical distribution management

Wholesalers are organizations who sell to retailers, other wholesalers, or industrial users but who do not sell in significant amounts to ultimate consumers.

The main function of a wholesaler is to buy in bulk and then distribute small orders to retailers, thereby realizing substantial savings on physical distribution costs.

The role of the wholesalers has resulted from:

(a) mass production in factories at a distance from the market;
(b) increased numbers of products manufactured on a speculative basis (that is, not on a job-order basis);
(c) increasing need to adapt products to the needs of intermediate and final users (for example, in terms of quality, shape, package and pricing);
(d) continuing increases in the quantities and varieties of products and services required by the customers.

Sorting is the key to the wholesaler's viability. The quantities in which products are produced or their natural characteristics often fail to match either the quantities in which they are demanded or the characteristics wanted by the customer.

7. Industrial wholesalers and physical distribution market

Most of the above applies only to the consumer market.

However, in the case of certain types of industrial goods, such as machine tools, industrial stockists are common. They buy from the producer and sell to other organizational buyers who require these goods. In these cases, both producer and buyer are unwilling to maintain large stocks.

8. Retailers and physical distribution management
Retail stores are important for most consumer goods. The retailer may offer some of the following advantages to manufacturers:

(a) bulk breaking;
(b) retailers can share some marketing tasks (such as advertising) with producers;
(c) retailers can act as a source of information between buyers and producers;
(d) retailers partly finance the storage of goods;
(e) retailers act as a buffer between buyers and producers. Sudden changes in demand for a product can be 'damped' by the existence of retail stocks.

9. Physical distribution and international distribution channels
Distribution channels that are specific to the international movement of goods can include:

(a) *Buying agencies* Large foreign companies may have agencies based in the UK through which they can purchase goods from UK firms and then arrange the transportation to the country involved. The main advantages of this system are that the agency will be aware of the reputation of the producer and the producer will have a simple means of export.
(b) *Export merchants.* The UK producer can sell his goods direct to the export merchant, who in turn sells the goods abroad. This system is the simplest for the UK producer.
(c) *Overseas branches.* Many large UK firms have set up offices in other countries. They can therefore set up a direct link between the UK producer and the foreign consumer, on the consumer's own territory.
(d) *Overseas agents.* Many organizations use the services of an overseas agent to act on their behalf in overseas markets. The

agent will normally stock and sell the goods and services of the organization, collecting a commission on sales as payment.

10. Efficiency of distribution channels
The efficiency of a distribution system can be analysed under three headings:

(a) *Cost.* You must consider both the capital/investment cost of developing a distribution channel and the cost of maintaining it. Your maintenance costs will cover either direct expenditure on transport or the margins and commissions of middlemen. Total distribution costs must be included in the final price to customers.
(b) *Coverage.* Full distribution coverage of your market means getting your products in the right quantities, where and when the customer requires them. Full coverage also means extra cost.
(c) *Control.* Using your own transport and distribution channels will give you maximum control. Many firms do not attempt to control the final destination of their products and are satisfied to place them under the control of middlemen.

In building and managing an overall distribution strategy, cost, coverage and control must be matched, balanced and harmonized with each other to field a customer-service-orientated and cost-effective distribution system. The integration of physical distribution management and channel strategy should aim to minimize distribution costs and maximize service.

11. Duties and responsibilities of materials management to distribution
Because distribution is involved in the administration and handling of materials there must be a relationship between materials management and physical distribution. The following are some of the duties and responsibilities of materials management in relation to distribution:

(a) *Marshalling and selection.* Stores is responsible for the selection and marshalling of the goods required for transport into the loading area (*see* 4:**21**). Stores must ensure that the correct items are marshalled as required by the sales advice note.
(b) *Quality control and inspection* (*see* 8:**1–10**). Distribution relies

upon stores to carry out regular checks of the goods marshalled to ensure that goods are in perfect condition. Delivery of faulty goods will mean a wasted trip and a loss of reputation for the organization.

(c) *Distribution documentation.* There are several documents involved in the process of marshalling and distribution of stock. All these documents must be properly completed and returned to the correct department or individual concerned. Materials management staff usually deal with this documentation and they must ensure that all the instructions contained within the document are noted and carried out (e.g. destination, quantities involved, handling requirements, etc.).

(d) *Management of warehouses.* This is the responsibility of stores management. The whole distribution system can be made inefficient if the supervision and management of the warehouse is less than professional.

(e) *Stock control.* Part of the task of stock control is to ensure that goods are stored in the correct location. It must therefore assist and instruct distribution as to what stock is required, where and when and in what quantities (*see* 13:2). It is vital that this task is performed properly, otherwise stock distribution will be inefficient and may result in loss of sales.

(f) *Stock records.* Stock records enable distribution to have a knowledge of the total stock situation, both at the factory and at the outside warehouses. This data will assist distribution in its task of ensuring a balanced spread of stock throughout the distribution network.

(g) *Security.* Materials management has a duty to maintain the security of stock. In many instances theft increases when goods leave the security of the store and before they are loaded and delivered. Security at the point of marshalling will help to reduce this stock loss.

(h) *Materials handling.* Materials management must ensure that the goods required for distribution are handled efficiently and that due notice is taken of any special handling requirements of the goods involved. This will ensure that goods arrive undamaged and therefore reduce the overall cost of distribution.

(i) *Indentification.* The distribution department is able to employ the materials coding system to identify the goods needed for distribution and therefore to ensure that the correct goods are selected and despatched. The codes also assist the processing of distribution documentation, especially when a computerized system is used (*see* 23:**9**).

12. Duties of distribution to materials management
Distribution has several duties in relation to materials management each of which will assist the relationship between the two departments and improve the overall efficiency of the distribution system. These duties will include the following:

(a) *Workable loading programmes*. Distribution must ensure that its programme for marshalling and loading is practical and avoids bottlenecks. The ideal situation is a steady work flow throughout the working period.

(b) *Due regard to stock levels*. Distribution must not programme loads from stocks which are insufficient to cover the quantities required. Materials management may have to waste a great deal of time and effort establishing that there are insufficient stocks.

(c) *Documentation*. Distribution must ensure that all the relevant documentation required is accurately prepared, complete and on time.

(d) *Notification of return loads*. In some cases loads will be returned to the store and these will often require unloading, storage and documentation. In view of the work involved for materials management, due notice of return loads must be given so that labour and space can be reserved to deal with the stock.

(e) *Special handling requirements*. In situations where the goods involved require special handling or loading (e.g. non-palletized) which is contrary to the normal loading techniques employed, distribution must ensure that stores management is given adequate notice and instructions. Distribution should, of course, wherever possible avoid circumstances where such special handling is required.

(f) *Overtime*. Distribution must make efforts to avoid marshalling and loading activities that will result in high overtime payments for the staff, especially if the staff are not fully utilized throughout the normal working period. Distribution should avoid evening and weekend working as well as late loading, other than for special one-off situations.

(g) *Communications*. It is vital that distribution and stock control are in constant communication with each other and keep each other fully informed about requirements and stocks. Distribution will have information from the sales department on future promotions and the expected effect upon sales in each area and the likely effects upon stocks. Stock control may also have this data. Nevertheless, an exchange of views and statistics is vital to ensure efficient distribution of stocks.

Organization of the physical distribution system

13. Selection of suitable systems of distribution

The organization has to take into account the following factors when selecting its distribution system:

(a) *The nature of the goods involved.* This will include the weight/size ratio, the conditions of transport required, and any special handling requirements.

(b) *Distances involved.* The further the goods have to be transported, the more the cost of distribution will rise. This distance will also include the mileage between the producer and the local rail, air or sea link.

(c) *Size of the market.* The size and demands of the market are very important. The more goods can be distributed to single areas having a demand for those goods, the more cost-efficient distribution will be. The cost of distribution is related to the number of units distributed and the cost of transportation. Bulk deliveries are more efficient than individual customers' deliveries.

(d) *Levels of competition.* The organization must be aware of the action of competitors in the market place and the extent to which their distribution system affects their final prices. If the competitor is based within the market area, then his distribution costs will be less.

(e) *Return on investment.* The setting up and running of a distribution system to take in another market place can be very expensive. The organization must be confident of making sufficient profit from this new market.

(f) *Local factors.* These can relate to land prices, government assistance, labour, transport, climate and levels of income within the area concerned. All these factors can affect the distribution of goods.

(g) *Exporting*. There are inherent difficulties relating to the process of exporting, e.g. export licences, shipping documents, exchange rates, payment, EC regulations, quotas and restrictions, all of which require skill and knowledge to tackle successfully.

14. The role of the warehouse in physical distribution management

The warehouse is a large centralized store, usually in a convenient location in relation to the market area to be served. The warehouse is basically designed to bridge the gap between the mass production of the producer and the batch requirements of the consumer. In most instances the warehouse will be managed by the stores. The warehouse has the following functions in relation to the overall distribution system:

(a) *Stockpiling*. The warehouse can be used to build up stocks to meet expected increases in demand arising from advertising, promotions, price cuts, changes in climate or seasonal factors. Stockpiling is vital if the organization is to benefit fully from increases in sales beyond its normal capacity.

(b) *Reducing the cost of transport*. Goods will be transported to the warehouse (which will be the furthest point from the factory) in bulk, therefore reducing the cost of distribution per unit.

(c) *Continuous supply*. It is important to maintain a continuous supply of products to the customer, as failure to do so will often mean a permanent loss of demand.

(d) *Control of goods*. The warehouse enables the goods involved to be properly handled and controlled before they reach the point of consumption.

(e) *Mixed loads*. Most organizations produce a range of products, and the customer will often require a mixture of all or some of the goods produced. The warehouse system enables the organization to deliver in bulk single-type loads, which can then be broken down and marshalled into mixed loads for the consumer.

15. Methods of transportation

There are several methods of transportation that can be employed to distribute the goods and services of the organization from the producer to the consumer. In many instances the total distribution system, from production to consumption, will embrace more than one method. (*See* 26:**4**.)

16. Cost of physical distribution

The following are some of the factors that contribute to the total cost of distribution for the organization:

(a) *Cost of transport*. Whichever method is employed there will be a cost and as the price of energy continues to rise, then the cost of transport will increase accordingly.

(b) *Maintaining warehouses*. This is a very expensive business and will include such costs as labour, rent, rates, heating, lighting and associated management costs.

(c) *Packaging*. This is a very expensive commodity. The more complex and involved the distribution system becomes, the more robust and protective the packaging will need to be.

(d) *Management costs*. These will cover stock control, materials handling, administration, traffic control, stock records and labour.

(e) *Cost of damages caused in transportation*. In some cases this can become a major cost, especially if the goods are very fragile and expensive.

It can be seen from this list that every effort must be made to reduce costs, if distribution is not to become excessively expensive.

17. Evaluation of distribution systems

To evaluate any system it is necessary to have a clear idea of what the organization expects of the system, the resources employed and the total cost of operating the system. To evaluate a distribution system we would have to examine the following criteria:

(a) The level of stocks needed at the warehouse.

(b) The total delivery period from the factory to the consumer.

(c) The total cost of distribution and the cost per unit transported.

(d) The number of nil-stock situations in any one period at the warehouse.

(e) Rate of stock loss due to damages in storage, handling or theft.

(f) The size of the distribution network in relation to the size of the market.

(g) The degree of liaison between distribution and production, marketing, stores and finance.

(h) Compatibility of the system with the materials handling system of the organization and its customers.

(i) Customer service levels achieved.

18. Improvement of materials management and physical distribution relationship

Physical distribution of stocks throughout the organization's warehouse system can greatly affect the level of sales and therefore profits. A lack of stock in any given area could lead to a loss of revenue in the short term and a loss of reputation in the long term. It is therefore vital that there should exist a sound working relationship between distribution and management. To improve and enhance this relationship, the following steps can be taken:

(a) *Joint meetings* between materials and distribution management on a regular basis to discuss problems and future requirements from both sides.

(b) *Involvement* of both sections in each other's long-term plans — materials in relation to the levels of stock and handling capacity, distribution for its future needs and delivery periods.

(c) *Professional and well-trained management* in both materials management and distribution.

(d) *Introduction of computer-based systems* where the volume of work justifies it.

(e) *Efficient transportation system.*

19. Computerized integration between materials management and physical distribution management

The control of the materials flow in materials requirement is controlled by the materials requirement planning system (MRP). Materials planning can also be part of the more complex manufacturing resource planning package called MRPII. These systems are referred to as 'push' systems in that they push materials forward to meet the master production schedule. Distribution management also have a role to play in the elimination of unnecessary finished goods within its system. The distribution resource planning system (DRP) was developed to assist in forecasting the demands for finished goods at the point of use.

20. Distribution requirement planning

DRP has been described by Christopher (1990) as 'being the mirror image of MRP in that it seeks to identify requirements for finished products at the point of demand and then produces aggregated, time placed requirement schedules for each echelon in the distribution system'. DRP differs from MRP in that it is a 'pull' system. It 'pulls' finished products in the exact quantities to the right place only when they are required. Effective integration between materials management, physical distribution management and production by using MRP, MRPII and DRP can ensure that customer needs are met with minimum finished goods and lower material stock.

Progress test 24

1. Describe the main channels of distribution. **(4)**

2. What factors have to be considered when selecting a suitable distribution system? **(14)**

3. What is the role of the warehouse in the distribution system? **(14)**

4. How would you attempt to measure the efficiency of an organization's distribution channels? **(10)**

5. What are the costs involved in maintaining a distribution system? **(16)**

6. By what criteria would you evaluate a distribution system? **(17)**

7. Outline the relationship between distribution and stores management. **(18)**

Despatch and packaging

Despatch

1. Definition
Despatch of stock refers to items being selected from stock and then marshalled, documented, loaded and subsequently delivered to their given destinations. These destinations can include the following:

(a) customers;
(b) suppliers (returns to suppliers);
(c) other departments in the organization;
(d) inspectors;
(e) export agents.

2. Types of items to be despatched
These will include the following:

(a) finished goods;
(b) repairs;
(c) returns;
(d) transfers;
(e) to be inspected.

3. Despatch documentation
To ensure efficient control of the despatch function a series of documents have to be employed:

(a) *Sales advice note* (*see* Fig. 25.1). In cases where the issues to be despatched are for customers, the issue or order will be made up against a copy of the sales order placed by the customer. This would have been acquired by the sales force and will be processed into individual requirements and the customers involved. Information contained within a sales advice note includes:

- (*i*) item involved and amount ordered;
- (*ii*) code number;
- (*iii*) destination;
- (*iv*) loading date;
- (*v*) loading dock number;
- (*vi*) customer's name and address;
- (*vii*) special handling or delivery instructions.

SALES ADVICE NOTE		Date _____
Customer J. Menzies Ltd.		
Address City Industrial Estate, West Walling.		
	GOODS TO BE DELIVERED	
Description	Copper rods 6m x 5mm Grade A	*Loading dock:* 7
		Special handling:
Quantity	500 rods	Fork lift truck
Loading date	2.1.— —	and pallets
Destination	Site No.6, City Industrial Estate, West Walling	*Code No.* RMMCRA 6mx5mm

Figure 25.1 *Sales advice note*

(b) *Return-to-supplier note.* This document is employed when items are to be sent back to suppliers for reasons such as the following:

- (*i*) damage;
- (*ii*) non-usage;
- (*iii*) sale or return agreements;
- (*iv*) faults.

A copy of the return-to-supplier note will be held by stores and a further copy will be sent to purchasing as a permanent record of the return.

(c) *Internal transfer notes.* These are employed when goods are being transferred from one part of the operation to another, usually in a different part of the country, but all within the same company or organization. Like the sales advice note, it will contain details of code number, amount and destination.

(d) *Loading sheet.* This is usually prepared by the transportation department which is responsible for the actual physical delivery of the items involved, by whatever method or methods the organization employs. The despatch staff are responsible for making up loads that are economical for lorries and which make full use of the vehicles' capacities. The loading sheet will be used by several different sections as follows:

    (*i*) Stores will marshal goods into the loading bay against the supplied loading sheet.

    (*ii*) Drivers will use the loading sheet to check on and off the loads they carry.

    (*iii*) The customer will use it to check the delivery; in some cases the loading sheet becomes the organization's delivery note.

    (*iv*) Sales will use the returned loading sheet as a confirmation of delivery.

    (*v*) Despatch will use the returned loading sheet as a permanent record of these activities.

4. Despatch of stock procedure

There can be no standard procedure, for every organization has its own individual needs and resources. However, the basic chain of events will be as follows in most typical organizations:

(a) *Original demand.* This can come from the sources mentioned in **1**.

(b) *Production of documentation (see **3**).*

(c) *Distribution of documentation.* Documents will be sent by the despatch department to the sections involved, whether stores, loading, sales, customers or suppliers.

(d) *Selection and marshalling of stock required.*

(e) *Checking and loading of stock by loading bay staff.*

(f) *Transportation to destination.*
(g) *Return of documentation and analysis to confirm procedure.*

5. Integration between PDM and despatch

In many organizations the finished goods store is a separate unit from the rest of the stores organization and is managed by the PDM function. This helps towards a greater integration between PDM and despatch. Integration will include the following:

(a) *Liaison* between loading and materials handling operations.
(b) *Checking and marshalling* of finished goods in predetermined areas within the loading bay.
(c) *Checking and compilation* of relevant documentation.
(d) *Provision of suitable alternatives* if the items required cannot be supplied.

6. Aims of the despatch department

The aims of the despatch department depend upon the overall aims and objectives of the organization and the resources employed. The following are some basic aims that every despatch department could identify with:

(a) *Analysis of orders* into economical loads for the methods of transport involved.
(b) *Provision of despatch control documentation* and loading/delivery instructions and details.
(c) *Analysis of goods* delivered and goods not delivered to customers.
(d) *Liaison with physical distribution management department* about the movement of finished goods throughout the network.

Packaging

7. Definition

Packaging is the general term applied to cover all aspects of the applications of materials and procedures in connection with them to the preparation of goods for handling, storage, marketing and despatch.

8. Functions of a package

The packaging of materials is of vital importance in relation to the tasks of transporting and storing the stock of the organization. Packaging has several very important functions, which can be divided into two main categories as follows:

9. Primary function

To provide adequate protection to the product by being of suitable strength and design to withstand the shocks, stresses and strains, climatic conditions and pressure of other goods stacked on top, encountered during transport or storage.

10. Secondary functions

These could involve some of the following:

(a) To provide a method of selling goods by weight quantities.

(b) As a form of advertising. The colour and design of packaging materials can be used to make the consumer aware of the organization and its products.

(c) To preserve the life of the product.

(d) To prevent product pilferage.

(e) To carry operating or safety instructions for the use of the product.

(f) To allow a hygienic method of handling food or medicines.

11. Requirements of a package

Packaging should fulfil the following requirements:

(a) It must be convenient to fill, close and open the package.

(b) It should be capable of being handled by the intended materials handling method.

(c) Due consideration should be given to the safety of the personnel who will come into contact with it.

12. Principles of packaging

Packaging should be designed to give maximum compatibility with the product. Considerations should include:

13. Product characteristics

(a) How fragile is the product?

(b) Does the product need to be rigid?
(c) Is it susceptible to water, heat and cold or other factors?
(d) Size and dimensions?
(e) If product will be moved as a unit load, what quantity will be in each movement pack?

14. Marketing needs of the product

(a) Will the product be delivered to an intermediary or directly to the customer?
(b) Must the product have an attractive appearance or other sales appeal?

15. Accurate information on handling, storage and mode of transport used

(a) *Mode of transport.* Will the product be transported by rail, road, sea or air, or a combination of these methods?
(b) *Handling.* What form of handling? Will it be manual, mechanical or automatic? How often will the product be loaded and unloaded?
(c) *Storage.* What length of time will the product be in storage?

16. Basic types of packaging material

The main consideration of which material to use depends on the handling, storage, market needs and the characteristics of the product. The amount of money that can be spent on the package depends to some extent on the value of the product.

The most common types of packages include the following:

(a) paper wrapping, bags and sacks;
(b) plastic bottles, tubes, jars and drums;
(c) metal kegs, drums, crates, cans, boxes and aerosols;
(d) fibreboard cartons, boxes, cases and drums;
(e) PVC and polythene films.

17. Package testing

Modern packaging designers are using an ever increasing range of new technology to simulate actual conditions the package will encounter on its journey. The three main causes of damage to cartons or containers in transit are:

(a) vibration;
(b) impact;
(c) dropping.

Standard tests include:

(a) *Vibration test.* Product is placed on a vibrating table for one hour.
(b) *Impact test.* The package is placed on a trolley which is allowed to run freely down a 10 degree inclined plane. The trolley is stopped by impact against a buffer stop at the bottom of the incline.
(c) *Drop test.* The container is dropped from a specific height onto a flat surface. The height depends on the weight of the container. It is dropped on one corner, three edges and six surfaces. If the contents are still undamaged it is considered to have passed the test.

Other forms of package testing include a revolving drum test, and a weaving test.

18. Physical distribution management and packaging
The design and characteristics of packaging have a major impact on physical distribution efficiency and costs. Poorly designed packaging can result in:

(a) poor load construction;
(b) damaged products resulting in poor customer service;
(c) unsafe or costly storage requirements.

Progress test 25

1. What information is contained on a typical sales advice note? **(3)**

2. List the basic elements in a despatch of stock procedure. **(4)**

3. What are the overall aims of the despatch department? **(6)**

4. What information would you expect to find on a typical return to supplier note? **(3)**

5. Who would make use of a loading sheet in the materials operation? **(3(d))**

6. Outline the primary functions of a package. **(8)**

7. What product characteristics have to be taken into account when selecting the appropriate form of packaging? **(13)**

8. List the basic types of packaging materials. **(16)**

9. How would you test packaging materials? **(17)**

10. What are the secondary functions of a package? **(10)**

Transportation

The role of the transport manager

1. Definition

Transportation is the process of transporting goods and materials either within a network of internal locations (i.e. depots) or to the customer. G.J. Murphy states: 'Industrial society rests on trade, that is the movement of materials from where they are found, to a processing point and then the finished product to the market.'

2. Essential features of a transport system

The factors which determine the effectiveness and efficiency of a transport system are as follows:

(a) *Cost.* Transport costs increase with distance so this is a vital factor in determining the limits of the area where the products can be sold.

(b) *Safety.* This factor is obviously vital when conveying people. In relation to goods a safe transport system involves handling, loading and unloading the goods safely, and more importantly safety from theft. The sender of the goods must cooperate fully by ensuring that the goods are properly packed.

(c) *Speed.* There may be times when speed is even more important than cost, e.g. drugs and computer components. A speedy system of transport is essential for the movement of perishable goods and products which have a short life span.

(d) *Convenience.* The transport system should be convenient to manufacturers, warehouses, wholesalers, retailers and customers. The transport system should be such that it should be possible to load and unload the goods cheaply and quickly. There is no point in importing goods unless there is the accessibility of terminals for unloading.

(e) *Flexibility.* An efficient transport system must be flexible and capable of carrying different kinds of goods, e.g. magazines, cars, electrical goods, cigarettes, etc. The flexible system can take both large and small consignments of goods.

(f) *Reliability.* Manufacturers must be able to distribute their goods as soon as possible after manufacture. If this were not the case the manufacturers would require very large warehouses. It is of equal importance that the manufacturer receives the raw materials on time.

3. Duties and responsibilities of the transport manager
The transport manager has a vital role to play in relation to the overall materials control of the organization and also to its total profitability. The duties and responsibilities of transport are listed below.

(a) *Selection* of most appropriate mode of transport, depending upon the materials to be moved and their destinations (*see* **4**).

(b) *Fleet management.* In some organizations a fleet of vehicles is owned for the transportation of the materials of the organization. The fleet manager is responsible for such factors as:

    (*i*) route planning;
    (*ii*) security;
    (*iii*) driver management.

(c) *Evaluation and control* of transport services used by the organization.

(d) *To work with stores, purchasing and marketing* to ensure that the transport service provided meets all the needs and goals of the organization.

(e) *To ensure the security of goods* while in transit and to select modes of transport that minimize the risk of stock loss.

(f) *To ensure that the organization functions as a legal operator.*

Methods of transport and their selection

4. Methods of transportation
There are several methods of transport that can be employed

to distribute the goods and services of the organization from the producer to the consumer. In many instances the total distribution system, from production to consumption, will embrace more than one method. The main methods are listed below.

(a) *Road transport.* Many organizations find the convenience of road transport so great that it outweighs the cost factor. In a distribution system, large, heavy lorries are used to transport the goods in bulk to the warehouse and smaller delivery vans are used to make the final delivery to the customer. In many cases the level of stock damages is reduced when using road transport, as the handling situations are minimized.

(b) *Rail transport.* In the UK we have a very sophisticated and complete rail network, designed to transport goods to and from the main centres of the country. It has the ability to handle bulk loads and is quite competitive in terms of cost. However, the railway system cannot deliver goods door-to-door (as can road transport), and it therefore involves more instances of materials handling.

(c) *Sea transport.* The UK has a tradition for seaborne trade and has the ports, docks and infrastructure to accommodate a very large volume of trade. Seaborne transport has the advantage of being relatively inexpensive in relation to bulk loads. However, it is a slow form of delivery and goods have to be collected at the docks and delivered to the warehouse by road.

(d) *Air transport.* This method involves the use of commercial passenger aircraft carrying extra freight and also aircraft used entirely for the transport of freight, usually via agencies. Air transport is very expensive, but it is also the quickest method of transport over long distances. It is usually used in cases where the goods involved are small, light and expensive, so that the cost of transport is only a fraction of the total cost of the item itself.

5. Selection of transportation mode

One of the main responsibilities of the transport manager is that of selecting the most appropriate means of transporting the goods of the organization, whether from the company to the customer or from the company to other depots and warehouses. The transport manager must constantly seek to improve the service provided to the organization by the modes of transport employed.

6. Reasons why organizations switch transport modes

The transport manager will be prompted to search for new modes of transport by the following:

(a) Desire to improve customer satisfaction in terms of time, method of materials handling, degree of security.

(b) Deterioration of service provided by existing mode.

(c) Desire to reduce overall costs of distribution.

(d) Desire to reduce transit time.

(e) Changing needs of the organization and/or the customer.

(f) Development of new products which require different modes of transport.

(g) Development of a new materials handling system that will not integrate with the existing mode of transport employed.

7. Sources of information concerning modes of transport

During the process of selecting modes of transport, the manager has to examine a number of considerations before making an effective decision. The sources of information available to him are as follows:

(a) *Past experience of the transport manager.* He will have dealt with a number of organizations and modes and will have a high degree of 'market' knowledge to refer to in his decision-making process.

(b) *Marketing departments* of the various modes and organizations in the field.

(c) *Trade directories and route maps.*

(d) *Trade magazines and journals* related to the transport business.

(e) *Specialist consultants* who will advise on the various modes of transport and the relative advantages and disadvantages of each.

(f) *Other transport managers.* If the transport or fleet manager is a member of the Chartered Institute of Transport information from fellow professionals is available.

8. Factors to be considered when selecting the mode of transport

The transport manager has to take into account a number of

factors before selecting the mode of transport for moving the goods of the organization. These include the following:

(a) *Relative costs* of each mode of transport.

(b) *Past experience* of the various modes of transport employed to date.

(c) *Relative delivery time.* In some instances the speed of delivery is a vital selection criterion, i.e. with perishable goods and high value goods.

(d) *Points served by the various modes.* In some instances the transport manager may require a mode that will serve particular destinations, i.e. overseas markets.

(e) *Loss or damage history of the mode.* In cases where delicate goods are involved the transport manager will seek a mode with a good record in relation to safe delivery.

(f) *Frequency of service offered by the mode.* The transport manager may require a regular collection and delivery service.

(g) *Adaptability to organizational needs.* Can the mode deal with the changing transport needs of a dynamic organization?

(h) *Prompt claim settlement.* To what extent does the mode deal with claims for loss or damage? The transport manager will require prompt payment of compensation (where due) from the carrier, once the claim has been investigated.

(i) *Integration between the mode and the materials handling system* presently employed by the organization.

All these factors have to be carefully considered before a decision on the mode of transport to be employed is made.

9.   Evaluation of mode performance
To enable the transport manager to effectively control the transport action operation, he must be able to evaluate the performance of the system employed. To enable him to do this, various measures can be examined in relation to mode performance.

(a) Analysis of on-time deliveries over a period of time, destinations and goods.

(b) Analysis of on-time collections by the organization operating the mode.

(c) Analysis of 'customer' complaints, in relation to such factors as damage, loss, delivery, materials handling and level of overall service.

(d) Overall costs of transportation as compared with budgeted costs.

(e) Analysis of claims for damages and losses over a period of time, and for ranges of materials and routes.

(f) Load placement, — to what degree can the operator of the mode pinpoint the location of loads during transit? This indicates the degree of control the operator has over the goods being transported.

The costs involved in transportation are very high and therefore every effort must be made to ensure that the most effective mode of transport is employed.

Transport costs

10. Costs involved in transport
There are a number of costs that have to be budgeted for in relation to transport. One of the functions of the transport manager is to ensure that such costs are controlled. They include the following:

(a) *Labour costs.* Drivers of vehicles are semi-skilled workers, but some of the large heavy goods vehicles require specially qualified drivers who will command higher salaries.

(b) *Energy costs.* The fuel used by vehicles will have to be paid for. In recent years energy costs have risen by substantial amounts on a regular basis.

(c) *Maintenance costs.* Where the organization operates its own vehicles, skilled personnel will have to service and maintain the vehicles.

(d) *Security costs.* The value of modern vehicles makes it vital that adequate security is maintained.

(e) *Administrative costs.* The system of transport control will involve staff management and records, route management and records, route planning activities, load planning and stock control. All of these will require an administrative system to ensure efficient operation.

(f) *Packaging (see* 25:**16**).

11. The fleet manager

In organizations where a number of vehicles are employed to transport materials, a fleet manager is required. The job of the fleet manager is vital to the overall efficiency of the distribution operation and the organization as a whole. The fleet manager is responsible for the aspects of transportation discussed in **12–17** below.

12. Vehicle replacement

It is the job of the fleet manager to select the most efficient and cost-effective vehicles for the needs of the organization. He has to take into consideration such factors as:

(a) costs of operation;
(b) nature of the goods to be transported;
(c) maintenance facilities required;
(d) materials handling systems employed by the organization and its customers;
(e) finance available for purchase;
(f) driver acceptability.

13. Maintenance

Vehicles need to be maintained and repaired during their working lives. The fleet manager must devise a system of planned maintenance whereby vehicles available for transportation can be regularly maintained. It is vital that this system enables the maintenance to be carried out without reducing the total effectiveness of the fleet. The advantages of a system of planned maintenance are:

(a) *Planned maintenance* will not disrupt the distribution system, whereas random breakdowns due to lack of maintenance will cause delay and non-delivery of goods.
(b) *Slack-time* within the distribution system can be used to complete maintenance work.

The fleet manager is also responsible for ensuring that maintenance costs are controlled.

14. Route planning

One of the most important tasks of the transport manager or

fleet manager's job is to ensure that the most effective route is employed, so that the costs of transport can be kept to a minimum and therefore improve overall profitability. A number of factors must be taken into account when deciding upon the most effective route. These will include the following:

(a) *Consultation* between transport, stores, distribution and marketing so as to ascertain the location of customers and the load-mix.

(b) *Lines of communication*, i.e. motorways, thus ensuring that the vehicle takes the route that makes maximum use of these efficient highways, reducing delivery time, energy costs and vehicle wear.

(c) *Time factor*. The fleet manager will always be concerned with journey time. To make maximum use of the vehicles within the fleet, he must pursue the objective of reducing the time vehicles are tied up for on any one delivery.

The fleet manager has a number of techniques which he can employ to help ascertain the most cost-effective route. These include transportation modes (*see* **4**).

15. Legal aspects of fleet management
The fleet manager has to ensure that the organization's vehicles are being operated in accordance with the national and international regulations that govern commercial transport.

16. Security
The fleet manager is responsible for the security of the vehicles within the fleet and also for the goods that are being transported. This task involves the following:

(a) *Ensuring that vehicles are secure* when not being used. In some cases organizations will have a 'vehicle compound', into which the vehicles are driven and stored when not being used. This compound is sometimes within the stockyard.

(b) *Ensuring that goods are properly checked* during loading, so that discrepancies due to faulty counting can be corrected.

(c) *Ensuring that vehicles are properly 'sealed'* so as to indicate unauthorized entry between destinations.

(d) *Training of staff*, including the drivers, to ensure that security procedures are carried out properly.

17. Driver management

It is the task of the fleet manager to ensure that all vehicle drivers are properly trained to use the vehicles within the fleet, that HGV licences are valid and that drivers are qualified to drive the class of vehicle used by the fleet.

Vehicle acquisition

18. Introduction

The fleet manager may be involved in deciding upon the most appropriate method of acquiring a fleet of vehicles or replacement vehicles for the organization. The method selected will be affected by the following major considerations:

(a) finance;
(b) operational skills;
(c) nature of the business.

The three options regarding equipment acquisition are:

(a) leasing;
(b) hiring;
(c) outright purchase.

19. Leasing

This is where the fleet manager leases a vehicle from a leasing company, for a set period of time (normally a minimum of three years) at a set fee. The equipment remains the property of the lessor but the responsibility for its maintenance is the duty of the lessee.

20. Advantages of leasing

There are several advantages to the leasing method and it is an increasingly popular option.

(a) *No capital commitment.* The organization will not have to find large sums of money to acquire the vehicle. The vehicle will, however, immediately begin to generate profit for the organization.
(b) *The fees for the lease* of the vehicle can be offset against tax and, therefore, the net cost of leasing the vehicle is reduced.

(c) *Low cost*. This method of acquiring a vehicle is the lowest of the three options and this is its main advantage.

21. Disadvantages of leasing

(a) *The lessee has to maintain the vehicle*. This can be very expensive, especially if the lessee does not have in-house maintenance skills.
(b) *Fixed-term contract*. The vehicle cannot be returned to the lessor in the event of changes in the lessee's business needs.

Chris Wyles states in *Works Management* (April 1980) that 'leasing can be summarized as best suited to high activity and application where in-house care and maintenance are of a good standard.'

22. Hiring of vehicles

The fee for hiring is normally set according to the type of vehicle, the period of hire and the routes to be covered. The vehicle remains the property of the rental company which also retains responsibility for maintaining the vehicle at all times.

23. Advantages of hiring

The main advantages of hiring are those of its flexibility.

(a) *Hire charges* can be planned and budgeted for.
(b) *No capital commitment is required*. Once the hire agreement is settled the vehicle can be put to work.
(c) *Flexibility*. The vehicle can be exchanged or returned at any time. If, therefore, the needs of the fleet manager change, the hire company can respond to that change and supply the type of vehicle required.
(d) *Maintenance* is the responsibility of the hiring company. Should the vehicle break down, the hire company must either repair the vehicle or supply a replacement. The company need have no in-house skills and still be able to operate a fleet of vehicles.
(e) *Hire payments* can be entirely set against revenue.

24. Disadvantages of hiring

The major disadvantage of hiring is that of cost in the long term.

(a) *Cost.* Hire charges will be designed to pay for the vehicle and then earn a return for the hire company. Therefore, the company could find that in terms of hire charges it has 'paid' for the vehicle, yet it remains the property of the hire company. The vehicle will now appear as an asset on the balance sheet of the company.

(b) *High usage premiums.* If the vehicle is going to be used for extended periods at a very high rate of usage, then the hire company can impose an extra charge known as a high usage premium.

The option to hire can be summarized as the best method in conditions of high usage, where no in-house skills exist and where a seasonal or innovative environment is the norm.

25. Outright purchase of the vehicle

This is the established method of vehicle acquisition, although in recent times there has been a shift away from the purchase option.

26. Advantages of outright purchase

(a) *Depreciation* on the total value of the vehicle is deducted from revenue. Therefore, tax advantages can be gained from the purchase option.

(b) *The vehicle belongs to the organization* and is therefore added to its list of assets and total worth. The organization has complete control over the vehicle and can thus use it as it sees fit.

(c) *Government development areas.* These are areas that the government has decided need special financial assistance to help promote growth and attract new industries. If the company operates in one of these areas then loans and grants may be available to assist in the purchase of vehicles.

27. Disadvantages of outright purchase

The main disadvantage of outright purchase is that of initial capital outlay. The organization must offset the 'opportunity costs' of using the cash required to purchase a vehicle in another part of the business. For example, a vehicle may cost £20,000. What if that sum was used to purchase new racking for the storehouse? The new racking could be so efficient as to save enough money to pay the hire charges on a hired vehicle. Therefore, the stores would have a new racking system *and* the use of a new vehicle.

The purchase option can be summarized as being the best method in conditions of a cash rich company.

28. Physical distribution and materials management

Transportation is a key sub-function of physical distribution management. Careful selection of the modes of transport is important if goods are to arrive where and when required in a condition suitable for use. Poor route planning or vehicle loading can increase the costs of transport and cause customer dissatisfaction.

Progress test 26

1. What are the essentials of a transport system? **(2)**

2. List the main methods of transportation. **(4)**

3. Outline the sources of information concerning modes of transport. **(7)**

4. What are the factors to be considered when selecting the mode of transport? **(8)**

5. List the main costs involved in transport. **(10)**

6. What are the advantages of leasing transport vehicles? **(20)**

7. List the advantages of hiring transport vehicles. **(24)**

Appendix 1
Bibliography

Ansoff, H. I., *Corporate Strategy* (Penguin, 1968)

Ansoff, H. I. (ed.), *Business Strategy* (Penguin, 1969)

Appleby, R. C., *Modern Business Administration* (5th edition) (Pitman, 1991)

Argenti, J., *Systematic Corporate Planning* (Nelson, 1974)

Baily, P. J. H., *Purchasing and Supply Management* (Chapman & Hall, 1990)

Baily, P. J. H. and Farmer, D., *Purchasing Principles and Management* (Pitman/Institute of Purchasing and Supply, 1990)

Betts, P. W., *Supervisory Studies: A Managerial Perspective* (5th edition) (Pitman, 1989)

Brech, E. F. L., *Organization — the Framework of Management* (Longman, 1957)

Burton, J. A., *Effective Warehousing* (3rd edition) (Pitman, 1981)

Cole, G. A., *Management Theory and Practice* (DP Publications, 1990)

Drucker, P. F., *The Practice of Management* (Pan Business Books, 1968)

Drucker, P. F., *Management* (Pan Business Books, 1979)

Fayol, H., *General and Industrial Management* (Pitman, 1949)

Fetherston, J. M., *Understanding the Freight Business* (Meadows Group, 1984)

Fulmer, R. N., *The New Management* (Macmillan, New York, 1978)

Graham, H. T., *Human Resources Management* (M & E) (7th edition) (Pitman, 1992)

Handy, Charles B., *Understanding Organizations* (Penguin Education, 1976)

Harding, H. A., *Production Management* (Macdonald & Evans, 1979)

Howard, K., *Quantitative Analysis for Planning Decisions* (Macdonald & Evans, 1975)

Humble, J., *Management by Objectives* (British Institute of Management, 1972)

Koontz, H. and O'Donnell, C., *Management: A System and Contingency Analysis of the Managerial Function* (McGraw-Hill, 1976)

Lester, G. C., *Data Processing* (Polytech Publishers Ltd, 1980)

Lysons, C. K., *Purchasing* (M & E) (2nd edition) (Pitman, 1989)

Proctor, Tony, *Management Theory and Principles* (Macdonald & Evans, 1982)

Shaw, Josephine, *Business Administration* (Pitman, 1991)

Simon, H., *Administrative Behaviour* (Macmillan, 1960)

Appendix 2
Examination technique

1. Preliminaries

Before you even reach the examination room, various preliminaries must be dealt with, so as to ensure that you are properly prepared for the coming examination. Sound preparation is the keystone to examination success: there is no substitute for simple, hard work. These preliminaries will include the following:

(a) *Revision.*

    (*i*) Revision is vital to examination success. You must ensure that all your notes are neat and in order. For the purpose of revision, you should be able to 'refine' your notes to the relevant points only.

    (*ii*) Revision must be organized on a long-term basis, so that all the material required is covered and you have time to clarify questions that may arise during the course of revision.

    (*iii*) Evaluation of the revision process is also very important. You must attempt to test yourself, with progress tests and sample questions.

    (*iv*) Seminar groups with fellow students are very useful during the period of revision, as problems and knowledge can then be shared.

(b) *Travel problems.* Wherever the examination is to be held, ensure that you know the best route to the examination centre, especially if you have never been to the area before. Always leave yourself plenty of time to get to the centre, especially when travelling through heavy traffic. Remember, examinations *always* start and end promptly!

(c) *Equipment.* Ensure that you have all the necessary pens, pencils, coloured pencils, rubbers, rules, etc., that you may need for the examination. There are several brands of typewriter masking fluid that can be used to mask-out errors neatly.

(d) *Correct frame of mind.* It is very important to adopt a positive frame of mind towards examinations. So long as you have worked on the course, completed the progress tests and spent time on revision, success in examinations is almost automatic, provided you remain *confident and determined.*

2. Examinations

Once you have entered the examination room, the second stage of the technique comes into action. Note the following points carefully.

(a) *Read instructions* given on the examination paper very carefully. Only answer the number of questions required. Never avoid compulsory questions. Note the time allowed for the examination and the marks per question (if not equal).

(b) *Allocate time* to each of the questions, ideally in equal parts. You should also allow time to read the paper several times over at the end of the examination to check through your answers. It is vital not to overrun on any of the questions. You must attempt all the questions required to ensure success.

(c) *Read the questions* very carefully and slowly, at least two or three times. Underline what you feel is the real 'core' of the question, and make sure your answer keeps on that theme and does not wander.

(d) *Plan your answer.* You should have an introduction/definition, then the main text and finally a conclusion. Planning will also assist you in allocating the time to spend on each point within the answer; obviously, a question that embraces a great many points will have less written work per point.

(e) *Make rough notes* on scrap paper before you begin to write your answer on the examination sheet. These should consist of single words, only taking a few moments. They will provide you with a checklist of points to refer to while completing the examination question. They will also give an indication of the amount of work required to cover the whole question carefully.

(f) *Improve your written style.* Examiners usually require the answers to be written in formal essay form and if you have not taken examinations for a long while you must practise this style of writing before the examination. Questions should only be answered in note form where the instructions state so or if you have run out of time and wish to complete the rest of the examination. You will lose marks for style, but will gain overall for at least attempting to answer all the questions.

(g) *Answer the question as set,* and not your own variation of the question. Marks are strictly allocated in examinations to pre-defined points: *stick to the question.*

Appendix 3
Stock control: a mathematical model

Below is a common mathematical 'model' which is used by stores management to calculate various costs and stock figures. This model can be extremely useful and is employed by the stock controller to help him control the stock held within the store.

1. Symbols
   In any system of equations we have to adopt a set of symbols to represent the individual elements of each equation. These symbols shall be as follows:

(a) Administration costs of ordering = AO
(b) Quantity ordered = QO
(c) Unit cost of materials = UM
(d) Cost of storage expressed as a percentage of unit costs = CS

2. Calculations
   Having established these basic symbols we can proceed to make the following calculations.

(a) Cost of purchasing one order = $AO + UMQO$

(b) Unit cost of purchased order = $\dfrac{AO}{QO} + UM$

(c) Cost of holding stock = $CS \left(\dfrac{AO}{QO} + UM \right)$

Appendix 4
Examination questions

We have selected below a number of past questions from the major professional bodies and associations that have materials related questions in their intermediate and final stages.

1. What are the main reasons for keeping stock records? (*ASPS, Stores, Administration and Control of Stock, November 1987*)

2. Describe the 'Just-in-Time' concept and explain how it will affect both the design and handling of stores. (*ASPS, Stores Design and Materials Handling, November 1987*)

3. Examine simply and clearly the advantages and disadvantages of using a computer for purchasing and stores records. (*ASPS, First Certificate, Business Procedures and Organizations, May 1982*)

4. As a departmental manager you are concerned about the performance of one of your section leaders. He seems to be a changed man. The morale of his section is affected by his irritable manner, by his inadequate and sometimes conflicting instructions, and by his exaggerated reaction to events.
    What do you see as the problem, and what action would you take to deal with this situation? (*Institute of Industrial Managers, Industrial Management and Organization, 1983*)

5. Your company is proposing to centralize the stores function in your organization. What advantages and disadvantages would you expect to arise if such a scheme were adopted? (*RSA, Storekeeping Stage II, 1981*)

6. Write what you know and discuss in detail in relation to the A, B, C analysis of stock holding in the stores. (*Institute of Production Control, Practical Stores Management, December 1982*)

7. The purpose of the storehouse is to provide an environment in which goods can be handled efficiently and stored satisfactorily, securely and safely. Many factors contribute to or militate against the achievement of these objectives. State what they are, giving reasons. (*IPS Diploma, Stores Management and Inventory Control, May 1983*)

8. What do you understand by the terms 'obsolete' and 'redundant'? How do you prevent stock from falling into these categories? (*ASPS, First Certificate, Stores Administration and Control of Stock, November 1982*)

9. Identify the characteristics of an efficient stock coding system and discuss the advantages which such a system can bring to a company. (*IPS Foundation Stage, Introduction to Purchasing and Supply, November 1987*)

10. You are asked to speak on 'The essential principles of stock control' to some new staff during their induction training. What are the principal points that you would include in your notes? (*ASPS, First Certificate, Stores Administration and Control of Stock, November 1982*)

11. (a) Describe the function and duties of a storekeeper in a medium sized engineering company.
(b) Explain how conflict may arise between stores and the production department.
(c) Indicate how the storekeeper can cope with this potential problem. (*AAT, Level III Business Organization, December 1982*)

12. Describe three distinct forecasting methods and give examples of fields in which they might be used. (*Institute of Industrial Managers, Autumn 1983*)

13. (a) Describe the various activities/functions of a manager, with a practical example of at least one function.
(b) Why is management considered so important in the effective running of an organization? (*AAT, Level III Business Organization, December 1983*)

14. Distinguish clearly between 'real time' and 'batch' methods of utilizing a computer. Describe an application for each method. (*ASPS, First Certificate Business Procedures and Organization, November 1982*)

15. To be fully effective those concerned with the stores function must cooperate with other departments and functions of the organization.
Outline the need for cooperation with only three departments, other than production. (*RSA, Storekeeping, Stage II, 1982*)

16. Examine the factors which need to be taken into account when considering the introduction of mechanical handling equipment into a store. (*IPS Foundation Stage, Introduction to Purchasing and Supply, May 1989*)

17. Discuss the principal objectives of:
(a) the stores function, and
(b) the purchasing function.
(*ASPS, Second Certificate, An Appreciation of Management of Materials, May 1982*)

18. Devise and explain a significant classification and coding system which would be appropriate for use in a large manufacturing organization. You may select whatever industry you like. (*IPS Diploma, Stock Management and Inventory Control, November 1983*)

19. Security of stock is of prime concern in any organization. Explain what methods are used to achieve this objective in a stores environment. (*ASPS, First Certificate, Stores Design and Materials Handling, May 1982*)

20. (a) In your opinion what is the difference between obsolete, redundant and surplus stock?
(b) At what periods is it advisable within a company to keep such stocks under review?
(*Institute of Production Control, Practical Stores Management, December 1982*)

21. The primary objective of the stores function is to provide a service to the operating functions. List and briefly describe five major activities that make up this service. (*RSA Storekeeping Stage I, June 1983*)

22. A supervisor has a responsibility for keeping costs down. How can this be achieved in either a purchasing office or a storehouse? (*ASPS, Second Certificate, Principles of Supervision, November 1982*)

23. Effective stores management and inventory control depend upon good relationships with other departments in an organization. How might these relationships make or mar stores management and inventory control operations? (*IPS Diploma, Stores Management and Inventory Control, May 1983*)

24. List four types of conveyor suitable for moving flat-based cartons. (*Institute of Materials Handling, June 1983*)

25. Distinguish between reorder level, minimum level and hastening level and comment upon the factors to be considered when determining these levels. (*RSA, Storekeeping, Stage II, June 1983*)

26. (a) Explain any methods of quality control in a production department.
(b) Describe any methods of quality control with which you may be familiar.
(*AAT, Level III, Business Organization, June 1983*)

27. 'A thorough investigation of each and every item of inventory with a view to determining whether we really needed to stock it, resulted in very considerable savings for our organization.' This quotation, from a supplier's director, reflects a fairly common experience. How would you organize a rationalization programme of this kind, and what steps would you take to prevent unnecessary additions to your stock range? *(IPS Diploma, Stores Management and Inventory Control, November 1983)*

28. 'The safekeeping of goods in stores can be divided into: security, preservation, care and cleanliness of buildings and stocks, maintenance.' Discuss the above statement and give specific examples of stores' responsibilities under each heading. *(ASPS, Second Certificate, An Appreciation of Management of Materials, November 1982)*

29. Product packaging and handling are principal factors in the physical distribution management function. What are the factors which govern the design and use of the transit package? *(ASPS, Second Certificate, Transport and Distribution, November 1982)*

30. (a) What is the role of good Stores or Warehouse Management in the overall structure of an organization?
(b) State in detail three areas where the stores or warehouse can make a significant contribution to the success of the organization.
(Institute of Production Control, Practical Stores Management, 1983)

31. 'Stockyards are either a neglected storage responsibility or organized and designed inefficiently.' Explain what is meant by this statement. *(ASPS, Stores Design and Materials Handling, May 1988)*

32. What factors must be borne in mind when planning a stock location system and what would be your objectives? *(ASPS, Stores Administration and Control of Stock, May 1988)*

33. There are certain basic objectives in planning a distribution system. Identify *three* of these and comment on them. *(ASPS, Transport and Distribution, May 1987)*

34. You have been asked to join a team to interview for a Stores Supervisor. What qualities would you look for? (*ASPS, Principles of Supervision, May 1987*)

35. Discuss the main considerations for siting a depot from which local deliveries can be made. (*ASPS, Transport and Distribution, May 1988*)

36. It has been said that the Japanese view inventory as an evil, whereas in the West inventory has been an asset. Discuss these views, with reference to raw materials, work in progress and finished goods inventories. (*IPS Professional Stage, Materials and Production Management, May 1990*)

37. Evaluate the nature and importance of logistics in relation to the supply chain. (*IPS Professional Stage, Logistics, May 1990*)

38. Explain how the techniques of standardization and variety reduction can benefit an organization and draw attention to any possible problems which might arise as a result of the application of these techniques. (*IPS Foundation Stage, Introduction to Purchasing and Supply, May 1986*)

On 15 July 1992 the Institute of Purchasing and Supply were granted chartered status, and are now the Chartered Institute of Purchasing and Supply (CIPS).

Index